# Fredericksburg City, Virginia

## Deed Book

## 1787–1794

**Ruth and Sam Sparacio**

HERITAGE BOOKS
2020

**HERITAGE BOOKS**
*AN IMPRINT OF HERITAGE BOOKS, INC.*


**Books, CDs, and more—Worldwide**

For our listing of thousands of titles see our website
at
www.HeritageBooks.com


Published 2020 by
HERITAGE BOOKS, INC.
Publishing Division
5810 Ruatan Street
Berwyn Heights, Md. 20740





International Standard Book Number
Paperbound: 978-1-68034-489-9

pp.
1-
4

THIS INDENTURE of three parts made this Fifth day of May in the year of our Lord Christ one thousand seven hundred and Eighty seven Between EDWARD SIMPSON of the Town of Fredericksburg in the County of Spotsylvania and State of Virginia of one part, CATHERINE his Wife of the Town, County and State aforesaid of the second part and CHARLES YATES, JAMES JULIAN, SAMUEL ABBOTT, CHARLES MORTIMER SENR. and JOHN ANDERSON of the Town County and State aforesaid, Trustees, of the third part; And Whereas some unhappy differences have lately arisen between the said SIMPSON and CATHERINE his Wife and they have mutually agreed to live seperate and apart from each other, and previous to such seperation, he the said EDWARD SIMPSON hath thereto consented and also agreed that he out of his own estate will allow & pay to the sd. CATHERINE his Wife during the term of her natural life for her support and maintenance the one half of the clear rents, profits and emoluments arising from the Lott No. 39 as per Deed of Indenture made to the said EDWARD SIMPSON by JOHN THORNTON and JANE his Wife, JOHN MANN SOWELL and ELIZABETH his Wife, THOMAS SOWELL and Ann his Wife bearing date the 7th day of April 1784, and ordered to be recorded in the Court of Hustings of the Town of Fredericksburg the 6th day of December 1784, and is now in the holding of SAMUEL ABBOTT aforesaid and WILLIAM JENKINS at the annual rent of One hundred and twenty pounds current money of Virginia for and during the term of one year and they the said CHARLES YATES, JAMES JULIAN, SAMUEL ABBOTT, CHARLES MORTIMER SENR. & JOHN ANDERSON or any three of them are hereby authorised and impowered to Lease rent and lett for the term of one year or more years or so long as ANN LEWIS, Relict of RICHARD LEWIS deceased, shall live, for the best price or most money that can be obtained for the rent of the premises aforesaid for the purposes before mentioned; And as by the Last Will and Testament of the said RICHARD LEWIS deced. it is expressed ordered that the Lott and premises aforesaid shall be sold after the death of the said ANN LEWIS and if at the time of such sale the said EDWARD SIMPSON shall become the purchaser, it is agreed that the one half of the clear rents and profits aforesaid shall continue and be applied to the sole use of CATHERINE his Wife for the term of her natural life, or if the premises shall be sold to another person or persons then one half of the money arising from such sale shall be put out to Interest with good & sufficient security and the interest arising therefrom shall be applied to the sole use of CATHERINE his Wife aforesaid, and during the term before mentioned. and which rents or interest shall be in quarterly payments, Vizt., commencing the first day of August, the first day of November, the first day of February and the first day of May annually, And also the property mentioned in the annexed Inventory is vested in her the said CATHERINE to sell devise or otherwise dispose off as she may think proper, except the Negro Woman named Milley, who is to revert to the said EDWARD SIMPSON after the decease of the said CATHERINE his Wife, And the said EDWARD SIMPSON at the decease of the said CATHERINE his Wife and the said EDWARD SIMPSON farther agrees that at the decease of the said CATHERINE his Wife, he the said EDWARD SIMPSON will pay to her Executors or Administrators the sum of Fifteen pounds current money of Virginia towards paying the expences of her funeral charges and that the said EDWARD SIMPSON will hereby ratify & confirm the herein recited settlement in such manner as is hereafter mentioned. NOW THIS INDENTURE WITNESSETH that EDWARD SIMPSON in pursuance of the aforesaid proposal and agreement doth hereby for himself his Executors and Admrs., promise and agree to and with CHARLES

YATES, JAMES JULIAN, SAMUEL ABBOTT, CHARLES MORTIMER & JOHN ANDERSON, Trustees, their assigns and doth also agree with said CATHERINE his Wife in manner & form following; (that is to say), that it shall be lawfull for the said CATHERINE his Wife and the said EDWARD SIMPSON shall permit & suffer her the said CATHERINE at all times from henceforth during her natural life to live seperate and apart from him and to reside and be in such place and places, family & familys, & with such relations friends & other persons & to follow & carry on such trade & business as the said CATHERINE from time to time at her will & pleasure (notwithstanding her present coverture and if as if she were a feme sole and unmarried), shall think fit and that EDWARD SIMPSON shall not at any time hereafter sue her in any Court whatever for living seperate and apart from him or at any time compel her to cohabit with him nor shall sue molest disturb or trouble her for such living seperate & apart from him or any other person or persons whatsoever for receiving harbouring or entertaining her, nor shall without the consent of the said CATHERINE visit her or come into her house or place where she may dwell reside or be nor send any letters messuages nor shall at any time claim or demand any of the monies, rings, Jewells, plate, clothes, linen, woolen, household goods or Stock in trace, which said CATHERINE now hath in her custody power & which shall be devised or given to her or shall otherwise acquire and that she shall enjoy and absolutely dispose of the same as if she were a feme sole & unmarried; AND FURTHER said EDWARD SIMPSON his Exors. or Administrators or some of them shall and will truly pay or cause to be paid unto said CATHERINE his Wife or her assigns during the term of her natural life for her support and maintenance the one half of the clear rent of Lott No. 39 in the Town of Fredericksburg as hereinbefore recited; And they the Trustees are hereby, or any three of them, impowered to receive the rents of the Lott and premises and pay the clear one half said rents to said CATHERINE or to her assigns quarterly; In Consideration of which rents so hereby made payable to said CATHERINE SIMPSON in manner aforesaid and of the provision so made for her by the said recited Indenture of Settlement in manner as aforesaid, the said CATHERINE SIMPSON doth hereby agree to accept and take in full satisfaction for her support and maintenance and alimony whatsoever during her coverture, PROVIDED ALWAYS and it is hereby expressly agreed and declared by and between all the parties hereto that in case EDWARD SIMPSON at any time shall be obliged and actually pay any debt or debts which said CATHERINE his Wife shall at any time hereafter during her present coverture contract with any person then in such case it shall be lawfull for EDWARD SIMPSON to deduct and reimburse to him and themselves out of the rent so hereby made payable to her the said CATHERINE as aforesaid; And Lastly EDWARD SIMPSON (in pursuance and full performance of his said recited agreement and divers other good and valuable causes and considerations him thereunto especially moving hath and by these presents doth confirm the before recited Indenture of Assignment and settlement made of the personal Estate of said CATHERINE his Wife & of the annual Rent by said EDWARD SIMPSON and CATHERINE his Wife so thereby respectively assigned to them by the Trustees aforesaid; In Witness whereof EDWARD SIMPSON and CATHERINE his Wife have hereunto set their hands and affixed their seals the day month & year first within written

Sealed and Delivered in presence of

WILLIAM WIATT,                          EDWD. SIMPSON
R. D. KENNY                             CATERINE her mark SIMPSON
HENRY WHITE

Inventory of Sundry Houshold and kitchen furniture the proper of EDWARD SIMPSON given to her by EDWARD SIMPSON her sd. Husband the 1st day of May 1787.

1 Maghoganet Beaureau or Chest of Drawers, 1 Chest, 3 Walnut Tables, 3 Walnut Chairs

2 Rush bottom chairs, 1 do. Buffet, 1 small looking glass, 1 case bottles, 2 feather beds, 1 bolster & pillow, 4 blanketts, 3 pr. sheets, 2 bed quilts, 1 counter pane, 3 pillow cases, 1 bed stead with curtains, 4 bed steads, 2 silver table spoons, 5 silver teaspoons, 1 pr. Silver tea tongs, 2 plated salts, 1 sett castors silver tops, 1 Mahogany Tea Chest with cannisters, 1 coffee pott, 1 tea kettle, 1 walnut teat board, 1 Japaned Tea board, 4 bowles with all the Tea cups saucers and sugar bowles I have, 3 oval dishes, 18 plates, 1 salad dish, 1 fruit plate and dish, 1 larg water Jugg, 1 small water Jugg, 1 Decanter, 1 tumbler, 1 Tureen, 1 butter tureen, 10 pictures in frames, 1 flower pott, 1 damask table cloth, 1 diaper table cloth, 8 knives and forks, 1 knive box, 1 pr. tongs, 1 fire shovel & 1 coal shovel For Kitchen use: 1 Servants bed with bedding and bedstead, 1 crock, 1 set fire irons with racks, 1 Spit, 2 pr. tongs & shovell, 2 dutch ovens, 1 tin oven, 1 frying pan, 1 grid iron, 1 tender, 2 potts, 1 skillett, 2 pr. pott hooks, 2 pine Tables, 5 pewter dishes, 7 pewter plates, 3 pewter basons, 2 smoothing irons and all tubs, pails &c. &c. &c. & sundry not inventories.
  Negro Woman Milly for and during CATHERINE SIMPSON's natural live

        At a Court held for the Town and Corporation of Fredericksburg on Monday September 3rd. 1787
  This Deed of Seperation between EDWARD SIMPSON and CATHERINE his Wife was proved by three of the witnesses thereto and ordered to be recorded
Ex. & Deld.
A. BUCHANAN                          Test. JNO: CHEW JR. Cl C.


pp.     THIS INDENTURE made the 21st day of May one thousand seven hundred and
5-      Eighty seven Between HENRY VOWLES of the Town of FALMOUTH of one part &
6       JAMES SLATOR of Town of Fredericksburg of other part; Witnesseth that said
        VOWLES hath for the consideration hereafter specified granted set & leased unto
said SLATOR during the term of twenty one years commencing the first day of January one thousand seven hundred & eighty five at which time he had possession of a certain piece or parcel of ground oposite the MARKET HOUSE in Fredericksburg now in occupation of said SLATER, containing Twenty feet front on the Main Street, Begining at the North corner of LEONARD PATTERSONs line or the South side of said SLATOR's Chimney & running up the said Main Street to the BRICK HOUSE at present occupied by Mr. ROBERT LILLY & to extend eighty feet back towards the River, the said SLATER is to pay said VOWLES his heirs the annual ground rent of Twenty dollars in Specie pay the Taxes of the ground & what houses he has or may put on this tenement during the term of his lease, the said SLATOR is to complete the addition to the House he now occupies on the walls now up & put a Dutch Roof to both the old Houses as well as the addition & finish off both in a good & workman like manner, these repairs to be made within the space of seven years from the date hereof. Its also agreed by the parties that said SLATOR shall not damage any buildings that has or may be putt on the premisses more than is customary by ware & natural decay & deliver up the said tenement to said VOWLES his heirs &c. at the expiration of said term of twenty one years with all houses &c., should said SLATOR sel or dispose of his lease during his natural live except by consent, the said VOWLES to receive the sum of Twenty pounds specie at the time of such disposal;
  It is further agreed that said SLATOR shall keep & fully perform each of the above covenants & obligations & should he fail or neglect to perform them, it shall be in the power of said VOWLES his heirs to re enter hold & possess the premisses in such manner as tho this lease had never been made; In performance of the above, the contracting parties bind themselves each to the other in the sum of one hundred pounds specie &

have interchangably set their hands & affixed their seals the day & date first above
written. P. S. the sd. SLATOR is to have a pass way of five feet to get into his Lott & to
extend thirty seven feet back.
Signed Sealed & Acknd. in presence of
    JOHN HOARES,                                HENRY VOWLES
    JOSEPH BERRY, WILLIAM JACKSON                JAMES SLATOR.
  At a Court held for the Town and Corporation of Fredericksburg on Monday Septr. 3rd.
1787. This Deed of Lease betweeen HENRY VOWLES & JAS. SLATER was proved by three
Witnesses and ordered to be recorded
Deld. SLATOR                              Teste JNO: CHEW JR. Cl.


p.    MEMORANDUM between JOHN TALIAFERRO of County of KING GEORGE and
6    JAMES HUNTER of County of NORFOLK, Witnesseth that Whereas JAMES HUNTER
    one of the Copartners of HUNTER & TALIAFERRO hath a ballance of Credit on the
Books of that Company, he doth hereby for himself his heirs relinquish all claim to said
ballance against the Company as well as all emoluments advantages or profits made or
to be made by said copartnary in any manner whatsoever; And said JOHN TALIAFERRO
for himself his heirs doth agree that he will hold harmless said JAMES his heirs against
all claims whatsoever which may any ways relate the said Copartnary; In Witness
whereof they have interchangeabley sett their hands and seals the 15th day of May one
thousand seven hundred and eighty seven
Teste  JOHN RUSSELL SPENCE              JOHN  TALIAFERRO
    JAS: TALIAFERRO              JAMES  HUNTER
  Duplicate of this is signed & sealed & left in the possession of Mr. JNO: TALIAFERRO.
                        JAMES  HUNTER
  At a Court held for the Town and Corporation of Fredg. on Monday Sept. the 3rd. 1787;
This Agreement between JOHN TALIAFERRO and JAMES HUNTER was proved by the oath
of JAMES TALIAFERRO a witness thereto and ordered to be recorded
Exd. & Deld. JAS. HUNTER              Teste JNO: CHEW JR. Cl Cur.


pp.    THIS INDENTURE made this 28th day of February one thousand seven hundred
7-    & Eighty seven Between THOMAS TURNER & JANE his Wife of the Parish of
8    WASHINGTON and County of WESTMORELAND of the one part and JOHN BROWN-
    LOW of the County of SPOTSYLVANIA of the other part; Witnesseth that THOMAS
TURNER and JANE his Wife in consideration of the sum of One hundred and fifty pounds
current money of Virginia to them in hand paid at the sealing & delivery of these presents by these presents do each of them bargain and sell unto said JOHN BROWNLOW his
heirs one half acre or lott of land lying & being in Town of Fredericksburg, & lying on
the River RAPPAHANNOCK and known by the number (4) together with all advantages
and profits thereunto belonging, and all the estate right and title of them said THOMAS
TURNER and JANE his Wife; To have and to hold the said lott or half acre of land to JOHN
BROWNLOW his heirs, and THOMAS TURNER and JANE his Wife for themselves and their
heirs doth covenant to and with JOHN BROWNLOW that they will warrent to said JOHN
BROWNLOW his heirs the before mentioned half acre of land against the claim of all
persons whatsoever; In Witness whereof they have hereunto sett their hands and seals
the day & year above written
Signed Sealed and delivered in presence of us
    WM. AUGT. WASHINGTON,                        J. TURNER
    DANL. McCARTEY, JAMES NEVISON               JANE TURNER
WESTMORELAND Sct. Received of the within named JOHN BROWNLOW the sum of One

hundred & fifty pounds being the full consideration for the within mentioned lott in
the same year & day of the date to the within Deed
Test  DANL. McCARTEY,                                                    J. TURNER
         WM. AUGT. WASHINGTON, JAMES NEVISON
  Commonwealth of Virginia to DANIEL McCARTY, WILLIAM A. WASHINGTON & BECK-
WITH BUTLER Gent., Justices of WESTMORELAND County Greeting, Whereas THOMAS
TURNER & JANE his Wife of the County of WESTMORELAND by an Indenture of Bargain &
sale bearing date the 28th day of February 1787, have conveyed unto JNO: BROWNLOW of
the Town of Fredericksburg in the County of Spotsylvania the fee simple estate of and
in one lott or half acre of land lying in said Town of Fredericksburg and by the plan of
said Town numbered Four and Whereas the said JANE TURNER cannot conveniently
travel to the Hustings Court of said Town and Corporation of Fredericksburg to make
her personal acknowledgement of the said Indenture, We do therefore authorize you or
any two or more of you to go to the said JANE TURNER and her examine seperate and
apart from her said Husband whether she doth freely and voluntarily acknowledge the
said Indenture hereunto annexed & that without the persuations or threats of her said
Husband & such acknowledgement as she shall be willing to make, you shall send certified under your hands & seals distinctly & plainly without delay sending therewith this
Commission. Witness HENRY ARMISTEAD, Clerk of our said Court, this 27th day of February 1787 in the 11th year of the Commonwealth
                                       HENRY  ARMISTEAD, Clerk
  Pursuant to this Commission, we did this day examine Mrs. JANE TURNER, Wife of the
within named THOMAS TURNER & she the said JANE TURNER did freely and voluntarily
acknowledge the said Indenture hereto annexed & declared that she did the same without the persuations or threats of her said Husband, Certified under our hands & Seals
this 28th day of Feby. 1787.                        DANIEL  McCARTY
                                                    WM. AUGT. WASHINGTON

  At a Court held for the Town and Corpo. of Fredg. on Monday Sept. 3rd. 1787
This Indenture was proved by one of the witnesses thereto and ordered to be certified;
And at a Court held for the sd. Corpo: October 1st 1787, This Indenture was fully proved
by two of the witnesses thereto and together with the Commission annexed and Certificate of the Execution thereof endorsed are ordered to be recorded
Examined and delivered JOHN BROWNLOE
   per Note                                    Teste  JNO: CHEW JR. Cl.


pp.      THIS INDENTURE made the Twenty sixth day of October in the year of our Lord
9-       one thousand seven hundred and Eighty seven Between EDWARD SIMPSON of the
10       City of PHILADELPHIA in the State of PENSYLVANIA, Merchant, of one part, and
         SAMUEL ABBOTT of Fredericksburg in the State of Virginia, Merchant, of the
other part; Witnesseth that EDWARD SIMPSON in consideration of the sum of Four hundred pounds current money of Virginia unto him in hand well and truly paid by said
SAMUEL ABBOTT before the sealing and delivery hereof by these presents doth bargain
sell release & confirm unto SAMUEL ABBOTT and to his heirs all the estate right title and
demand either in Law or Equity which EDWARD SIMPSON now hath or may have in a
certain lot of ground situate in the Town of Fredericksburg in said State of Virginia and
marked in a plot of said Town No. 39, now in the tenure and possession of said SAMUEL
ABBOTT his under Tenants PAYNE, THOMPSON & WM. JENKINS and bounded by a lott of
WILLIAM JACKSON on the South, by a lot belonging to the Estate of JOHN BAGGOTT deceased on the West, by other part of the sd. lot marked No. 39 now in possession of the
heirs of the said JOHN BAGGOTT deced., on the North and by CAROLINE STREET on the East

together also with all buildings improvements streets lanes alleys water courses privi-
leges and appertenances whatsoever thereunto belonging; To have and to hold the said
hereby bargained and sold premises with the appertenances unto SAMUEL ABBOTT his
heirs, SUBJECT NEVERTHELESS to the payment of the sum of Thirty pounds current
money of Virginia yearly unto Mistress ANN LEWIS, Relict of RICHARD LEWIS deceased,
during her natural life and after her decease to the claim of HANNAH FANT, one of the
heirs of the said RICHARD LEWIS deceased to one undivided fourth part of the net rent
issues and profits of the premises as the same shall arise to CATHERINE SIMPSON, Wife of
the said EDWARD SIMPSON, of the Town of Fredericksburg during her natural life and
the sd. EDWD. SIMPSON for himself his heirs doth hereby covenant promise and agree
with SAMUEL ABBOTT his heirs in the manner following, that is to say, that said
EDWARD SIMPSON & his heirs the hereby bargained & sold premises with the appertenances hereby granted or mentioned or intended so to be (subject as aforesd.) unto said
SAMUEL ABBOTT his heirs against him the sd. EDWD. SIMPSON & his heirs & against
every person whatsoever shall and will warrent and forever defend by these presents;
In Witness whereof the said parties to these presents have interchangeably set their
hands & seals hereunto the day & year first above written
Sealed and Delivered in the presence of us
    SAML. KINGSLEY,                                        EDWD. SIMPSON
    SAML. HILL,  WM. ABBOTT
Received the day of the date of the above written Indenture from the therein named
SAMUEL ABBOTT the sum of Four hundred pounds current money of Virginia being the
full consideration money therein mentioned.
Test SAML. KINGSLEY,                                        EDWD. SIMPSON
    SAML. HILL,  WM. ABBOTT


    PHILADELPHIA County. Ss.  Before us the Subscribers two of the Justices of the
County Court of Common Pleas for the County of PHILADELPHIA & also Justices of the
peace for the same County, personally appeared EDWARD SIMPSON in the within Indenture named and acknowledged the same Indenture as his act & deed.  In Testimony
whereof and in order that the same may be recorded as such according to the Laws of
Virginia, we have hereunto set our hands seals the 27th day of October in the year of
our Lord 1787                                        ROBT. McKNIGHT
                                                ALEXANDER TODD
PHILADELPHIA County Ss.
    I JONATHAN BAYARD SMITH Esquire, Prothonotary of the County Court of Com-
mon Pleas for the County of PHILADELPHIA do hereby certify that ROBERT McKNIGHT
and ALEXANDER TODD, Esquires, the persons taking the foregoing acknowledgement are
Justices of the peace and of the County Court of Common Pleas for the County of PHILA-
DELPHIA as by their Commission remaining of Record in my Office fully appears, & that
to all acts & deeds by them done and subscribed full credit is & ought to be given.  In
Witness whereof I have hereunto affixed the Common Seal of the said County Court of
                      of Common Please and sett my hand the Twenty seventh day of
    SEAL              October in the year of our Lord One thousand seven hundred &
                Eighty seven                                        J. B. SMITH
At a Court of Hustings held for the Town and Corporation of Fredericksburg on Monday
November the 5th 1787
    This Indenture from EDWARD SIMPSON of the one part and SAMUEL ABBOTT of
the other part and a Certificate of the acknowledgment thereof from under the hands
and seals of ROBT. McKNIGHT and ALEXANDER TODD, two of the Justices of the County

Court of Common Pleas for the County of PHILADELPHIA, also Justices of the peace for
the sd  Coty., and also a Certificate from under the hand and seal of JONATHAN BARYARD
SMITH Esqr., prothonotary of the County Court of PHILADELPHIA aforesaid, certifying
that the sd. ROBT. McKNIGHT and ALEXANDER TODD are Justices as aforesaid; Upon which
Certificate the said Indenture is ordered to be recorded
Exd. & Deld. SAML. ABBOTT                    Teste    JNO: CHEW  JR., Cl Cur.


p.          THIS INDENTURE made the 16th day of March one thousand seven hundred and
11          Eighty seven Between MARY SULLIVAN of the one part and WILLIAM REATT of
            the other part, both of the Town of Fredericksburg; Witnesseth that the said
MARY SULLIVAN in consideration of the sum of Thirty pounds current money to her in
hand paid by said WILLIAM REAT, the receipt is hereby acknowledged, she the said
MARY SULLIVAN by these presents doth demise grant and to farm lett unto said WM.
REATT his heirs part of a lot of land situate and being in Town of Fredericksburg on
CAROLINE STREET and is known & distinguished in the plan of the said Town by No. 258,
and is part of the said Lott unoccupied by the said WILLIAM REATT and is conveyed by
Deed in fee with that part in the occupation & possession of said WM. REATT by ROGER
DIXON to MARY SULLIVAN as by a Deed recorded in the Hustings Court of Fredericksburg, refference thereto being had may more fully appear; To have and to hold the said
part of the Lott and premises with the appurtenances unto said WILLIAM REATT his
heirs from the date of these presents untill the 7th day of March which shall happen in
the year of our Lord 1793, And if it shall happen that said WM. REATT shall leave unpaid
the sum of Fifteen pounds part of the consideration within mentioned more than thirty
days from the date hereof then and from thence forth shall and may be lawfull for said
MARY SULLIVAN into the said premises to re enter & the same to repossess as if this
Indenture had never been made; And MARY SULLIVAN for herself her heirs doth covenant and grant to and with said WILLIAM REATT his heirs that they shall occupy possess and enjoy all the premises and appertenances during said term without hindrance
of any person whatsoever; In Witness whereof the parties to these presents have interchangeably set their hands & seals the day and year first above written
Signed Sealed & Delivered in presence of
        MARY  WALKER,                            MARY  SULLIVAN
        JOHN BOOK, JOHN BAGGOTT                  WILLIAM  REATT
   At a Court held for the Town and Corpo. of Fredg. on the 5th day of November 1787;
This Deed of Lease was acknowledged by sd. WILLM. REATT and proved by one of the
witnesses as to MARY SULLIVAN


pp.         THIS INDENTURE made the 19th day of September in the year of our Lord 1787
12-         Between JAMES DUNCANSON of Fredericksburg and MARY his Wife of the one
13          part and CHARLES URQUHART of the said Town, Merchant, on the other part;
            Witnesseth that JAMES DUNCANSON & MARY his Wife in consideration of the sum
of Five shillings current money of Virginia to them in hand paid by said CHARLES
URQUHART at and before the ensealing and delivery of these presents; by these presents do fully & absolutely grant bargain sell & confirm to the said CHARLES URQU-
HART his heirs one lott or half acre of Land lying in Town of Fredericksburg and is
numbered  119; And bounded by GEORGE STREET on the South, extends Eastward to Lott
No. 59, thence Northward by a corner of a Lott No. 60 & Lott No. 120; thence it extends
Westward to CHARLES STREET, thence with the said Street to the begining, which said
Lot of ground was purchased by said DUNCANSON of JOHN ATKINSON, Wheel Wright, &by
ATKINSON of JOHN WALLER of Spotsylvania & all the houses gardens priviledges &

appertenances to the same belonging; To have and to hold the said Lott of Ground to said CHARLES URQUHART his heirs & JAMES DUNCANSON & MARY his Wife agree with sd. CHARLES URQUHART his heis that the said CHS. hold use occupy & possess the said lott of ground with the appertenances free and discharged from the claim & interruption of said JAMES DUNCANSON and MARY his Wife or any other person whatsoever lawfully claiming the same by from or under them; and JAMES DUNCANSON & MARY his Wife do for themselves their heirs the sd. lot of ground with the appertenances to said CHARLES URQUHART his heirs against themselves their heirs shall & will warrent & for ever defend by these presents, Provided always & it is the true intent & meaning of JAMES DUNCANSON & CHARLES URQUHART that if the said JAMES should depart this life intestate that then the said premises above mentioned by this Deed bargained and sold to said CHARLES URQUHART shall be appraised in its unimproved state together with the other part of his the said JAMES's Estate & that the value thereof affixed by the said appraisment shall make a part of that proportion of the Estate of the said JAMES DUNCANSON which the said CHARLES URQUHART will be intitled to in right of his Wife, FINNELLA, Daughter of the sd. JAMES; Provided the said JAMES DUNCANSON shall depart this life intestate as aforesaid; In Witness whereof said JAMES DUNCANCON and MARY his Wife have hereunto set their hands & seals the day & year first above written Signed Sealed & Delivered in the presence of us

    (no witnesses shown)          JAMES  DUNCANSON
                               MARY  DUNCANSON

Received of the within named CHARLES URQUHART the sum of Five shillings current money being the consideration money within mentioned as witness my hand this 19th day of September 1787               JAMES  DUNCANSON

The Commonwealth of Virginia to WILLIAM HARVEY and GEORGE FRENCH of the Corporation of Fredericksburg Gent., Greeting; Whereas JAMES DUNCANSON and MARY his Wife by the certain Deed of bargain & sale bearing date the 19th day of September have sold and conveyed to CHARLES URQUHART the fee simple estate of one lot or half acre of land lying and being in the Corporation aforesd., & Whereas the said MARY DUNCANSON cannot conveniently travel to our said Court to make acknowledgment of the said conveyance (The Commission for the privy Examination of MARY, the Wife of JAMES DUNCANSON); Witness JOHN CHEW JR., Clerk of our said Court, the 5th day of Novr. 1787, in the 12th year of the Commonwealth        JNO: CHEW JR.

In Obedience to the within Commission, we the Commissioners therein named have examined the said MARY DUNCANSON in the manner therein directed who assents to the bargain & sale therein contained and is willing the same should be recorded in the Court of Hustings for Corporation of Fredg., Given under our hands & seals this 5th day of Novr. 1787            WILLIAM  HARVEY
                               GEO: FRENCH

Square of Lotts behind THE CHURCH & MARKET HOUSE
contg. the following numbers;

Lot No. 59 WILLIAM  JACKSON
       60 JAMES  DUNCANSON
    119 CHARLES  URQUHART
    120 The Representatives of the late
BENJA: PIPEMAN & the late ALEXR. CRUCKSHANKS

|  CHARLES  STREET |      |
|:---:|:---:|
| 119 | 120 |
| 59 | 60 |
| PR. ANN STREET | |

At a Court held for Town & Corpo. of Fredg. November 5th 1787
This Indenture was acknowledged by the sd. DUNCANSON & together with the Comm. annexed and Certificate of the Execution thereof Indorsed, were ordered to be recorded

p.     TO ALL PEOPLE to whom these presents shall come, I JAMES DUNCANSON of the
14    Town of Fredericksburg send Greeting.  Know ye that I the said JAMES DUNCAN-
SON as well in consideration ofthe love & affection which I have & bear unto my
Son in Law, CHARLES URQUHART, as also the sum of Five shillings to me in hand paid by
the said CHARLES URQUHART the receipt whereof I hereby acknowledged, and also for
other good causes & considerations me hereunto moving by these presents do give
grant & confirm unto said CHARLES URQUHART the following slaves Viz., Milly & her
two Children named Grace & Will, to have & to hold the said three slaves together with
their increase or children of the female slaves unto the said CHARLES URQUHART his
heirs and I said JAMES DUNCANSON the said three slaves above mentioned against the
claim of all persons whatsoever do warrant & forever defend, Provided always & it is
the true intent and meaning of the said JAMES DUNCANSON & CHARLES URQUHART that
if the said JAMES DUNCANSON should make no will but depart this life intestate that
then the slaves above mentioned by these presents conveyed shall be appraised in the
same manner with the other Estate of the said JAMES DUNCANSON and shall be considered as so much of that or whatever proportion of said JAMES's Estate the said
CHARLES URQUHART will be intitled to in right of his Wife, (the Daughter of the said
JAMES DUNCANSON), provided the said JAMES die intestate as aforesaid; In Witness
whereof I have hereunto set my hand & seal this 21st day of Septr. Anno Domini one
thousand seven hundred & Eighty seven
In presence of (no witnesses shown)        JAMES  DUNCANSON
At a Court held for the Town and Corporation of Fredericksburg November 5th 1787
This Deed of Gift was acknowledged by the said JAMES DUNCANSON and ordered to be
recorded


p.     THIS INDENTURE made the 22nd day of October in the year of our Lord one
15    thousand seven hundred and Eighty seven Between WILLIAM JACKSON of the
Town of Fredericksburg and County of Spotsylvania, Gent., of the one part and
WILLIAM LOVELL of the Town & County aforesaid, Merchant, of the other part;  Witnesseth that WILLIAM JACKSON in consideration of the rents and covenants herein after
mentioned on the aprt of WILLIAM LOVELL his heirs to be paid done and performed,
said WILLIAM JACKSON hath demised and to farm let unto WILLIAM LOVELL his heirs
one certain tenement or part of a lot of land in Town of Fredericksburg containing
twenty four feet front on CAROLINE STREET and running back one hundred and thirty
two feet and adjoins the STORE HOUSE now occupied by MESSRS. YATES and LOVELL, and
that part of the HOUSE at present occupied by Mr. WILLIAM SMOCK (Sadler), together
with all profits commodities and appertenances to the same belonging; To have and to
hold the said tenement or part of a Lott with the appertenances unto WILLIAM LOVELL
his heirs from the first day of January next ensuing the date hereof and during the
term of Sixteen years to be fully ended & compleated; Yielding and paying unto WIL-
LIAM JACKSON his heirs during the term on the first day of January each year the sum
or yearly rent of One shilling current money of Virginia if the same shall be demanded
and WILLIAM LOVELL doth hereby covenant and agree to and with WILLIAM JACKSON
that in consideration of the premises, said WILLIAM LOVELL will build or cause to be
built upon the Lott of Ground hereby demised within the term aforesd. one house fifty
feet in length and twenty two feet wide and two story high, to be finished in a substantial workmenlike manner & will at the expiration of the term of Sixteen years deliver
up to said WILLIAM JACKSON his heirs the peaceably possession of the hereby demised
premises In Witness whereof the parties to these presents have hereunto set their
hands & seals the day & year first above written

Sealed & Delivered in the presence of
    ROBERT  WALKER,                                    WILLIAM  JACKSON
    ROBERT  GRIGG,  WM.  SMOCK                           WILLIAM  LOVELL
  At a Hustings Court held for the Town & Corpo: of Fredg., on Monday the 5th February
1787    This Deed of Lease between WILLIAM JACKSON & WILLIAM LOVELL was proved
by three witnesses thereto and ordered to be recorded
Deld. WM. LOVELL                              Teste    JNO: CHEW  JR., Cl Cur


pp.        THIS INDENTURE made the 13th day of August one thousand seven hundred &
16-        Eighty seven Between ELISHA HALL and CAROLINE his Wife of the Town and
17         Corporation of Fredericksburg in the State of Virginia of one part and JOHN
           LEWIS of the County of CULPEPER and State aforesaid of the other part; Whereas
the said ELISHA HALL in and by his Bond or obligation bearing even date with these
presents became bound unto said JOHN LEWIS in the penal sum of Two thousand two
hundred pounds Specie at the rate of Six Shillings per Dollar with a condition there-
under written that if the said ELISHA HALL or his heirs should well and truly pay to the
said JOHN LEWIS or his certain Attorney or assigns the sum of Eleven hundred pounds
like money in manner following, to wit, Three hundred and twenty pounds on or before
the 6th day of September 1786, Five hundred and fifty five pounds on or before the 6th
day of April 1787; Two hundred and twenty five pounds on or before the 6th day of
September 1789 with legal interest on the several sums (Eleven hundred pounds) from
the Sixth day of September 1785 till paid, then the said Bond or obligation to be void or
else to remain in full force. NOW THIS INDENTURE WITNESSETH that said ELISHA HALL
and CAROLINE his Wife as well for the better securing the payment of the said Eleven
hundred pounds in manner aforesaid with legal interest on the same unto JOHN LEWIS
as also in consideration of the sum of Five shillings current money to said ELISHA HALL
in hand paid by said JOHN LEWIS at and before the sealing and delivery of these presents, by these presents do bargain and sell unto said JOHN LEWIS his heirs all the Lotts
of Ground with the appurtenances thereunto belonging as are specified in a Deed of
Bargain & Sale from JOHN LEWIS and MARY ANN his Wife unto the said ELISHA HALL
bearing date the first day of March 1786 situate in the Town of Fredericksburg and by
plan of said Town are numbered as follows, to wit, 142, 144, 145, 146, 147 & 148; & by
refference to the same will more fully appear; To have and to hold the several lots of
land lying in the Corporation & Town of Fredericksburg and numbered as heretofore
mentioned with all appurtenances thereunto belonging unto JOHN LEWIS his heirs for
the better and more perfect secureing the payment of the said Eleven hundred pounds
with legal Interest from the said 6th day of September 1785 unto said JOHN LEWIS his
certain attorney his heirs, the said ELISHA HALL do by these presents convey and
assigns unto JOHN LEWIS his heirs all his right to & interest in the several Bonds and
Claims against the respective persons following, to wit, a Bond to ROBERT B. CHEW of the
Corporation of Fredericksburg payable unto said ELISHA HALL for the condition of One
hundred and forty pounds bearing date the first day of October 1785; ANN HACKLEY's
Bond of the Corporation of Fredg. payable unto ELISHA HALL for the condition of
Ninety pounds bearing date the 9th day of November 1785; SAMUEL & WILLIAM DU-
VALL's Bond payble unto ELISHA HALL on or before the first day of April 1787 condi-
tioned for the payment of five hundred and fifty five pounds which several Bonds I do
hereby convey & warrent unto said JOHN LEWIS his heirs against the claim of me or my
assigns or any other person whatsoever; PROVIDED Always, that if ELISHA HALL his
heirs do pay or cause to be paid unto JOHN LEWIS or assigns the sum of Eleven hundred
pounds with legal Interest thereon in manner following, that is to say, (in the three

payments set out above); said JOHN LEWIS his heirs will at the request cost and charges of
ELISHA HALL his heirs transfer all the premises and their appertenances and several
Bonds mentioned herein unto ELISHA HALL his heirs and he shall his heirs the lots &
appertenances the same as if this Instrument had never been made;  In Witness where-
of the said parties to these presents set their hands and seals the day & year first above
written
Sealed & Delivered in presence of
        FONTAINE MAURY, WILLIAM LEWIS,                    ELISHA HALL
        ROBT. PATTON, R. D. KENNY,
        EDWD. SINGLETON, JAMES NEWTON, Z. LUCAS
  At a Court held for the Town and Corpo: of Fredg. November 5th 1787
This Deed of Trust from ELISHA HALL to JOHN LEWIS was acknowledged by the said HALL
and ordered to be recorded
Examined and Delivered                    Teste   JNO: CHEW JR., Cl Cur.


pp.       THIS INDENTURE made the first day of May in the year of our Lord one thou-
18-       sand seven hundred & Eighty seven Between PHILIP LIPSCOMB of Spotsylvania
19        County of the one part and GEORGE McCUTCHAN of said County of other part; Witnesseth that PHILIP LIPSCOMB in consideration of the sum of Two shillings current money of Virginia to him in hand paid by GEORGE McCUTCHEN. the receipt whereof he doth hereby acknowledge, by these presents do bargain & sell unto GEORGE
McCUTCHEN a certain lott or parcel of land situate in Town of Fredericksburg being Lot
No. (blank) Begining onthe North end of CAROLINE STREET and joining the said LIPS-
COMB's lott where he now lives, thence runing N. E. 58 feet, thence S. E. 132 feet, thence
S. W. 58 feet thence N. W. to CAROLINE STREET, 65 1/2 feet to the first station; And all
houses orchards ways profits commodities and appertenances whatsoever to said
premises belonging; To have and to hold the said lott of land together with the use of
the Well in the said LIPSCOMB's Lott and all other the premises hereby granted unto
GEORGE McCUTCHING his heirs from the first day before the date of these presents
during the full term of twelve years from thence next ensuing and GEORGE McCUTCHEN
do further bind & oblige himself his heirs to build on the front of the said Lott a House
20 by 16 feet with a Shed 9 by 16 with one Chimney, the said McCUTCHEN finding bricks
& lime for the Chimney, bricknocking & plastering (and the said LIPSCOMB to do the
work at his own expence); and said McCUTCHEN further agrees to take the Stable now on
the ground which is 20 by 12 feet & fronted to the Street, then pulling a Dutch Roof to
it, also a Sheld 10 by 20 feet, the hole to be done in a workman like manner and also to
find lime and bricks as before and the said LIPSCOMB to do the work at his own expence
of brick noging &c. as before. And GEORGE McCUTCHEN his heirs do agree to give up the
said land and houses at the expiration of twelve years from the date above mentioned to
PHILIP LIPSCOMB his heir;  In Witness whereof we bind our selves each unto the other
in the penal sum of five hundred pounds current money of Virginia to be paid by the
first failure thereof; As Witness our hands & seals this 13th day April 1787.
Signed sealed & delivered in presence of
        TULLY WHITHURST, W. SKINNER,            PHILIP LIPSCOMB
        BENJAMIN ELLIS, JOHN MUNFORD            GEORGE McCUTCHEN
  At a Court held for the Town and Corporation of Fredericksburg December the 3rd.
1787    This Deed of Lease between PHILLIP LIPSCOMB and GEORGE McCUTCHEN was
acknowledged by the parties and ordered to be recorded
Deld. G. McCUTCHEN                       Teste  JNO: CHEW JR., Cl. Cur.

pp.     THIS INDENTURE made this 13th day of August 1787 Between JOHN LEWIS and
19-    MARY ANN his Wife of the Town of Fredericksburg in State of Virginia of one
20      part and ELISHA HALL, Doctor of Physic, of Town of Fredericksburg, in the State
       of Virginia of the other part; Witnesseth that JOHN LEWIS in consideration of
Eleven hundred pounds current money to him paid or secured to be paid by ELISHA
HALL, the receipt of which is hereby acknowledged, do by these presents bargain & sell
unto ELISHA HALL Six lotts of ground with all the Improvements thereon lying & being
in the Town of Fredericksburg containing Three acres & distinguished in the Plot of
the sd. Town by the following numbers, 142, 144, 145, 146, 147 & 148; To have and to hold
the lotts of ground free from all rents Incumbrances & charges whatseover unto
ELISHA HALL and to his heirs; and said JOHN LEWIS doth hereby covenant and promise
for himself his heirs that he will forever warrent and defend a just right and title in
the said lotts unto ELISHA HALL his heirs; In Witness whereof the said JOHN LEWIS and
MARY ANN his Wife have hereunto set their hands & affixed their seals the day & year
first above written
Signed Sealed and Delivered in presence of
      R. D. KENNY,  EDWD. SINGLETON,        JOHN LEWIS
      JAMES NEWTON, Z. LUCAS           MARY ANNE LEWIS
 The Commonwealth of Virginia to GEORGE FRENCH & BENJAMIN DAY, Justices of the
Corporation of Fredericksburg Greeting; Whereas JOHN LEWIS & MARY ANN his Wife of
Town of Fredericksburg have by Indenture of bargain & sale bearing date the 13th day
of August 1787, conveyed unto ELISHA HALL of the same Town the fee simple Estate of
and in six lotts of ground lying in said Town containing three acres with all buildings &
improvements thereon, And whereas the said MARY ANN cannot conveniently tracel to
our Court of Hustings of the Corporation of Fredericksburg to make acknowledgment of
the said conveyance (The Commission for the privy Examination of MARY ANN, the Wife of JOHN
LEWIS); Witness JOHN CHEW JUNR., Clerk of our said Court of Hustings, this 14th day of
August 1787 in the 12th year of the Commonwealth      JNO: CHEW JR.
      Corporation of Fredericksburg to wit:
 In Obedience to the within Commission to us directed, we the Subscribers, two of the
Commissioners therein named, have privately examined the within mentioned MARY
ANN LEWIS in the manner therein required who assents to the Bargain & Sale therein
contained and is willing the same should be recorded in the Court of Hustings of the
Corporation of Fredericksburg, Certified under our hands & seals this 14th day of
August 1787                   GEO: FRENCH
                               BENJN. DAY
  At a Court held for the Corporation of Fredg. December 3rd 1787
This Deed for Lotts from JOHN LEWIS to ELISHA HALL was acknowledged by the said
JOHN LEWIS and together with the Commission annexed and Certificate of the Execution
thereof indorsed, were ordered to be recorded
Examd. & Delivered WM. A. GREGORY      Teste JNO: CHEW JR. Cl Cur.

pp.     THIS INDENTURE made the 4th day of July in the year of our Lord one thousand
20-    seven hundred and Eighty seven Between CHARLES CARTER of Spotsylvania
21      County of one part and GEORGE McCUTCHEN of said County of other part; Witnes-
       seth that CHARLES CARTER in consideration of the sum of Two shillings current
money of Virginia to him in hand paid by GEORGE McCUTCHEN, the receipt whereof he
doth hereby acknowledge, by these presents doth bargain & sell unto GEORGE
McCUTCHEN Twenty seven and a half feet of ground in front situate and being in Town
of Fredericksburg joining & being a part of the square on which the said CARTER lives,

to be extended one hundred and thirty two feet back, And all houses orchards ways profits commodities and appertenances whatsoever belonging; To have and to hold the Lott or parcel of land as described with the appertenances unto GEORGE McCUTCHEN his heirs from the date of these presents during the full term of Twenty years from thence next ensuing, And GEORGE McCUTCHEN do further bind and oblige himself his heirs to build on the front of the said land a House 20 by 16 feet with a shed 10 by 16 with one chimney, the said McCUTCHEN finding all materials except the frame of an old house 32 by 16, twenty feet of which is to be put on the lott with a Dutch Roof and sheld as the above to be done in a workman like manner, And the said GEORGE McCUTCHEN for himself his heirs do agree to give up the sd. land and houses in good order at the expiration of Twenty years from the date hereof to sd. CHARLES CARTER his heirs, In Witness whereof we bind ourselve each to the other in the penal sum of Five hundred pounds current money of Virginia to be paid by the first failure thereof; As Witness our hands and seals the date above mentioned

Signed Sealed and Delivered in the presence of

JNO: RICHARDS, RICHD: SIMCOCK,          CHAS. CARTER JUNR.
JOHN MUNFORD, CHARLES T. McCARTY     GEO: McCUTCHEN

At a Court held for the Town and Corporation of Fredericksburg December 3rd 1787 This Deed of Lease was proved by the oath of JOHN RICHARDS, JOHN MUNFORD and CHARLES T. McCARTY, three of the witnesses thereto and ordered to be recorded

Teste JNO: CHEW JR., Cl. Cur.

pp.  THIS INDENTURE made the 4th day of July in the year of our Lord one thousand
21-  seven hundred and Eighty seven Between CHARLES CARTER of Spotsylvania
22   County of one part and JOHN MUNFORD of the said County of the other part; Witnesseth that CHARLES CARTER in consideration of the sum of Two shillings current money of Virginia to him in hand paid by JOHN MUNFORD, the receipt whereof he doth hereby acknowledge, by these presents doth bargain and sell unto JOHN MUNFORD Twenty seven and a half feet of Ground in front, situate lying and being in the Town of Fredericksburg joining and being part of the square on which the said CARTER lives, to be extended one hundred and thirty two feet back, & all houses orchards, profits and appertenances whatsoever to said premises belonging; To have and to hold the abovesd. lott of land with the appertenances unto JOHN MUNFORD his heirs from the date of these presents during the full term of Twenty years; And JOHN MUNFORD do further bind & oblige himself his heirs to build on the front of the said land a House 30 feet by 18, two story high with one Chimney, the said MUNFORD finding all materials & being at the whole expence, all which to be done in a workman like manner, & JOHN MUNFORD his heirs do agree to give up the said land and houses in good orders at the expiration of Twenty years above mentioned to said CHARLES CARTER his heirs; In Witness whereof we bind ourselves each to the other in the penal sum of five hundred pounds current money of Virginia to be paid by the first failure thereof; As Witness our hands and seals the date above mentioned

JNO: RICHARDS, RICHD. SIMCOCK,          CHARLES CARTER
GEO: McCUTCHAN,   CHARLES T. McCARTY     JOHN MUNFORD

At a Court held for the Town and Corporation of Fredg. December 3rd 1787 This Deed of Lease between CHS. CARTER JUNR. and JOHN MUNFORD was proved by three witnesses thereto and ordered to be recorded

Exd. & Deld. J. MUNFORD          Teste JNO: CHEW JR., Cl Cur

pp.      THIS INDENTURE Bipartite made this sixth day of Augsut Anno Domini one
22-     thousand seven hundred and Eighty seven Between JOHN LEGG of the Town of
23      Fredericksburg and County of Spotsylvania of one part and FONTAIN MAURY of
the Town and County aforesaid of the other part; Witnesseth that said JOHN in
consideration of Ninety pounds Virginia Currency to him in hand paid, the receipt
whereof is hereby acknowledged, by these presents doth bargain and sell unto FON-
TAINE MAURY his heis all that parcel of ground containing about one fourth of an acre
lying and being on the Street called CHARLES STREET in the Town of Fredericksburg,
and being part of the Lott known by the number One hundred and thirty three in the
plan of the aforesaid Town, purchased of the Executors of MICHAEL ROBINSON deced., by
the said JOHN and bounded; Begining where the said Lott number One hundred and
Thirty three is cornered by CHARLES STREET & AMELIA STREET, thence along CHARLES
STREET half way to the line deviding the lots number one hundred and thirty three &
thirty five, thence at right angles with CHARLES STREET to the line deviding the lotts
number one hundred & thirty three and one hundred and thirty four; thence along the
said line to AMELIA STREET and from thence along the said Street to the begining; comprehending the compleat half of the aforesaid lot numbered one hundred and thirty
three and also all houses orchards, gardens profits advantages and hereditaments to the
premises belonging; To have and to hold the premises above mentioned with the appertenances unto FONTAINE MAURY his heirs, And the sd. JOHN for himself his heirs doth
covenant and grnt to and with sd. FONTAINE MAURY his heirs that said JOHN hath not
done or committed any act whereby or wherewith the said premises or any part thereof
are or may be charged or incumbered in title or Estate, and the said JOHN against all
persons whatsoever to said FONTAIN his heirs will warrent and forever defend by these
presents; In Witness whereof I have hereunto set my hand and seal the day and year
abovesaid
Signed Sealed & Delivered in presence of
     (no witnesses shown)                        JOHN LEGG
At a Court held for the Town and Corporation of Fredg., January the 7th 1788
This Indenture for Land from JOHN LEGG to FONTAINE MAURY was acknowledged by the
said LEGG and ordered to be recorded
Exd. and deld. FONT. MAURY          Teste   JNO: CHEW Cl Cur.


pp.      THIS INDENTURE made this first day of January in the year of our Lord Christ
24-     one thousand seven hundred and Eighty eight Between JOHN LEWIS and MARY
25      ANN LEWIS, his Wife, of Town and Corporation of Fredericksburg in the County
of Spotsylvania of the one part and JOHN FERNEYHOUGH of the Town and Corporation of the other part; Witnesseth that in consideration of the sum of Five hundred
pounds current money of Virginia to him the said JOHN LEWIS in hand paid at and before the sealing and delivery of these presents by said JOHN FERNEYHOUGH, the receipt
whereof said JOHN LEWIS doth hereby acknowledge, they the said JOHN LEWIS and
MARY ANN his Wife by these presents do bargain and sell unto JOHN FERNEYHOUGH his
heirs all that lott or parcel of ground lying in Town and Corporation of Fredericksburg
known and described in the plan of said Town by the lott number 68, contains by survey seventy six square poles and is bounded; Northerly by HAWKE STREET, Easterly by
RAPPAHANNOCK RIVER, Southerly by Lott No. 67 and Westerly by SOPHIA STREET, Together with all houses orchards profits and appertenances belonging; To have and to hold
the lands hereby bargained and sold and every of their appertenances unto JOHN
FERNEYHOUGH his heirs, And JOHN LEWIS for himself his heirs doth covenant and
agree to and with JOHN FERNEYHOUGH his heirs that JOHN LEWIS hath good and lawful

power and authority to grant and convey the same to JOHN FERNEYHOUGH in manner
and form aforesaid and that the premises now are and forever hereafter shall remain
free & clear of and from all gifts, grants, bargains, sales dower right and title of dower
and Incumbrances whatsoever suffered by JOHN LEWIS and MARY ANNE his Wife or
any person (the Quitrents that may hereafter become due only excepted & foreprized),
And JOHN LEWIS and MARY ANN his Wife and their heirs against all persons shall
warrent and forever defend by these presents; In Witness whereof JOHN LEWIS & MARY
ANN his Wife have hereunto set their hands & affixed their seals the day & year first
above written
Sealed and Delivered in presence of
      WILLIAM WIATT,                    JOHN LEWIS
      JAMES WEIR, FIELDING LUCAS         MARY ANNE LEWIS
 Received the day of the date of the within written Indenture from the within named
JOHN FERNEYHOUGH Five hundred pounds current money of Virginia being in full the
consideration within mentioned
Teste   BENJA: DAY,                       JOHN LEWIS
      GEO: FRENCH
 At a Court held for the Town and Corporation of Fredg. Jany. 7th 1788
This Indenture was proved by the three witnesses thereto and together with a
Commission annexed & Certificate of Execution thereof Indorsed were ordered to be
recorded
Exd. & Deld. J. FERNEYHOUGH          Teste JNO: CHEW Cl. Cur
Commission recorded in /45/ folio


pp.          THIS INDENTURE made this Twenty fourth day of December in the year of our
26-          Lord one thousand seven hundred and Eighty seven Between JOHN BENSON of
27           Town of Fredericksburg and County of Spotsylvania and ELEANOR his Wife of the
        one part and RICHARD PEACOCK of the other part; Witnesseth that JOHN BENSON
and ELEANOR his Wife in consideration of the sum of Seventy pounds current money of
Virginia to him in hand paid by RICHARD PEACOCK, the receipt of which the said JOHN
BENSON doth hereby acknowledge, by these presents doth bargain sell and confirm
unto RICHARD PEACOCK his heirs one half of the Lott in the Town & numbered in the
plan Eleven and contains in front on PRINCESS ANN STREET, Eighty two and a half feet
and runs back the full depth of the said Lott on PRUSSIA STREET, together with all the
appertenances thereunto belonging; and all Estate right claim or demand of them the
said JOHN BENSON & ELEANOR his Wife to the same; To have and to hold the said half a
lott of ground with the appertenances unto RICHARD PEACOCK his heirs, And JOHN
BENSON and ELEANOR his Wife do further covenant to & with RICHARD PEACOCK his
heirs that they will warrent and forever defend the said half lott of ground unto
RICHARD PEACOCK against the claim of all persons whatsoever, In Witness whereof the
said JOHN BENSON & ELEANOR his Wife have hereunto set their hands & seals the day &
year first within written
Sealed & Delivered in presence of
      WM. JACKSON,                       JOHN BENSON
      JOS: CHRISTY,  WM. SMITH           ELEANOR BENSON
(Comm. recorded in (44).
 At a Court held for the Town and Corporation of Fredg. Jany. 7th 1788
This Indenture was proved by two witnesses thereto and ordered to be recorded
Exd. & Deld. RD. PEACOCK              Teste JNO: CHEW, Cl Cur

At a Court held for the sd. Corpo: the 26th March 1790
This Indenture was further proved by one other witness & ordered to be recorded
(Commission recorded in (44)          Teste  JNO: CHEW, Cl Cur

pp.      KNOW ALL MEN by these presents that I BURGES BALL of Town of Fredericks-
27-      burg in the County of Spotsylvania, Surviving Administrator of Colo. BURGESS
28       SMITH deced., late of County of LANCASTER, by these presents do make ordain &
         appoint & in my place and stead put and depute LeROY PEACHY of County of
RICHMOND, Attorney at Law, my true and lawfull Attorney for me and in my name and
the use of the Estate of BURGES SMITH to ask demand recover and receive all sums of
money debts & demands whatsoever which now are or hereafter shall be due and owing
to the said Estate from any person whatsoever and sufficient discharges for the same
either in my name or in his own name; and after receipt of the same or any part thereof to pay it away towards discharging the Debts due from the Estate of said BURGES
SMITH deced; And I do further impower my said Attorney to make sale of any part of the
said BURGES SMITHs Estate that he may think requisite towards discharging the said
Debts and to apply the money arising from such sales in the same manner and to take
receipts and acquitances for all moneys paid by him to the Creditors of BURGES SMITH
and in my name to do all other acts & things whatsoever concerning the premises as
fully in every respect as I the said BURGESS BALL might or could do if I were personally
present, hereby ratifying and confirming all my said Attorney shall lawfully do or
cause to be done in the premises by virtue of these presents;  In Witness whereof I have
hereunto set my hand & seal this 4th day of February in the year of our Lord 1788
Signed Sealed Published & Delivered in presence of
         (no witnesses shown)                          B. BALL
  At a Court held for the Town and Corporation of Fredericksburg February 4th  1788
This Power of Attorney from BURGESS BALL Gent. to LeROY PEACHY Gent. was acknow-
ledged by the said BALL and ordered to be recorded
Deld. Colo. BALL                     Teste  JNO: CHEW JR. Cl Cur.

pp.      THIS INDENTURE made this 28th day of December in the year of our Lord Christ
28-      one thousand seven hundred and Eighty seven Between GEORGE WEEDON and
29       CATHERINE WEEDON his Wife of the Town and Corporation of Fredericksburg and
         County of Spotsylvania and State of Virginia of the one part and JOHN LEGG of
the Town County and State aforesaid of the other part; Witnesseth that GEORGE WEEDON
and CATHERINE his Wife in consideration of the rents conditions & agreements in this
Indenture contained on the part of JOHN LEGG to be paid and performed by these presents do bargain Lease and let to JOHN LEGG his heirs a certain parcel of land situate
and lying in the Town and Corporation of Fredericksburg on CAROLINE STREET and is
part of Lott number 26, as described in the plan of the Town, Begining at the upper corner of the said Lott No. 26 on CAROLINE STREET, thence down the said Street twenty one
& one half feet, thence back sixty six feet, thence up the said Lott paralel to CAROLINE
STREET twenty one and one half feet, thence sixty six feet adjoining the lott number 28,
to the beginning; To have and to hold the parcel of land with the appertenances to said
JOHN LEGG his heirs, yielding and paying for the same on the first day of January in
the year of our Lord Christ 1789, yearly unto GEORGE WEEDON his heirs the sum of
Eleven pounds five shillings and nine pence in half yearly payments, vizt., half the
said sum to be paid on the first day of July next and the other half on the first day of
January following issuing out of the hereby demised premises, And JOHN LEGG doth
hereby covenant & grant to and with GEORGE WEEDON his heirs that he will in half

yearly payments and every year hereafter truly pay the sum of Eleven pounds five
shillings and nine pence current money of Virginia to be discharged in Gold at Five
shillings and four pence the penny weight or in Silver at Six shillings & Eight pence
the ounce, /any act to the contrary hereafter to be made & provided regulating the
current exchange of the state aforesaid shall in no wise effect the parties to these
presents notwithstanding, And they GEORGE WEEDON and CATHERINE his Wife do for
them doth for themselves their heirs covenant grant and agree to and with JOHN LEGG
his heirs that he paying and performing the covenants and agreements by him to be
performed shall and may at all times hereafter occupy possess and enjoy all the above
mentioned parcel of land and premies with appertenances without the hindrance or
disturbance of them the said GEORGE WEEDON and CATHERINE his Wife their heirs and
that free from all incumbrances whatsoever (the growing Taxes which may hereafter
become due excepted), In Witness whereof the parties to these presents have hereunto
interchangeably set their hands & affixed their seals the day & year above written
Sealed & Delivered in presence of
      (no witnesses shown)                                      G. WEEDON
                                                      JNO: LEGG

   At a Court held for the Town and Corporation of Fredg. 4th Febry. 1788
This Deed of Lease from GEORGE WEEDON to JOHN LEGG was acknowledged by the parties
and ordered to be recorded
Deld. Capt. LEGG                              Teste  JNO: CHEW JR. Cl Cur


p.        I JOHN HARDIA of the Town of Fredericksburg do hereby oblige myself my
30       heirs & assigns to permit and suffer WILLIAM ALEXANDER Gent., of STAFFORD
         County his heirs and assigns to enjoy and make use of without interruption or
molestation at all times hereafter six feet width of ground upon my part of the Lott
Number (blank) in the said Town to run contiguous and paralel to the half or moiety of
the said Lott which I have heretofore conveyed to the said WILLIAM ALEXANDER by
Deed, the said six feet to run the whole length of the said Lott from the Main Street of
said Town to the back line of the Lott aforesd., which six feet width of ground is always
to be left open & free for the use occupation ingress, egress & regress of said WILLIAM
ALEXANDER his heirs without obstruction of said JOHN HARDIA his heirs, In Witness
whereof I have hereunto set my hand & seal this 17th day of Jany. 1788
Sealed & Delivered in presence of
   WILLIAM LOVELL,                                      JOHN HARDIA
   RICHD: GARNER,   THOMAS SIMPSON
 Memo. It is agreed that the cross paling seperating the property of the parties shall
be put up and kept in repair at their joint expence
  At a Court held for the Town and Corporation of Fredericksburg February 4th 1788
This Agreement between JOHN HARDIA & WILLIAM ALEXANDER was proved by three
witnesses and ordered to be recorded
                      Teste JNO: CHEW Cl.


pp.       THIS INDENTURE made the 29th day of January in the year of our Lord one
31-      thousand seven hundred and Eighty eight Between JOHN LEWIS of the Corpora-
33       tion of Fredericksburg in the Commonwealth of Virginia and MARY ANNE his
         Wife of the one part and JACOB KUHN of the Corporation aforesaid of the other
part; Witnesseth that in consideration of the sum of Ninety pounds current money of
Virginia to said JOHN LEWIS in hand paid by JACOB KUHN, at or before the sealing and
delivery of these presents; the receipt whereof he doth hereby acknowledge, said JOHN

LEWIS and MARY ANN his Wife by these presents do bargain sell & confirm unto JACOB KUHN and his heirs two compleat lotts of land containing half an acre each lying and being in the Corporation of Fredericksburg described and known in the plan of the said Corporation by Nos. 105 & 106; bounded Westerly by CHARLES STREET, Northerly by PITT STREET and Easterly by PRINCIS ANN STREET, Together with all houses and buildings thereon erected and all priviledges profits and appertenances to the said two lotts belonging; To have and to hold the above two lotts of land above mentioned unto JACOB KUHN his heirs and JOHN LEWIS for himself his heirs doth covenant promise and grant to and with JACOB KUHN his heirs that the said premises now are & so forever shall remain and be free & clear from all former and other gifts sales dower right and title of dower and incumbrances whatsoever suffered by said JOHN LEWIS or any other person whatsoever; and that JOHN LEWIS and his heirs the bargained and sold premises with the appertenances unto JACOB KUHN his heirs against said JOHN LEWIS and MARY ANN his Wife and their heirs shall warrent and forever defend by these presents; In Witness whereof JNO: LEWIS and MARY ANN his Wife have hereunto set their hands and seals the day & year above written

Sealed and Delivered in the presence of

  FONTAINE MAURY,        JOHN LEWIS

  CHS. CARTER JUNR., WILLIAM HARVEY  MARY ANNE LEWIS

 The Commonwealth of Virginia to CHAS. MORTIMER, BENJAMIN DAY and WM. HARVEY Gent., of the Corporation of Fredericksburg Greeting; Whereas JOHN LEWIS and MARY ANNE his Wife by their Deed of Bargain and Sale dated the 29th day of January have sold and conveyed unto JACOB KUHN the fee simple estate of two compleat lotts lying and being in the Town of Fredericksburg, And whereas the said MARY ANN cannot conveniently travel to our sd. Court of Hustings to make acknowledgment of the said conveyance (the Commission for the Privy Examination of MARY ANNE, Wife of JOHN LEWIS); Witness JOHN CHEW JR. Clerk of our said Court this 2nd day of Feby. 1788 in the 12th year of the Commonwealth         JNO: CHEW JR. Cl. Cur

 In Obedience to the within Commission to us directed, we the Subscribers have privately examined the within named MARY ANN LEWIS in the manner therein directed who assents to the bargain & sale therein contained and is willing that the annexed Deed should be recorded. Certified under our hands & seals this 4th day of Feby. 1788

 At a Court held for the Townand Corpo: of Fredg. Feby. 4th 1788

This Indenture was proved by three of the witnesses thereto and together with the Commission annexed and Certificate of the Execution thereof endorsed, were ordered to be recorded

Deld. J. KUHN       Teste JNO: CHEW Cl Cur H.


pp.  KNOW ALL MEN by these presents that I JAMES WEIR of the County of Spotsyl-
33-  vania Virginia in consideration of the sum of Three hundred & twenty pounds
34  Five shillings and Three pence Sterling to me in hand paid at and before the
   sealing and delivery of these presents by JAMES SOMERVILLE, Merchant of Fredericksburg, the receipt whereof I do hereby acknowledge, by these presents do bargain and sell unto sd. SOMERVILLE the following slaves; to wit, Moll, Jeanie, Jeanie the Child of Moll, Patty, Fanny the Child of Patty, George the Child of Phillis & Isaac which slaves are already sold and made over by said JAMES WEIR to the sd. SOMERVILLE by Bill of Sale dated the 13th day of July 1784 and recorded in the Court of Hustings for the Corporation of Fredericksburg on the Seventh day of March 1785; which will appear by the Record of said Court reffering thereto; And as a further security for the said Debt, by these presents do bargain & sell to the said SOMERVILLE the following

slaves, to wit, Lucy a Negro woman and her Children, Edmund, Suckey & Collin and
Nancy a slave with the increase of the aforementioned slaves and every of them and
the said JOHN WEIR for himself his heirs doth covenant and agree to and with said
SOMERVILLE his heirs that sd. JAMES WEIR now at the making and delivering of these
presents hath full right & lawfull authority to bargain and sell the slaves Mill, Jeanie,
Jeanie, Patty, Fanny, George and Isaac, also Lucy, Edmund, Suckey, Collin and Nancy
unto said SOMERVILLE in manner and form above expressed; and JAMES WEIR for himself his heirs the above named slaves unto the said SOMERVILLE his heirs will warrent
& for ever defend by these presents; In Witness whereof I have hereunto set my hand &
seal this 14th day of December  1787
Signed Sealed & Delivered in the presence of
    HENRY MITCHELL,                   JAMES  WEIR
    JOHN MILLEN,  GEORGE HUTCHERSON
 At a Court held for the Town and Corporation of Fredg. February 4th 1788
This Bill of Sale was proved by three witnesses thereto and ordered to be recorded
Exd. & Deld. J. SOMERVILLE         Teste JNO: CHEW C. C. H.


p.        THIS INDENTURE made the third day of December in the year of our Lord one
35      thousand seven hundred and Eighty seven; Witnesseth that GEORGE SWEATMAN
      of County of STAFFORD hath of his own free & voluntary will placed and bound
himself an Apprentice unto JAMES SMOCK, Sadler, of the Town of Fredericksburg to be
taught in the said Trade, Science or Occupation of a Sadler which said JAMES SMOCK now
useth; and with him as an Apprentice to dwell continue and serve from the day of the
date hereof unto the full end and term of Three years, three months & twenty days,
during which term the said Apprentice his said Master well & faithfully shall serve, his
secrets keep, his lawfull commands gladly do, hurt to his said Master he shall not doe
nor willingly suffer to be don by other but of the same to his power shall forthwith
give notice to his said Master, the goods of his said Master he shall not Imbezzel or waste
or lend them without his consent to any person whereby his Master may be damaged in
his own goods or the goods of others, at cards, dice or any other unlawfull games he
shall not play, Taverns or Ale Houses he shall not frequent, Matrimony he shall not
commit withint the said Term, he shall contract from the service of his said Master by
day or night, he shall not at any time depart or absent himself without his said Masters
leave; But in all things as a good and faithfull Apprentice shall demean and behave
himself towards his said Master and all his during the said Term, And the said Master
his said Apprentice the Trade, Science or Occupation of a Sadler with all things thereto
belonging shall and will teach and instruct or cause to be well & sufficiently taught
after the best way and manner that he can and shall also find and allow his said
Apprentice sufficient meat, drink washing lodging & apparel both Linen and Wollen &
allother necessarys fit and convenient for such an Apprentice during the term, And
the said Master doth promise to give his Apprentice Six months Schooling, the said
Apprentice to be under no one, corrected by any one during the said Term but his said
Master. In Witness whereof the parties to these presents have hereunto interchange-
ably set their hands and seals the day month & year first above written
Signed sealed & Delivered in presence of
    (no witnesses shown)            JAS. SMOCK
                         GEORGE his mark ✕ SWEATMAN
 At a Court held for the Town and Corporation of Fredg. Feby. 4th 1788
This Indenture of Apprenticeship was acknowledged by the parties and ordered to be
recorded             Teste JNO: CHEW Cl.

pp.     THIS INDENTURE made the 17th day of December in the year of our Lord one
36-    thousand seven hundred and Eighty seven Between JAMES TAYLOR, late of the
37      Town of ALEXANDRIA of the Commonwealth of Virginia, Merchant, of the one
        part and SAMUEL ABBOTT of the Town of Fredericksburg, Mercht., of the other
part; Witnesseth that JAMES TAYLOR in consideration of the sum of Two hundred and
fifty pounds current money to him in hand paid by SAMUEL ABBOTT at and before the
ensealing and delivery of these presents, by these presents doth bargain and sell unto
SAML ABOTT his heirs a certain lott or parcel of ground lying in Town of Fredericksburg, and described in the plan of said Town by No. 257, (and now in the tenure and
occupation of said SAML ABBOTT), bounded on the West by CAROLINE STREET, on the
North by PRUSIA STREET, on the East by JAMES HUNTER's Lott, and on the South by
JAMES HEATH's lott, which said lott of ground was sold and conveyed by JOHN WELCH
and NELLY his Indenture bearing date twenty sixth day of December 1782, and recorded
in the Clerks Office of the Corporation Court of Fredericksburg, and the moity of the sd.
SAMUEL RODDY was granted and conveyed to said JAMES TAYLOR by the said SAMUEL
RODDY and MARY his Wife by Indenture bearing date the fourth day of November in
the year of our Lord 1783 and recorded in the Clerks Office of the Corporation Court of
Fredericksburg, together with all houses streets lanes alleys profits commodities and
appertenances whatsoever belonging; To have and to hold the said lott of ground with
all the appertenances thereunto belonging unto SAMUEL ABBOTT his heirs; and the said
JAMES TAYLOR for himself his heirs doth covenant and agree to and with said SAMUEL
ABBOTT his heirs that SAMUEL ABBOTT his heirs shall peaceably and quietly hold and
possess all the granted premises with interruption or denial of said JAMES TAYLOR and
JAMES TAYLOR his heirs the said lott of ground unto SAMUEL ABBOTT his heirs against
the claims of every persons shall and will warrent and forever defend by these
presents; In Witness whereof JOSIAH WATSON of the Town of ALEXANDRIA by virtue of a
Power of Attorney to him granted by the said JAMES TAYLOR bearing date the 28th day
of October 1786, hath hereunto affixed the hand & seal of the sd. JAMES TAYLOR, the day
and year first above written
Sealed and Delivered in presence of us
     WM. WADDLE, B. HYDE,                   JAMES TAYLOR
     JAMES MADDEN
Received the day of the date of the above SAMUEL ABBOTT the sum of Two hundred and
fifty pounds current money of Virginia being in full of the consideration money
therein mentioned
Teste WM WADDLE.                       J. TAYLOR
     B. HYDE,  JAMES MADDEN
At a Court held for the Town and Corporation of Fredericksburg on Monday the 3rd day
of March 1788         This Indenture was proved by the oath of WILLIAM WADDLE,
BENJAMIN HYDE and JAMES MADDEN, the witnesses thereto, and ordered to be recorded
Exd. & Delivered S. ABBOTT       Teste JNO. CHEW JR. Cl Cur.

pp.     THIS INDENTURE made the 25th day of February in the year of our Lord one
38-    thousand seven hundred and Eighty eight Between the Honble. JAMES MERCER
39      of County of Spotsylvania, Executor and Devisee of Majr. ALEXANDER DICK, late
        of the Town of Fredericksburg deced, of the one part and WILLIAM LOTSPEICH of
the Town of FALMOUTH in the County of STAFFORD of the other part; Whereas CHARLES
DICK Esqr. was in his lifetime and at the time of his death seized and possessed of certain lotts of land in the Town of Fredericksburg being situate, as also other real and
personal Estate, and being so seized and possessed, made his last Will and Testament in

Writing and therein devised his whole Estate to the aforenamed ALEXANDER DICK his only Son and heir at Law in fee upon the express condition of his paying the debts of him the said CHARLES and the Legacies in the said Will mentioned; And Whereas the said ALEXANDER having entered into the said Estate devised to him by his said Father & the said ALEXANDER having in his life time taken upon the Execution of the said Will as may appear by his Will & Probate thereof now of Record among the Records of the Corpo: Court of the Town of Fredericksburg, departed this life on the 17th day of March 1785, seized and possessed of the same Estate so devised him by his Father, except so much thereof as he had disposed of by sale without having paid any of his Fathers Debts or Legacies & well knowing the same were considerable, & that he the said ALEXR. had contracted several Debts on his own account which were then due & owing, by his last Will and Testament bearing date (blank) 1785, devised his whole Estate & Interest both real and personal to the aforenamed JOHN MERCER in fee simple upon Trust, to wit, for the purpose of paying his own & his Fathers Debts with certain limitations over and appointed the said JAMES MERCER sole Executor thereof with power to secure the paymt. of the debts by sale mortgage or otherwise, as he the said JAMES MERCER should think proper, as by the said Will also of Record among the Records of the said last mentioned Court may also appear, And also whereas the debts of the said CHARLES being con-fessedly more than the value of the whole Estate & the Debts of the said ALEXANDER being also above the supposed value of the Estate of his own acquiring (then which however consisting of Locations or Entries for Lands on the Western Waters which would not sell previous to being Pattented and then at a price inferior to what they might raise at some future day) the said JAMES determined to sell and dispose of the proper Estate of said CHARLES in the first place (the same being then at its full value & more likely to fall than raise in value), and to that end the said JAMES MERCER adver-tized a sale of all the Estate which was of the said CHARLES in his lifetime & being in the Town of Fredg. and County of Spotsylva: in both the VIRGINIA GAZETTE & also in the PUBLIC PAPER in the State of MARYLAND, to be as on the sixth day of June which should be in the year of our Lord 1785; then next coming by way of public auction and upon Eighteen months credit; And Lastly, whereas the aforenamed WILLIAM LOTSPEICH at a public sale made persuant to the said advertisements became a Purchaser of a certain part of a lot in the Town of Fredericksburg situate and herein after particularly described (being part of the Estate which devised the sd. ALEXANDER DICK by his Father), for the price of Thirty eight pounds current money, the most that was bidden for the same, NOW THIS INDENTURE WITNESSETH that JAMES MERCER in consideration of the sum of Thirty eight pounds now reced., of the said WILLIAM LOTSPEICH pursuant to his Bond entered into at the day of the sale, by these presents doth bargain and sell unto WILLIAM LOTSPEICH all that lot of land so purchased at the sale aforementioned being the upper part of a lot known in the plan of the Town of Fredericksburg by number Five and bounded by WILLIAM STREET on the North West by SOPHIA STREET, on the South West and on the South East by one other part of said Lott No. 5, which the sd. ALEXANDER DICK sold and conveyed in his lifetime to a certain (blank) ARRELL of the Town of ALEXANDRIA and on the North East by the RIVER RAPPAHANNOCK; the part now sold to WILLIAM LOTSPEICH being the upper moiety of said lott No. 5; as to Length on the said Street called SOPHIA STREET and being as to breadth between the said Street last mentioned and the River whatever it may turn out, be the same more or less, so as that the said LOTSPEICHs part of said lott No. 5 shall extend along SOPHIA STREET as far as the lot number twenty three which lies next to and opposite to the same, to the South West and no more, so as to reserve to the aforenamed (blank) ARRELL & those who claim or hereafter may claim under him the lower moiety of lott No. 5; as to length on SOPHIA

STREET, that is to say, the same length as the lott numbered Twenty one which lies to the Southwest side of SOPHIA STREET & opposite to the part sold the said ARRELL, And also all Estate right title and demand of said JAMES MERCER in the premises; To have and to hold the said premises unto WILLIAM LOTSPEICH his heirs forever. In Witness whereof the aforenamed JAMES MERCER hath hereunto set his hand & affixed his seal the day & year first before written
Sealed & Delivered in presence of
     JNO: CHEW JR., JOHN T. BROOKE,        JS. MERCER
   JAMES LILLY, JAMES POTINGER,
   CHS. CARTER
  At a Court held for the Town and Corporation of Fredericksburg on the 3rd March 1788 JAMES MERCER Esqr. acknowledged this his Deed for Land to WILLIAM LOTSPEICH which is ordered to be recorded
Exd. & deld. WM. LOTSPEICH       Teste  JNO: CHEW JR., Cl Cur

p.     EXTRACT of a LETTER from Mr. WILLIAM HORNER dated in LONDON December
40     31st 1787 to CHARLES YATES, Fredericksburg, Virginia
     I am exceeding glad to find that Minney has so far given you satisfaction and as it was always my inclination that you should have him knowing him to be a good Servant and his inclination at the same time to serve you rather than any other person, I therefore willingly accepted of your offer and accordingly wrote to your Brother concerning it, who immediately remitted me a Bill for Fifty pounds Sterling which I received in this Town on the 15th ulto. Minney is therefore your Servant for the term of Ten years to commence from the 20th of June last during which time I hope he will proved a good and faithfull Servant and at the expiration of the said term of Ten years which will be on the 20th of June 1797, I give him his Freedom in consideration of his faithfull services and the dislike I have to Bondage
  At a Court held for the Town and Corpo. of Fredg. March 3d. 1788
This Extract of a Letter from WILLIAM HORNER to CHS. YATES Gent. is at the motion of said YATES ordered to be recorded

pp.    THIS INDENTURE made this 25th day of January in the year of our Lord one
40-   thousand seven hundred and Eighty eight Between GEORGE WEEDON and CATHE-
42    RINE his Wife of Town & Corporation of Fredericksburg in the County of Spotsyl-
     vania of one part and WALTER GREGORIE of the Town and County aforesd., of the other part; Witnessesth that GEORGE WEEDON and CATHERINE his Wife in consideration of the rents conditions and agreements in this Indenture contained on the part of sd. GEORGE GREGORIE to be paid and performed by these presents do bargain lease unto the sd. WALTER GREGORY his heirs a certain parcel of land lying in said Town and Corporation of Fredericksburg on CAROLINE STREET and being part of the Lott No. 26, Begining twenty one and a half feet below the upper corner of the sd. Lott No. 26 on CAROLINE STREET, thence running down sd. Street twenty one & a half feet, thence back and paralel with Lott No. 28 sixty six feet; thence up the sd. Lott paralel to CAROLINE STREET twenty one and a half feet, thence sixty six feet to the begining; To have and to hold the parcel of ground with the appertenances to said WALTER GREGORIE his heirs, yielding and paying from the first day of this present month (January) yearly unto GEORGE WEEDON his heirs the sum of Twelve pounds Eighteen shillings, one moiety of the sd. Sum on the first day of January and the other moiety on the first day of July in each year, and WALTER GREGORIE doth promise and grant with GEORGE WEEDON his heirs that he the said WALTER GREGORY his heirs will every year pay the aforesd. sum to be dis-

charged in Gold at the rate of Five shillings and four pence the penny weight or in
Silver at Six shillings & eight pence the ounce (any Act to the contrary to be made &
provided regulating the current exchange of the rate aforesaid shall in no wise or ever
effect the parties to these presents nowithstanding) And they the sd. GEORGE WEEDON
and CATHERINE his Wife do and each of them doth for themselves their heirs the said
WALTER GREGORIE his heirs paying and performing the covenants and agreements to
be performed shall at all time hold and possess the parcell of land without the
hindrance of them the sd. GEORGE WEEDON and CATHERINE his Wife their heirs or any
other person claiming under them (the growing taxes which may hereafter become
due excepted) In Witness whereof the sd. parties to these presents have interchangeably set their hands and affixed their seals the day & year above written
Sealed and Delivered in presence of
(CATHERINE WEEDON signed sealed &c. before us)
    CHS. MOIRTIMER,             G. WEEDON
    WILLIAM HARVEY           C. WEEDON
                              WALTER GREGORY

  The Commonwealth of Virginia to CHAS. MORTIMER, WILLIAM HARVEY & BENJA> DAY
Gent. of the Corporation of Fredg. Greeting; Whereas GEORGE WEEDON & CATHERINE his
Wife by their Deed of bargain and sale bearing date eht 25th day of January have
Leased and conveyed unto WALTER GREGORY one lott of land lying in Town of Fredg.
and Whereas the said CATHERINE cannot conveniently travel to our said Court of Hustings to make acknowledgment of the said conveyance (the Commission for the privy Examination of CATHERINE, the Wife of GEORGE WEEDON). Witness JOHN CHEW JUNR., Clerk of our
sd. Court this 7 day of April 1788 in the 12th year of the Commonwealth
                              JNO: CHEW JR.

  Corporation of Fredericksburg, to wit
  In Obedience to the within Commission, we the Subscribers have privately examined
the within named CATHERINE, Wife of GEORGE WEEDON, in the manner therein directed
who assents to the within conveyance by Lease forever, is willing the same should be
recorded; Given under our hands & seals this 7th April 1788
                        CHS. MORTIMER
                        WILLIAM HARVEY
  At a Court held for the Town & Corpo: of Fredg. April 7th 1788
This Deed of Lease was acknowledged by the parties and together with the Commission
annexed and Certificate of the Execution thereof endorsed were ordered to be recorded


p.       THIS INDENTURE made the 25th day of March in the year of our Lord one thou-
43      sand seven hundred and Eighty eight Between JOHN LEWIS & MARY his Wife of
        the Town of Fredericksburg of the one part and PHILIP EVANS of the same place
of the other part, Witnesseth that JOHN LEWIS and MARY his Wife in consideration of
the sum of Seventy nine pounds current money of Virginia to them in hand paid by sd.
PHILIP EVANS at & before the sealing and delivery hereof, by these presents doth bargain sell and confirm unto PHILIP EVANS and to his heirs all the Estate right title and
demand whatsoever either in Law or Equity which they the sd. JOHN LEWIS & MARY his
Wife now have or may hereafter have in two certain lotts of ground lying in the Town
of Fredg. and marked in the plan of the sd. Town No. 104. bounded by CHARLES & HAWK
STREETs and No. 168 bounded by CHARLES STREET, Together also with all the improvements streets passages rights liberties and appertenances thereunto belonging; To
have and to hold the sd. bargained & sold premises with the appertenances unto PHILIP
EVANS his heirs and JOHN LEWIS & MARY his Wife for themselves their heirs doth

covenant and promise PHILIP EVANS his heirs that JOHN LEWIS & MARY his Wife &
their heirs the hereby bargained and sold premises will warrant and forever defend by
these presents; In Witness whereof the sd. parties to these presents have interchange-
ably set their hands and seals hereunto the day and year first above written
Sealed and Delivered in the presence of
    WILLIAM LOVELL,                          JOHN LEWIS
     JOS: CHRISTY,  G. HEISKELL          MARY ANNE LEWIS
 Reced. the day of the date of the within written Indenture from the within named
PHILIP EVANS Seventy nine pounds current money of Virginia being in full of the
consideration within mentioned
Teste WILLIAM LOVELL                        JOHN LEWIS
 At a Court held for the Town and Corporation of Fredericksburg  April 7th  1788
This Indenture for Lotts from JNO: LEWIS to PHILIP EVANS was proved by two witnesses
thereto & ordered to be certified
 At a Court held for the said Corporation October the 6th 1788
This Indenture further proved by another witness thereto and ordered to be recorded


p.     The Commonwealth of Virginia to CHARLES MORTIMER,  WILLIAM HARVEY &
44    GEO: FRENCH of the Corporation of Fredg., Gent., Whereas JOHN BENSON &
     ELEANOR his Wife by their certain Deed of bargain and sale bearing date the
24th day of December 1787 have sold and conveyed unto RICHD. PEACOCK the fee simple
Estate of one half of the lott of land lying and being in the Corpo: afsd., & numbered in
the plan of the said Town 11.11, And Whereas the said ELEANOR cannot conveniently
travel to our said Hustings Court to make acknowledgment of the said conveyance (the
Commission for the privy Examination of ELEANOR, the Wife of JOHN BENSON), Witness JOHN
CHEW JR., Clk. of our sd. Court this 3rd May  1788     JNO: CHEW JR.
 In Obedience to the within Commission to us directed, we the Subscribers have privately examined the within named ELEANOR, Wife of the sd. J. BENSON in the manner
therein directed, who assents to the bargain therein mentioned and is willing the same
should be recorded; Given under our hands and seals this 3rd of May  1788
                     CHS. MORTIMER
Truly recorded                              WILLIAM HARVEY
    Teste  JNO: CHEW JR., Cl Cur.


p.     The Commonwealth of Virginia to CHARLES MORTIMER,  GEORGE FRENCH &
45    BENJA: DAY of the Corporation of Fredericksburg Gent., Greeting; Whereas JOHN
     LEWIS and MARY ANN his Wife by their certain Deed of bargain and sale dated
the 1st day of January last have sold and conveyed unto JOHN FERNEYHOUGH one certain
lott of ground in the Corporation aforesaid and known by the number 68, And whereas
the said MARY ANN cannot conveniently travel to our said Corporation Court to make
acknowledgment of the said conveyance (the Commission for the privy Examination of MARY
ANN, the Wife of JOHN LEWIS); Witness  JOHN CHEW JR., Clerk of our said Court this 7th day
of March 1788 in the 12th year of the Commonwealth        JNO: CHEW JR.
 Corporation of Fredericksburg Sct.
 In Obedience to the within Commission to us directed, we the Subscribers have privately examined the within named MARY ANN LEWIS, Wife of JOHN LEWIS, in the manner therein directed who assents to the bargain and sale therein containing and is wil-
ling the same be recorded, Certified this 29th day of March 1788
                     GEO: FRENCH
Truly recorded Teste  JNO: CHEW JR., Cl Cur.        BENJA: DAY
Exd. & Deld. JNO. FERNEYHOUGH

pp.      TO ALL TO WHOM these presents shall come, JAMES INNES and JAMES BEVERIDGE
46-      of the City of LONDON, Merchants and Partners carrying on Trade under the
48       firm or title of INNES BEVERIDGE and COMPANY severally send Greeting: Know
         ye that JAMES INNES and JAMES BEVERIDGE by these presents do and each of
them doth make appoint & fully impower ROBERT DUNLOP of LONDON, Merchant, now
shortly bound to North America, tob e their true and lawfull Attorney for them in their
names to ask demand recover and receive all such sums of money debts goods wares
merchandize and effects whatsoever as is are shall be due owing payable or belonging
to them and if needful to commence sue & prosecute to final Judgment &c. any action
touching the premises, to give sign execute and sufficient acquittances & discharges
for the same promising hereby to ratify and confirm all ROBERT DUNLOP shall lawfully
do or cause to be done concerning the premises; In Witness whereof the said JAMES
INNES and JAMES BEVERIDGE have hereunto severally set their hands and seals the 20th
day of July 1787
Sealed and delivered in presence of
        GEORGE  JOYNER                            JAMES  INNES
                                                  JAMES  BEVERIDGE
    GEORGE JOYNER, Clerk to JAMES SUTHERLAND of BIRCHIN LANE in the City of LONDON,
Notary Public, maketh oath and saith that he was present and did see JAMES INNES and
ROBERT BEVERIDGE of the City of LONDON, Merchants and Partners carrying on trade
under the firm of INNES BEVERIDGE and COMPANY sign seal and deliver the Deed Poll or
Letter of Attorney hereunto annexed to ROBERT DUNLOP, In Testimony thereof this Deponent doth subscribe his name as witness to the Execution of the sd. Deed Poll or Letter
of Attorney
Sworn at LONDON the 1st day of August  1787                GEO: JOYNER
  before me THO: SAINSBURY, Mayor
    I JAMES SUTHERLAND, Notary Public, dwelling in LONDON duly admitted and sworn, do
hereby certify and attest that I was present and did see GEORGE JOYNER, the Deponent
named in the affidavit hereto annexed set and subscribe his name thereunto and afterwards on the Holy Evangelists of Almighty God solemnly declare to be true the several
things in the sd. affidavit mentioned before the Right Honourable THOMAS SAINSBURY
Esquire, Lord Mayor of the City of London
              SEAL                                JAS. SUTHERLAND, Not. Pub.
    To all to whom these presents shall come I THOMAS SAINSBURY Esqr., Lord Mayor of
LONDON, do hereby certifie that on the day of the date hereof personally came and
appeared before me, GEORGE JOYNER, the Deponent named in the affidavit hereunto
annexed being a person well known and worthy of good credit and by solemn oath
which the said Deponent took upon the Holy Evangelists of Almighty God did solemnly
declare to be true the several matters mentioned in the sd annexed affidavit
    Dated in LONDON the 1st day of August in the year of our Lord one thousand seven
hundred & Eighty seven                            BEACH
    At a Court of Hustings held for the Town & Corporaltion of Fredericksburg on Monday
June 2nd 1788.        This Power of Attorney from JAMES INNIS & JAMES BEVERIDGE of
the City of LONDON, Merchants & Partners, to ROBERT DUNLOP, with the proof and acknowledgment thereof before THOMAS SAINSBURY Esqr. Lord Mayor of the City of LON-
DON and also the Certificate signed by JAMES SUTHERLAND Esqr., Notary Public, of sd.
City are ordered to be recorded
Exd. & deld. Mr. H. MITCHELL            Teste   JNO: CHEW JR., C. C. H.,

pp.      THIS INDENTURE made the 14th day of June in the year of our Lord one thou-
49-      sand seven hundred and Eighty eight Between JOHN BAYLOR of NEW MARKETT
50      and County of CAROLINE Gent. of the one part and GEORGE FRENCH of the Town of
Fredericksburg and County of Spotsylvania, Phisician, of the other part;  Witnesseth that JOHN BAYLOR in consideration of the rents and covenants herein after
mentioned on the part of said GEORGE FRENCH to be paid and performed, hath granted
and to farm let unto GEORGE FRENCH his heirs one certain part of a lott of land in the
Town of Fredericksburg containing Twenty feet front on CAROLINE STREET and running back thirty four feet and adjoins the House now occupied by MRS. PATTERSON, and
that Lott now occupied by JOHN LEGG together with all profits commodities and appertenances belonging;  To have and to hold the part of a lott unto GEORGE FRENCH his
heirs from the 14th day of July next ensuing the date hereof during the term of Fifteen
years paying unto JOHN FRENCH his heirs on the 14th day of July each year the yearly
rent of one shilling current money of Virginia if demanded and GEORGE FRENCH doth in
consideration of the premises agree to build upon the lott of ground one house twenty
feet in front & sixteen feet back one story high as also a shed twenty feet long & ten
feet wide to be finished in a substantial workman like manner In Witness whereof the
parties to these presents have hereunto set their hands & seals the day & year first
above written
Sealed and Delivered in the presence of
  Witness to GEO: FRENCH acknowledgment          JOHN BAYLOR
      WILLIAM HARVEY,  JAMES GILLES          GEO: FRENCH
  At a Court held for the Town and Corporation of Fredericksburg on Monday July 7th
1788   This Deed of Lease was acknowledged by the parties and ordered to be recorded
Examd. & deld. GEO: FRENCH       Teste   JNO: CHEW C. C. H.

pp.      THIS INDENTURE made the 24th day of June in the year of our Lord one thou-
50-      sand seven hundred & Eighty eight Between JOHN BENSON of the Town of
51      Fredericksburg and ELEANOR his Wife of one part and WALTER PAYNE of said
      Town of other part;  Witnesseth that JOHN BENSON and ELEANOR his Wife in con-
sideration of the sum of One hundred pounds current money of Virginia by said WAL-
TER PAYNE unto JOHN BENSON in hand paid before the sealing and delivery of these
presents; by these presents doth bargain sell and confirm unto WALTER PAYNE his
heirs part of the lott of ground in Town of Fredericksburg known by the name of Lott
number Eleven Eleven (11.11), adjoining ground sold by JOHN BENSON and ELEANOR his
Wife unto RICHARD PEACOCK and being also a part of the above mentioned lott number
Eleven Eleven (11.11) containing in front on PRINCESS ANN STREET Thirty nine feet
and to extend back its full breadth of thirty nine feet, the distance of onehundred and
thirty two feet being the whole depth of my Lott on PRINCESS ANN STREET, whereof this
was a part, Together with all buildings gardens and trees; To have and to hold the said
lott with the appertenances unto WALTER PAYNE his heirs and JOHN BENSON and
ELEANOR his Wife for themselves their heirs do agree they will warrant and forever
defend the lott and premises unto WALTER PAYNE his heirs against the claims of all
persons whatsoever; In Witness whereof JOHN BENSON and ELEANOR his Wife have
hereunto set their hands & seals the day & year above written
Signed Sealed and Delivered in presence of
      JOHN COAKLEY,           JOHN BENSON
      WILLIAM WINSLOW
  Received the day & year within written from the within named WALTER PAYNE the
sum of One hundred pounds being the whole consideration money within mentione

JOHN COAKLEY, WILLIAM WINSTON                    JOHN BENSON
At a Court held for the Town and Corporation of Fredg. July 7th 1788
This Indenture was acknowledged by the said JOHN BENSON and ordered to be recorded
Exd. & Deld. WM. PAYNE                    Teste    JNO: CHEW JR., Cl Cur.


pp.        THIS INDENTURE made this 18th day of December in the year of our Lord one
52-        thousand seven hundred and Eighty seven Between ROBERT SCOTT & JEAN SCOTT
54         his Wife of County of Spotsylvania of one part & JOHN BROWNLOW of Town of
           Fredericksburg of County aforesd., of other part Witnesseth that ROBERT SCOTT
and JEAN his Wife in consideration of the sum of Nine hundred pounds current money
of Virginia to receipt whereof is hereby acknowledged by these presents do each of
them bargain & sell unto JOHN BROWNLOW his heirs the upper half of two lotts or half
acre of ground situate and lying in Town and Corporation of Fredericksburg and known
by the numbers 79 and 80, and bounded, Westerly by CAROLINE STREET, 82 1/2 feet,
Northerly by the Lotts No. 81 & 82; 264 feet; Easterly by SOPHIA STREET 82 1/2 feet, and
Southerly by the aforesaid two lotts 79 and 80, 264 feet; together with all houses priviledges and appertenances belonging; To have and to hold the premises with appertenances unto JOHN BROWNLOW his heirs, and ROBERT SCOTT and JEAN his Wife their
heirs and every other person claiming under them will forever warrant and defend
the said hereby bargained and sold premises unto JOHN BROWNLOW his heirs; In Witness whereof ROBERT SCOTT and JEANE his Wife have hereunto set their hands and
affixed their seals the day & year first above written
Sealed & Delivered in presence of
           WILLIAM WIATT,                              ROBERT SCOTT
           FRANCIS TOMPKINS, RICHARD SIMCOCK           JANE SCOTT
 Fredg. 18th December 1787. Received of JOHN BROWNLOW the sum of Nine hundred
pounds current money of Virginia being in full of the consideration within mentioned
Witness WM. WIATT, FRANCIS TOMPKINS,                   ROBT. SCOTT
           RICHD. SIMCOCK
The Commonwealth of Virginia to BEVERLEY WINSLOW, JOSEPH BROCK & JAMES LEWIS
of County of Spotsylvania Gent., Gent. ((The Commission for the privy Examination of JEAN, the
Wife of ROBERT SCOTT), Witness JOHN CHEW JR., Clerk of our said Court this 24th day of
June 1788 in the 12th year of the Commonwealth          JNO: CHEW JR.
 In Obedience to the within Commission we this day privately examined the within
named JANE SCOTT (the return of the Execution of the privy Examination of JANE SCOTT); Certi-
fied this 2d. day of July 1788                          JOSEPH BROCK
                                                        JAS: LEWIS
 At a Court held for the Town and Corporation of Fredg., July 7th 1788
This Indenture was proved by three of the witnesses thereto and together with the
Commission annexed and Certificate of the Execution thereof endorsed, were ordered to
be recorded
Exd. & Deld. JNO: BROWNLOW          Teste    JNO: CHEW JR., C. C. H.


pp.        THIS INDENTURE made the 22nd day of July in year of our Lord one thousand
55-        seven hundred and Eighty eight Between JOHN LEWIS of Town of Fredericksburg
56         and County of Spotsylvania, Eldest Son and heir at Law of FIELDING LEWIS, late
           of same place Esqr. deced., and one of the acting Executors of said FIELDING
LEWIS deced., of one part and GUINN PAGE of same County Esqr., of other part. Whereas
FIELDING LEWIS deced. in his lifetime having bargained and sold unto MANN PAGE of
MANSFIELD in aforesaid County, Esqr., since deceased, eight certain lotts or half acres

of land lying in Town of Fredericksburg for the consideration of One hundred and sixty pounds current money, which FIELDING LEWIS received, and MANN PAGE in consequence of said purchased entered into possession from time of the purchase to time of his death and being so seized made his last Will and Testament in Writing now of Record in County Court of Spotsylvania and therein devised the said Eight lotts to his Son, the aforenamed GUINN, his heirs; And whereas Deeds of conveyance for said Eight lotts never having been made to said MANN PAGE in his lifetime by FIELDING LEWIS whereby the title still remained in said FIELDING LEWIS and whereas FIELDING LEWIS dyed so intitled having before his death duly made and published his last Will and Testament in writing now also of Record in the aforesaid County Court, and therein having devised all the lotts unto JOHN LEWIS, party to these presents in fee simple, whereby the legal Interest of FIELDING LEWIS in the eight lotts so sold to MANN PAGE became vested in the said JOHN LEWIS, NOW THIS INDENTURE WITNESSETH that JOHN LEWIS in consideration of the premises and the intent that the title of said GUINN PAGE (agreeable to the devise of MANN PAGE) in said eight lotts may be fully confirmed, in consideration of the sum of Twenty shillings current money to JOHN LEWIS in hand paid by GUINN PAGE by these presents JOHN LEWIS doth bargain and sell unto GUINN PAGE his heirs all the eight lotts or half acres of ground aforementioned being two whole squares numbered 149, 150, 151 and 152; and bounded by FAUQUIER STREET, PRINCE EDWARD STREET, HAWKE STREET and the back line of the Town; And JOHN LEWIS and his heirs shall warrent and defend against the claims of all persons, In Witness whereof JOHN LEWIS hath hereunto set his hand and seal the day & year first above written
Sealed and delivered in presence of
     WILLIAM LEWIS,                              JOHN LEWIS
     JNO: CHEW JR., JOHN MINOR JR.
 At a Court of Hustings held for the Town and Corporation of Fredericksburg on Monday the 1st of September 1788        This Indenture for Lotts from JOHN LEWIS to GUINN PAGE was proved by three witnesses thereto and ordered to be recorded

pp.     THIS INDENTURE made the Second day of June in the year one thousand seven
57-    hundred and Eighty eight Between JOHN ATKINSON of Town of Fredericksburg
58     and MARGARETT his Wife of one part and CHARLES YATES, EDMUND WINDER
       and CHARLES MORTIMER of the same place of other part; Witnesseth that JOHN ATKINSON & MARGARETT his Wife in consideration of the sum of Five pounds to them paid, do by these presents bargain and sell unto CHARLES YATES, EDMUND WINDER and CHARLES MORTIMER their heirs all that part of a lott number Forty three in Town of Fredericksburg which was sold and conveyed by GEORGE MITCHELL to JOHN ATKINSON by Deed dated the 20th day of March 1771, and recording in the County Court of Spotsylvania, and which is bounded, Begining at the lower or Southeast Corner of said Lott on CAROLINE STREET being the uper corner of a lott called LONG ORDINARY LOTT, thence with the same Westward one hundred and thirty two feet to the Lotts called the COURT-HOUSE LOTTS, thence with the same thirty seven feet & one half, thence in a direction nearly parralell with the first Course to CAROLINE STREET, so as to make the last Course upon & along the said Street to the begining; a distance of thirty three feet; together with all houses gardens profits & hereditaments to the same belonging; To have and to hold the said aprt of the lott unto CHARLES YATES, EDMUND WINDER and CHARLES MORTIMER their heirs upon Trust that they or any two of them shall as soon as convenient sell and dispose of said part of the lott afsd. at public auction for the best price that can be gotten therefor on twelve months Credit having first given reasonable notice of the time and place of such sale and out of the money arising therefrom the said Trustees do

pay unto the several persons their Exers. or assigns agreeable to the annexed list, the sums of money respectively affixed to their names as soon as the purchase money can be collected; And JOHN ATKINSON doth hereby impower the Trustees to make good and sufficient Deeds or Conveyances to the purchasers; In Witness whereof the parties have hereunto interchangeably set their hands & affixed their seals the day & year first within written
Sealed and delivered in presence of

    ALEXR: ROANE JR.,                    JOHN ATKINSON
    ROBT. GILLIS                         MARGRET her mark X ATKINSON
    CHS. ATKINSON                        CHS. YATES
                                         EDMD. WINDER
                                         CHS. MORTIMER

  THOMAS MIDDLETON a Bond assigned to him by ARCHIBLD. McCALL amount with Credits deducted exclusive of any interest which is to be added L. 213...18...4.
  At a Court of Hustings held for the Town and Corporation of Fredericksburg September 1st 1788        This Deed of Trust from JNO: ATKINSON and MARGRET his Wife to CHS. YATES, EDMD. WINDER & CHS. MORTIMER was proved by three witnesses thereto and acknowledged by the said MARGRETT, she being first privately examined and ordered to be recorded
Examined and sent Mr. YATES by R. B. CHEW        Teste JNO: CHEW, Cl Cur


p.      THIS INDENTURE made and entered into this 31st day of December in year of our
58      Lord one thousand seven hundred and Eighty seven Between CHARLES CARTER
        of County of Spotsylvania of one part and TULLY WHITHURST of same County of other part; Witnesseth that CHARLES CARTER in consideration of the sum of Three pounds Twelve shillings current money annually, the receipt whereof the said CHARLES CARTER doth acknowledge, by these presents doth bargain and sell unto TULLY WHITHURST nine and a half feet in front adjoining the Lott leased by GEORGE McCUTCHAN from said CHARLES CARTER to be extended One hundred and thirty two feet back, lying in Town of Fredericksburg, together with all houses gardens, trees water profits and appertenances thereunto belonging; To have and to hold the granted premises during the full term of Twenty years commencing from the date of these presents; In Witness whereof we bind ourselves each to the other in the penal sum of Five hundred pounds current money to be paid by the first failure, In Testimony whereof we have fixed our hands & seal the date above mentioned
Signed Sealed and Ackd., in presence of

    BENJA: ELLIS,                        CHARLES CARTER,
    JNO: HAMILTON,  WILLM. PAYNE         TULLY WHITHURST

  At a Court of Hustings held for the Town and Corporation of Fredericksburg September the 1st 1788   This Deed of Lease from CHARLES CARTER to TULLY WHITHURST was proved by two witnesses thereto and ordered to be certified


pp.     THIS INDENTURE made the 15th day of April in the year One thousand seven
60-     hundred and Eighty eight Between JOSEPH JONES of County of KING GEORGE of
61      one part and WILLIAM BANKHEAD of County of WESTMORELAND of other part;
        Witnesseth that JOSEPH JONES in consideration of the sum of Five hundred pounds in hand paid by WILLIAM BANKHEAD, by these presents doth bargain sell & make over unto WILLIAM BANKHEAD his heirs all that lott of ground in Town of Fredericksburg being number in the platt (blank) lying between the lots numbered (blank) now in occupation of JAMES MUNROE and Doctr. LAWRENCE BROOKE with the

buildings and Improvements thereon together with an unfinished House now on the lott occupied by the said JAMES MUNROE and which is to be moved and place on Lott No. (blank). To have and to hold the said lot with the rights and appertenances thereunto belonging (the rents thereof due to the date hereof excepted) unto WM. BANKHEAD his heirs; said JOSEPH JONES doth covenant that the same is now free and clear of all charges and encumbrances whatsoever and will warrent and forever defend. In Witness whereof JOSEPH JONES hath hereunto set his hand and seal the day and year above written

Sealed and Delivered in the presence of

    JNO: CHEW JR.,                                    JOS: JONES
    WILLIAM WIATT, THOS: COCHRAN

At a Court of Hustings held for the Town and Corporation of Fredg. Octo. 6th  1788 This Indenture was proved by three of the witnesses thereto and ordered to be recorded

pp.      THIS INDENTURE witnesseth that JOHN PARKER hath put himself and by these
61-    presents with the consent of the Worshipfull Court of Hustings for the Corpora-
62     tion of Fredericksburg doth voluntarily and of his own free will put himself Apprentice to JOSEPH CHRISTY of the Corpo. of Fredg., to learn his trade and mystery and after the manner of an Apprentice to serve JOS: CHRISTY from the day of the date hereof during the full term of Six years; And the said Master shall use the utmost of his deneavours to teach or cause to be taught and instructed the said Apprentice in the Trade and mystery of a Hatter and teach sd JOHN PARKER in reading writing and arithmatick within the said Term and for the true performance of the covenants and agreements the parties bind themselves each to the other firmly by these presents, In Witness whereof the parties have interchangeabley set their hands and seals hereunto dated the 6th day of Octr. in the year of our Lord  1788

Sealed and delivered in presence of                      JOS: CHRISTY
    (no witnesses shown)                               JOHN  his mark  X  PARKER

At a Court of Hustings held for the Town and Corporation of Fredericksburg October 6th 1788        This Indenture of Apprenticeship was acknowledged by the parties, approved of by the Court, and ordered to be recorded

pp.      THIS INDENTURE made this 16th day of June in year of our Lord one thousand
62-    seven hundred and Eighty Eight between WILLIAM JACKSON of Town of
63     Fredericksburg, Gentleman, of one part and JAMES BROWN SENR. and HENRY WHITE of Town aforesaid of other part; Witnesseth that WILLIAM JACKSON in consideration of the Rents and Covenants herein after mentioned on the part of JAMES BROWN SENR. and HENRY WHITE to be paid and performed, hath demised and to farm lett unto JAMES BROWN SENR. and HENRY WHITE their heirs one certain part of a lott of land in Town of Fredericksburg lying between the Houses at present occupied by SAMUEL ABBOTT & YATES & LOVELL and containing Fifty seven feet front on CAROLINE STREET and extending the full breadth back to the next paralel street, To have and to hold the part of a lott with the appertenances unto JAMES BROWN SENR. and HENRY WHITE their heirs from the first day of December last past during the term of Twenty one years paying unto WILLIAM JACKSON his heirs on the first day of December each year the yearly rent of Twenty pounds current money of Virginia; In Witness whereof the parties have hereunto sett their hands and seals the day and year first mentioned

Sealed and delivered in the presence of

    WILLIAM LOVELL,                                    WILLIAM JACKSON
    ROBT. WALKER,                                      JAMES BROWN
    THOMAS SIMPSON                                     HENRY WHITE

At a Court held for the Town and Corporation of Fredericksburg October 6th 1788
This Deed was proved by three witnesses thereto and ordered to be recorded
Teste JNO: CHEW JR. C. C. H.


p.      THIS INDENTURE made this 21st day of February in year of our Lord one thou-
63      sand seven hundred and Eighty eight Between MICHAEL RYAN of County of
        Spotsylvania of one part and DANIEL McCARTY of County of WESTMORELAND of
other part; Witnesseth that MICHAEL RYAN in consideration of the sum of Five shillings to him in hand paid by DANIEL McCARTY by these presents doth bargain and sell
unto DANL: McCARTY and his heirs a lott of land lying in and being parcel of a tract of
land purchased by MICHAEL RYAN of Doctr. CHAS. MORTIMER and lately laid off for a
Town called & known by the name of NEW MARKETT containing Forty feet on SECOND
STREET and runing quite back to the Third Street bounded on the South by a Lot of
GENERAL ALEXANDER SPOTSWOOD and by a Lott of CAPT. PRESLY THORNTON's on the
North, Together with all houses ways, priviledges commodities and appertenances belonging; To have and to hold the said lott and every of their members and appertenances unto DANL. McCARTY and his heirs, And MICHAEL RYAN for him and his heirs
the said premises against all persons to DANL. McCARTY his heirs will warrent and
forever defend; In Witness whereof the said MICHAEL RYAN hath hereunto set his
hand and seal the day & year first above written in presence of
Witness  JOHN W. WILLIS                              M. RYAN
        JNO: RICHARDS,  JOHN DOWSON
 At a Court of Hustings held for the Town and Corporation of Fredericksburg Octr. 6
1788    This Indenture for a Lott from MICHAEL RYAN to DANL. McCARTY was acknowledged by the sd. RYAN and ordered to be recorded
Exd. & deld. Mr. JOHN RYBURN for Mr. McCARTY      Teste  JNO: CHEW  C.C. H


p.      THIS INDENTURE made the 21st day of February in the year of our Lord one
64      thousand seven hundred and Eighty eight Between MICHAEL RYAN of County of
        Spotsylvania of one part and PRESLEY THORNTON of County of NORTHUMBER-
LAND of other part; Witnesseth that MICHAEL RYAN in consideration of Five shillings
in hand paid by PRESLEY THORNTON by these presents doth bargain and sell unto
PRESLEY THORNTON his heirs a lott of land lying in and being part of a tract of land
purchased by MICHAEL RYAN of Doctr. CHARLES MORTIMER & lately laid off for a Town
called NEW MARKETT, the said lott containing forty feet front on SECOND STREET
running back within paralel lines quite to THIRD STREET bounded on the South by
DANL. McCARTYs lott and on the North by lotts No.. 7, 15, 17 & 29; together with all lands
common of pasture, profits and appertenances belonging; To have and to hold the said
lott with the appertenances unto PRESLEY THORNTON his heirs, And MICHAEL RYAN for
himself and his heirs the said lott to the said PRESLEY THORNTON his heirs will warrent
and forever defend by these presents; In Witness whereof MICHAEL RYAN hath hereunto set his hand and seal the day & year first above written, In presence of
Witness  JOHN W. WILLIS,                             M. RYAN
        J. DAWSON, JNO: RICHARDS
 At a Court of Hustings held for the Town & Corporation of Fredericksburg Octr. 6th
1788, This Indenture for Lotts from MICHAEL RYAN to PRESLEY THORNTON was acknowledged by the sd. MICHL. RYAN & ordered to be recorded


pp.     THIS INDENTURE made this 28th day of June in year of our Lord one thousand
65-     seven hundred and Eighty eight Between CHARLES URQUHART and FANNY his
66      Wife of Town of Fredericksburg of one part and WILLIAM LOVELL of the Town

aforesd. Witnesseth that CHARLES URQUHART and FANNY his Wife in consideration of
the sum of Ninety pounds Specie by WILLIAM LOVELL to CHARLES URQUHART and
FANNY his Wife in hand paid by these presents do bargain sell and confirm unto
WILLIAM LOVELL his heirs part of a lott of ground in Town of Fredericksburg which is
numbered 77, begining at the South corner of the lott now owned by WILLIAM LOVELL
which he purchased of RICHARD KENNY, runing thence one hundred and ten feet
along SOPHIA STREET until it joins the corner of Lott No. 75; thence along the line that
devides Lotts No. 77 and 75 one hundred and twenty five feet to the corner of an Alley
that devides Lott 77 from Lott 78, thence along the said Alley one hundred and ten feet
until it joins the South boundary of the lott sold by RICHARD KENNY to said WILLIAM
LOVELL and thence to the begining; Together with all houses, stables, gardens, profits
and appurtenances to the same belonging; To have and to hold the said part of a lott of
ground with the appertenances unto WILLIAM LOVELL his heirs and CHARLES URQU-
HART and FANNY his Wife for themselves their heirs do agree to warrant and forever
defend against the claim of all persons; In Witness whereof the said CHARLES URQU-
HART and FANNY his Wife have hereunto sett their hands and seals the day & year first
above written
Sealed and Delivered in presence of
     G. HIESKELL,                           CHAS. URQUHART
     JAMES BROWN JR., JAMES BROWN SENR.    FINNELLA URQUHART
  At a Court of Hustings held for the Town and Corporation of Fredericksburg October
6th 1788      This Indenture p. Lott from CHAS. URQUHART to WILLIAM LOVELL was
proved by three witnesses thereto and ordered to be recorded
Examd. & deld. W. LOVELL               Teste   JNO: CHEW JR., C. C. H.


pp.      THIS INDENTURE made this 31st day of January Anno Domini one thousand
66-      seven hundred and Eighty eight Between CHAS. URQUHART and RICHARD KENNY
67       Trustees of BENJAMIN WICKS of Town of Fredericksburg, of one part and FON-
         TAINE MAURY of the aforesaid Town of other part; Witnesseth that CHAS. and
RICHARD in consideration of the sum of Two hundred and Eighty four pounds Virginia
money to them in hand paid by FONTAINE MAURY by these presents do bargain and sell
unto FONTAINE MAURY his heirs all that parcel of ground containing one quarter of an
acre of land being in Town of Fredericksburg and knwon by Lott number 133; which
was purchased by MICHAEL ROBINSON in his lifetime, together with the Lott No. 134, of
JAMES DUNCANSON, the said parcel of ground hereby transferred being bounded, begining at JOHN LEGG's Corner of Lott No. 133, thence along CHARLES STREET to Lott 135;
thence running back to corner of the lotts No. 134 & 136, thence along one half of lott
134 to JOHN LEGG's Lott, & thence along JOHN LEGG's lott to the begining, comprehending the compleat half of the aforesd. Lott No. 133; with all houses orchards profits &
hereditaments to said premises belonging; To have and to hold the premises with every
appertenances unto FONATAINE MAURY his heirs, And the said CHARLES and RICHARD
for them and their heirs the said premises against all persons to FONTAINE MAURY his
heirs will warrent and forever defend by these presents; In Witness whereof the said
parties have hereunto affixed their hands & seals the year & day above said
Signed sealed and delivered in presence of
     JNO: CHEW JR., as to R. K.                    CHAS: URQUHART
     EDMD. BERKELEY JR. as to do.                  R. D. KENNY
     BEVERLEY CHEW as to R. K.
  At a Court of Hustings held for the Town and Corporation of Fredg. Octr. 6th 1788
This Indenture for Lott from CHAS. URQUHART & RICHD. KENNY to FONTAINE MAURY
was acknowledged by the sd. URQUHART, And at at Court held for the Corporation

December 2d. 1788, This Indenture was proved by the oath of three witnesses as to the
Execution of the said KENNY and ordered to be recorded
Examined & deld. FONTAINE MAURY          Teste  JNO: CHEW C.C.H.

p.        LIST of MEMBERS belonging to the VIGILANT FIRE COMPANY of the Corpora-
68        tion of Fredericksburg                    18th Octr. 1788

| | | |
|---|---|---|
| ROBERT PATTON | JAMES PETTIGREW | JOHN WELCH |
| WM. McWILLIAMS | THOMAS MILLEN | WILLIAM PEARSON |
| CHARLES URQUHART | JAMES SLATOR | DAVID HENDERSON |
| JOHN RICHARDS | JOHN FERNEYHOUGH | FIELDING LUCAS |
| WILLIAM SMITH | RICHARD SIMCOCK | STANDISH FORD |
| FONTAINE MAURY | THOMAS COCHRAN | CHS. CROUGHTON |
| JOHN MUNFORD | ELIEZER CALLENDER | |
| ROBERT GALLOWAY | WILLIAM WIATT | WILLIAM WIATT |
| JOSEPH CHRISTIE | LEONARD PATTERSON | Secry. to the |
| JOHN NEWTON | JAMES POTTINGER | VIGILANT FIRE DE- |
| RICHARD GARNER | JOHN DALRYPLE | PARTMENT |
| TULLY WHITHURST | JOHN CALLENDER | |
| JOHN PROUDFIT | WILLIAM FRENCH | |
| TIMOTHY GREEN | ZACHY. LUCAS | |
| THOMAS MIDDLETON | ELISHA HALL | |
| EDWARD ROBERTS | BENJAMIN DAY | |
| WILLIAM S. STONE | JOHN LEGG | |
| WALTER GREGORY | GODLOVE HIESKELL | |

pp.        THIS INDENTURE made the 3rd day of April in year of our Lord one thousand
69-        seven hundred and Eighty eight and the Twelvth year of AMERICAN INDEPEN-
71         DENCE between JOHN LEWIS of the Corporation of Fredericksburg and MARY
           ANN his Wife of one part and JOHN CALLENDER of said Corporation of other part;
Witnesseth that in consideration of the sum of Fifty pounds in hand paid by JOHN CAL-
LENDER by these presents JOHN LEWIS and MARY ANN his Wife do bargain sell and confirm unto JNO: CALLENDER and his heirs all that lott or half acre of land lying in the
Corporation of Fredg., No. (103), bounded Easterly by PRINCESS ANNE STREET and
Southerly by HAWKE STREET, together with all houses and buildings thereon; To have
and to hold the parcel of land unto JOHN CALLENDER his heirs and JOHN LEWIS for
himself his heirs doth promise the premises now are and forever hereafter shall remain free & clear of and from all other gifts sales dowers right and title of dower and
incumbrances whatsoever suffered by JOHN LEWIS or any other person; In Witness
whereof JOHN LEWIS and MARY ANN his Wife have hereunto set their hands and seals
the day & year first above written
Sealed & Delivered in presence of
        GEO: FRENCH,                        JOHN LEWIS
        JAMES HOWORTH,                      MARY ANNE LEWIS
        WILLIAM HARVEY, BENJA: DAY
  The Commonwealth of Virginia to BENJAMIN DAY, WILLIAM HARVEY & GEORGE
FRENCH of the Corporation of Fredg. Gent. Greeting; (the Commission for the privy Examina-
tion of MARY ANNE, Wife of JOHN LEWIS); Witness JOHN CHEW JR., Clerk of our said Court this
4th April 1788 and in the 12th year of the Commonwealth
  Corporation of Fredg. Sct.
  In Obedience to the within Commission (the return of the execution of the privy Examination

of MARY ANN LEWIS), Given under our hands and seals this 15th day of November 1788
BENJA: DAY
WILLIAM  HARVEY
At a Court of Hustings held for the Town and Corporation of Fredg. December 1st 1788
This Indenture was acknowledged by the said JOHN LEWIS and together with the Com-
mission annexed & Certificate of Execution thereof endorsed, were ordered to be
recorded
Examined & delivered  J. CALLENDER          Teste    JNO: CHEW  JR. Cl Cur

pp.        THIS INDENTURE made this 15th September Anno Domini one thousand seven
72-        hundred and Eighty eight by JOHN BENSON of County of Spotsylvania and Town
73         of Fredericksburg of one part & AMBROSE LEWIS of County and Town aforesaid
           of other part; Witnesseth that the said JOHN in consideration of the payment of
the Rent hereafter to be mentioned by these presents doth demise and bargain unto
said AMBROSE a certain parcel of ground lying in County and Town afsd., and described
bounded above by HENRY CHILES line intersecting PRINCES ANN STREET at right angles,
thence by said Street Twenty feet and then extending back One hundred and thirty two
feet the full depth of the lott, to which the said parcel of ground belonged; To have and
to hold the parcel of ground unto the said AMBROSE & assigns during the full term of
Twenty years from thence next ensuing paying said JOHN and assigns the Annual Rent
of Six shillings current money for every foot contained in the front of the parcel of
ground upon PRINCES ANN's Street, And the said AMBROSE for himself his assigns will
and at his own costs in all things make and sett up one or more houses as said AMBROSE
his assigns may or shall convenient or suitable for his habitation and abode; In Witness
whereof we have hereunto set our hands and seals the day and year above said
Signed sealed & delivered in presence of          JOHN BENSON
     (no witnesses shown)                          AMBROSE his mark ⳾ LEWIS
  At a Court of Hustings held for the Town and Corporation of Fredericksburg December
1st 1788          This Deed of Lease from JOHN BENSON to AMBROSE LEWIS was acknowledged by the parties and ordered to be recorded
Exd. & delivered to AMBROSE LEWIS          Teste  JNO: CHEW  Cl Cur

pp.        THIS INDENTURE made the 21st day of April in year of our Lord one thousand
74-        seven hundred and Eighty eight Between JOHN LEWIS & MARY ANNE LEWIS his
75         Wife of County of Spotsylvania and Town of Fredg., of one part and GEORGE
           AUGUSTINE WASHINGTON of County of FAIRFAX of other part; Witnesseth that
JOHN LEWIS and MARY ANNE his Wife in consideration of the sum of Ninety pounds
current money of Virginia to them in hand well and truly paid by said GEORGE AUGUS-
TINE WASHINGTON by these presents doth bargain sell release and confirm unto said
GEORGE AUGUSTINE WASHINGTON and to his heirs all the estate right title and demand
either in Law or Equity which they the said JOHN LEWIS and MARY ANNE his Wife now
have or may hereafter have claim or demand in two certain lotts of ground lying in the
Town of Fredericksburg and marked in the plott No. 169 bounded by PITT and CHARLES
STREETs and No. 171, bounded by PITT and PRINCESS ANN STREETs which said lotts by
plott of said Town will appear; Together with all the Improvements streets allies rights
and appurtenances thereunto belonging; To have and to hold the premises with appertenances unto GEORGE AUGUSTINE WASHINGTON his heirs, And JOHN LEWIS and MARY
ANNE his Wife and their heirs the premises hereby granted unto GEORGE AUGUSTINE
WASHINGTON his heirs against every other person shall warrent and forever defend by
these presents; In Witness whereof the said parties to these presents have interchangeably sett their hands and affixed their seals the day & year first above written

Signed Sealed and Delivered in the presence of
  Z. LUCAS, GEO: McCUTCHEN     JOHN LEWIS
  FIELDING LUCAS, JNO: MUNFORD   MARY ANNE LEWIS
 Received the day of the date of the within written Indenture from GEORGE AUGUSTINE
WASHINGTON the sum of Ninety pounds current money of Virginia being in full of the
consideration within mentioned
Teste FIELDING LUCAS,        JOHN LEWIS
  ZACHARIAH LUCAS
 At a Court of Hustings held for the Town and Corporation of Fredericksburg December
1st 1788   This Indenture for Lotts from JOHN LEWIS to GEORGE AUGUSTINE
WASHINTON was acknowledged by the said JNO: LEWIS and ordered to be recorded
Commission Recorded in 98.
Exd. & Deld. G. A. WASHINGTON    Teste JNO: CHEW JR. Cl.


pp.  THIS INDENTURE made the 23rd day of April Anno Domini one thousand seven
76-  hundred and Eighty eight Between RICHARD KENNY of Town of Fredg. of one
77   part and STANDISH FORD of same Town of other part; Whereas said RICHARD
    KENNY by a Decree of the Honourable the High Court of Chancery held in RICH-
MOND on the 27th day of November last and decreed and ordered to pay to REID and FORD
Merchants and Partners, the sum of Four hundred and seventeen pounds one shilling
and three pence, And said STANDISH FORD, one of the Partners of said House or Firm of
REID and FORDE is unwilling to enforce the said Decree by coersive methods provided
the benefit of it can be otherwise obtained, And whereas the said RICHARD KENNY
being desirous and willing to secure the payment of the aforesaid Decree together with
the Interest thereon from the 27th day of November last did on the 22nd day of this
month convey a part of his real property for the aforesaid purpose and being also
willing more fully to confirm and secure the payment of the aforesaid Decree by sub-
jecting a part of his other property to the payment of the same; NOW THIS INDENTURE
witnesseth that RICHRD KENNY for and in consideration that the said REID and FORDE do
and shall withhold all coersive processes on the Decree (which they might otherwise
issue and send out agst. the said RICHARD KENNY on the said Decree) during the term of
two years next ensuing from the 22nd day of this present month and in consideration
of the sum of Five shillings lawfull money to RICHARD KENNY in hand paid, doth by
these presents sell and confirm unto said STANDISH FORDE his heirs the Good Sloop or
Vessell commonly called *THE UNITY,* together with her tackle, apparel & furniture as
she lays in the RIVER RAPPAHANNOCK near Fredericksburg, UPON THE TRUST and to the
uses herein mentioned, that is to say, Upon Trust that if RICHARD KENNY shall not have
paid One hundred pounds in part of the Decree to said REID and FORDE or in some manner have satisfied them for the same before the first day of December next that then
STANDISH FORDE shall as soon as conveniently he can sell the said Sloop or Vessell *THE*
*UNITY,* together with her tackle apparel and furniture for the raising the aforesaid
sum, Provided always that the said Sloop shall be sold for the purpose aforesaid at public
auction and the time and place of sale shall be advertised for three weeks in the VIR-
GINIA GAZETTE, Provided always that RICHARD KENNY shall have full power and
authority to man and navigate the said Sloop to such places within the State of Virginia
or MARYLAND as he may think for the interest or convenience untill the first day of
December next ensuing the date hereof; In Witness whereof the parties hereunto have
interchangeably set their hands and seals the day & year above written
Sealed and delivered in presence of
  ALEXR: ROAN JR., GUST: B. WALLACE,   R. D. KENNY
  JAMES POTTINGER, CHS. URQUHART   STANDISH FORDE

At a Court of Hustings held for the Town and Corpo: of Fredericksburg December 1st 1788   This Deed of Trust from RICHD. KENNY to STANDISH FORDE was proved by three of the witnesses thereto and ordered to be recorded
Deld. FORDE                            Teste   JNO: CHEW JR. Cl. Cur.

pp.        THIS INDENTURE (bipartite) made this 22d day of April Anno Domini one thou-
78-        sand seven hundred and Eighty eight Between RICHARD KENNY of Town of
81         Fredericksburg of one part and STANDISH FORDE of same Town of other part.
          Whereas RICHARD KENNY by a Decree of the Honourable the High Court of Chancery held in RICHMOND on the Twenty seventh day of November Anno Domini 1787, was decreed and ordered to pay MESSRS. REID and FORDE, Merchants and Partners, the sum of Four hundred and seventeen pounds one shilling and three pence and the said STANDISH FORDE, one of the Partners of the said House or Firm of REID and FORDE is unwilling to enforce the said Decree by coercive methods provided the benefit of it can be otherwise obtained, And Whereas the said RICHARD KENNY is desirous and willing to subject a part of his real property to the discharge and payment of the same, NOW THIS INDENTURE WITNESSETH that RICHARD KENNY in consideration of said REID & FORDE do withhold all coercive processes for two years and in consideration of the sum of Five shillings of lawfull money to him in hand paid by these presents doth bargain sell and confirm unto said STANDISH FORDE and to his heirs the following Lots of ground lying in the Town of Fredericksburg, to wit, all that lot of ground lying on CAROLINE STREET in the plott of said Town begining where HAWKE STREET intersects CAROLINE STREET, then along the sd. CAROLINE STREET sixteen feet, thence back from said Street and paralel with HAWKE STREET one hundred and twenty feet, from thence at right angles to HAWKE STREET and from thence to the begining; making an oblong of sixteenfeet by one hundred and twenty feet on which there is a framed dwelling, Also one other lott of ground adjoining the just described which has forty feet front on CAROLINE STREET & extends back One hundred & twenty feet making an oblong of forty by one hundred and twenty feet on which there is a large house or dwelling; And also one other lott of ground adjoining the one last described which has a front on CAROLINE STREET of Twenty feet and extends also back one hundred and twenty feet making an oblong of twenty by one hundred and twenty feet on which there is a framed dwelling Bakehouse &c., To have and to hold the said several lotts of ground and appertenances unto STANDISH FORDE his assigns UPON TRUST, that is to say, if RICHARD KENNY shall not have paid and discharged the one half of the sum afsd. to said REID and FORDE before the 22nd day of April next ensuing the date of these presents that then STANDISH FORDE shall as soon as conveniently he can convey in fee simple as much of the premises to him granted by these presents as will pay and content the said REID and FORDE for the said half of the sum of money decreed to them; In Witness of all and singular of which said premises the parties thereto interchangeably have sett their hands and seals the day and year first above written
Sealed and Delivered in presence of
          ALEXR: ROAN JR. GUS. B. WALLACE          RICHARD KENNY
          JAMES POTTINGER, CHS: URQUHART          STANDISH FORDE
   At a Court of Hustings held for the Town and Corporation of Fredericksburg December 1st 1788;          This Deed of Trust from RICHARD KENNY to STANDISH FORDE was proved by the oath of three of the witnesses thereto and ordered to be recorded
Deld. S. FORDE                    Teste JNO: CHEW JR. Cl Cur

pp.     THIS INDENTURE made the first day of January one thousand seven hundred
81-    and Eighty seven Between JOHN BENSON of one part and JOHN COAKLEY of the
82     other part, both of Town of Fredericksburg; Witnesseth that JOHN BENSON in
      consideration of Fifty pounds Virginia currency hath demised and to farm
letten unto JOHN COAKLEY and assigns that part of my Lott whereon stands a BRICK
HOUSE with two rooms below stairs and two rooms above stairs being in Town of
Fredericksburg on CAROLINE STREET; To have and to hold the said part of the lott unto
JNO: COAKLEY and assigns from the date of these presents and during the term of Five
years; and JOHN BENSON doth covenant that JOHN COAKLEY and assigns shall quietly
occupy the said premises without hindrance interruption or denial of said JOHN BENSON
his heirs or any other person whatsoever. In Witness whereof the parties to these
presents interchangeably set their hands and their seals the day and year first written
Signed Sealed acknowledged & delivered in presence of
     WILLIAM REAT,          JOHN  BENSON
     JAMES SLATOR, JOSEPH STEWARD    JOHN COAKLY
  At a Court of Hustings held for the Town and Corporation of Fredericksburg December
1st 1788      This Deed of Lease from JOHN BENSON to JOHN COAKLEY was acknowledged
by the parties and ordered to be recorded


pp.     THIS INDENTURE made the 21st day of April in year of our Lord one thousand
82-    seven hundred and Eighty eight Between JOHN LEWIS and MARY ANN his Wife
83     of Town of Fredericksburg of one part and SMITH, YOUNG and HYDE of the same
      place of other part; Witnesseth that JOHN LEWIS & MARY ANN his Wife in con-
sideration of the sum of Eighty pounds current money to them in hand paid by the said
SMITH, YOUNG and HYDE by these presents doth bargain sell release and confirm unto
the said SMITH, YOUNG and HYDE and to their heirs all the estate right title and demand
either in Law or Equity which JOHN LEWIS and MARY ANN his Wife now have in a certain lott of ground lying in Town of Fredericksburg and marked in the platt Number 65
bounded by LEWIS & SOPHIA STREETs, Together with all buildings improvements rights
priviledges and appurtenances whatsoever belonging; To have and to hold the hereby
bargained premises with the appertenances unto said SMITH, YOUNG and HYDE and
their heirs, And JOHN LEWIS and MARY ANN his Wife for them selves their heirs doth
hereby promise that the hereby bargained premises unto said SMITH, YOUNG and HYDE
their heirs against JOHN LEWIS and MARY ANN his Wife their heirs will warrent and
forever defend by these presents; In Witness whereof JOHN LEWIS and MARY ANN his
Wife have hereunto set their hands & seals the day and year above written
Sealed & Delivered in the presence of
     EDMD. WINDER,  T. GREEN,        JOHN LEWIS
     SAM: RODDEY, CHS: CARTER,     MARY  ANNE  LEWIS
     JNO: STEWARD, JOHN ROBINSON,
     TULLY  WHITHURST
  At a Court of Hustings held for the Town and Corpo: of Fredg. December 1st 1788
This Indenture for Lott from JNO: LEWIS to SMITH, YOUNG and HYDE was proved by
three witnesses thereto and ordered to be recorded


pp.     THIS INDENTURE made this 6th day of December in year of our Lord one thou-
84-    sand seven hundred and eighty eight Between  JOHN LEWIS and MARY ANN his
87     Wife of Town of Fredericksburg of one part and GEORGE AUGUSTINE WASHING-
      TON of County of FAIRFAX of other part; Witnesseth that JOHN LEWIS and MARY
ANN his Wife in consideration of the sum of Ninety pounds current money of Virginia
unto them in hand paid by GEORGE AUGUSTINE WASHINGTON by these presents doth

bargain sell quit claim and confirm unto GEORGE AUGUSTINE WASHINGTON and to his
heirs all the estate right title and demand either in Law or Equity which JOHN LEWIS
and MARY ANN his Wife now have or may hereafter have in two certain lotts of ground
lying in Town of Fredericksburg and marked in the plott No. 170 bounded by CHARLES
STREET and the upper extremity of the Town and No. 172 bounded by PRINCESS ANN
STREET and upper extremity of the Town, which said Lotts which said lotts by Plott of
said Town will fully appear; Together with all buildings improvements rights and
appertenances belonging; To have and to hold said premises with the appertenances
unto GEORGE AUGUSTINE WASHINGTON his heirs and JOHN LEWIS and MARY ANN his
Wife and their heirs the sold premises against all persons whatsoever will warrant and
forever defend by these presents; In Witness whereof the parties to these presents
have hereunto interchangeably set their hands and affixed their seals the day and year
first above written
Signed Sealed and Delivered in presence of
    ZACHARIAS LUCAS,                          JOHN LEWIS
    THO: VOWLES, JOHN CALLENDER,               MARY ANNE LEWIS
    FIELDING LUCAS
  Received the day of the date of the within written Indenture from GEORGE AUGUSTINE
WASHINGTON the sum Ninety pounds current money of Virginia being in full of the
consideration within mentioned
Teste FIELDING LUCAS, ZACHARIAH LUCAS,              JOHN LEWIS
    THOMAS VOWLES, JOHN CALLENDER
Exd. & Deld. G. A. W.

  The Commonwealth of Virginia to CHARLES MORTIMER, BENJAMIN DAY & WILLIAM
HARVEY of the Corporation of Fredericksburg Gent., Greeting (The Commission for the
privy Examination of MARY ANNE, the Wife of JOHN LEWIS); Witness JOHN CHEW JR. Clerk of
our said Court this 6th day of Decr. 1788 in the 13th year of the Commonwealth
  Corporation of Fredericksburg, to wit: In Obedience to the within commission we the
Subscribers (the return of the execution of the privy examination of MARY ANN LEWIS); Certified
under our hands and seals this sixth day of December 1788
                 WILLIAM HARVEY
                 BENJA: DAY
  At a Court of Hustings held for the Town and Corporation of Fredericksburg being the
5th day of January 1789;     This Indenture was proved by three witnesses thereo and
together with the Commission annexed and Certificate of the Execution thereof
endorsed were ordered to be recorded
Exd. & deld. G. A. W.                    Teste   JNO: CHEW JR., Cl. Cur

pp.    THIS INDENTURE made the 19th day of August in year of our Lord Christ one
88-    one thousand seven hundred and Eighty eight Between JOHN DAWSON of the
91    Corporation of Fredericksburg of one part and JAMES JULIAN of the other part;
     Witnesseth that said JAMES JULIAN hath at the special instance and request of
said JOHN DAWSON paid and advanced to JOHN DAWSON the sum of Seventy two pounds
nineteen shillings and four pence current money of Virginia and being desirous to
secure the payment thereof to JAMES JULIAN these presents therefore witnesseth that
in consideration of the premises as also for the sum of Five shillings current money to
said JOHN DAWSON in hand paid by JAMES JULIAN, JOHN DAWSON doth bargain and sell
unto JAMES JULIAN his heirs the five following slaves namely Captain, a Negroe Fellow
about forty five years of age, Renah, a Negroe Woman twenty two years of age with her
two children namely Oliver aged five years old and Sam one year of age and CHARLOTTE,
a Negro Woman about twenty years of age; To have and to hold the Negroe slaves unto

JAMES JULIAN his heirs in Trust for the use of JOHN DAWSON his heirs provided JOHN
DAWSON his heirs shall truly pay JAMES JULIAN his heirs the aforesaid sum before the
Tenth day of January next, And if JOHN DAWSON shall make default in payment JAMES
JULIAN shall sell the slaves together with their future increase either for ready money
or upon credit and the surplus of any there be remaining out of the sale of the said
slaves shall be paid to JOHN DAWSON and assigns; In Witness whereof JOHN DAWSON
hath hereunto set his hand and affixed his seal the day and year first written
Sealed and delivered in presence of
    WILLIAM WIATT,                                    J. DAWSON
    JOHN HARDIA, THO: WALLER SR.
  At a Court of Hustings held for the Town & Corporation of Fredericksburg being the
5th January 1780      This Deed of Trust from JOHN DAWSON to JAMES JULIAN was
proved by one Witness thereto, And at a Court held for sd. Corporation the 24th April
1789, This Deed of Trust was acknowledged by JOHN DAWSON and ordered to be recorded
Examined and Deld. JAS. JULIAN      Teste   JNO. CHEW Cl.


p.     Be it resolved that GENL WEEDON, Messrs.  SUNDERLAND & EDDY be a Committee
91    to collect the lower subscription of the Town to rais two Fire Companies agreable
     to Act pased the last session at Assembly
     We the Subscribers whose names are underwritten oblige ourselves to become
members of the Fire Companies to be established in the Town & Corporation of
Frederickburg                    June 25th  1788

| | | |
|---|---|---|
| G. WEEDON | SAM: RODDY | WILL: LOVELL |
| THOMAS EDDY | JOHN BROWNLOW | WM: SMOCK |
| JNO: SUNDERLAND | CHARLES LEEMONS | WM. JACKSON |
| ROGER DIXON | JAMES SOMERVELL | JAMES BOWIN |
| ROBT. BROOKE | ROBT. JOHNSON | JAMES ABBOTT |
| JNO: CHEW | JOHN COAKLEY | JAMES BROWN JR. |
| R. B. CHEW | J. KUHN | AARON McCLINTOCK |
| JOHN HARDIA | WILLIAM HARVEY | ROBT. RITCHEE |
| JOHN MINOR JR. | F. TOMPKINS for | WM. DRUMMOND |
| BENJA: HAZELGROVE | JACOB WHITLER | JAMES GILLIS |
| WILLIAM REAT | ROBT. WALKER | WM. JENKINS |
| WM. McAUSLAND | DA:D EASTON | HENRY WHITE |
| WALTER PAYNE | JAMES BLAIR | STEPHEN LACOSTE |
| | DAVID BLAIR | JOHN BENSON |


pp.    THIS INDENTURE made this 25th day of July in year of our Lord one thousand
92-   seven hundred and Eighty eight Between GUIN PAGE of County of Spotsylvania
94    Gentleman of one part and LARKIN SMITH of County of KING and QUEEN and
     JOHN CHEW JUNR. of Town of Fredericksburg Gentleman of other part; Witnes-
seth that GUINN PAGE in consideration of the sum of Four hundred pound current
money to him in hand paid by LARKIN SMITH and JOHN CHEW JR. by these presents doth
bargain sell and confirm unto said LARKIN and JOHN their heirs all those eight lotts or
half acres of ground lying in Town of Fredericksburg numbered in the Plan of said
Town 149, 150, 151, 152, 153, 154, 155 & 156, being the same lotts conveyed to GUINN PAGE
as devisee under the Will of his Father, MANN PAGE Esquire deced., by JOHN LEWIS,
Eldest Son and heir at Law of FIELDING LEWIS Esquire deced., by Indenture bearing date
the 22nd day of this Intant (July) and entered to be recorded in Court of Hustings for
the Town and Corporation of Fredericksburg, the bounds of which said eight lotts were
by the said Indenture more fully and at large appear; Together with all the appurti-

nances thereto belonging; To have and to hold the said eight Lotts or half acres of ground with appurtenances unto LARKIN SMITH and JOHN CHEW JR., or assigns as Tenants in Common and not as Joint Tenants; In Witness whereof GUIN PAGE hath hereunto set his hand and affixed his eal the year first before written
Sealed and Delivered in presence of
    THOMAS HUGHES,                                    GWYN PAGE
    BEVERLEY CHEW, CHS. MORTIMER
At a Court of Hustings held for the Town and Corporation of Fredericksburg being the 5th day of January 1789      This Indenture for Lotts from GWYN PAGE to LARKIN SMITH and JOHN CHEW JR., was proved by the oaths of three witnesses thereto and ordered to be recorded


pp.      THIS INDENTURE made this Seventeenth day of December in year of our Lord
95-      Christ one thousand seven hundred and Eighty eight Between PHILIP LIPSCOMB
97       and JANE his Wife of Town and Corporation of Fredericksburg of one part and
    WILLIAM STANARD of County of Spotsylvania of other part. Witnesseth that in consideration of the sum of Eighty pounds current money of Virginia to him the said PHILIP LIPSCOMB in hand paid by WILLIAM STANARD by these presents the said PHILIP LIPSCOMB and JANE his Wife do bargain sell & confirm unto WILLIAM STANARD and his heirs one square of lotts lying in Town aforesaid known in the plan by numbers 157, 158, 159 and 160; bounded; Northward by PITT STREET, Eastwardly by PRINCE EDWARD STREET, Southwardly by HAWKE STREET and Westwardly by the land of the late FIELDING LEWIS deced., containing by survey Two acres of ground, Together with all houses, profits and appurtenances belonging; To have and to hold the land hereby conveyed with appertenances unto WILLIAM STANARD his heirs; that the said premises now are and forever hereafter shall remain free and clear of all incumbrances whatsover and PHILIP LIPSCOMB and his heirs the premises unto WILLIAM STANARD his heirs will warrent and forever defend by these presents; In Witness whereof the said PHILIP LIPSCOMB and his Wife have hereunto interchangeably set their hands and affixed their seals the day and year first above written
Sealed and delivered in the presence of
    B. HYDE, ALEXR: ROANE JR.,               PHILIP LIPSCOMB
    JOHN PROUDFIT                             JANE LIPSCOMB
Recd. the day and date within written of WILLIAM STANARD the sum of Eighty pounds current money of Virginia being the full consideration for the within granted land
At a Court of Hustings held for the Town and Corporation of Fredericksburg the 27th day of February 1789      This Indenture for Lotts from PHILIP LIPSCOMB to WIL- LIAM STANARD was by the oaths of three witnesses thereto and ordered to be recorded
Commission Folio 212; Exd. & Deld. W. STANARD    Teste JNO: CHEW C.C.H.


p.       KNOW ALL MEN by these presents that I ISAAC TAYLOR of County of LANCASTER
97       in consideration of sum of Eleven pounds Thirteen shillings & four pence, have
    this day by these presents sold and delivered unto JOHN LEGG of Fredericksburg my wright title & claim in a certain Negro wench Nancy & her two Children, Lewis & Clarissa together with their future increase; for the true and faithful performance of these presents I do bind myself my heirs in the penal sum of One hundred pounds Virginia Currency; Given under my hand & seal this twentyeth day of Decr. 1788
Teste KEMP HURST                                    ISAAC TAYLOR
At a Court of Hustings held for the Town and Corporation of Fredericksburg the 27th day of February 1789      This Bill of Sale was proved by the oath of KEMP HURST a witness thereto and ordered to be recorded

p.      The Commonwealth of Virginia to CHARLES MORTIMER, BENJA: DAY & WIL-
98      LIAM HARVEY of the Corporation of Fredericksburg Gent., Gent. (The Commission
        for the privy Examination of MARY ANN the Wife of JOHN LEWIS for sale of two lotts, No.
169 & 171 to GEORGE AUGUSTINE WASHINGTON); Witness JOHN CHEW JR., Clerk of our said
Court the 6th day of December 1788 in the 13th year of the Commonwealth
  Corporation of Fredericksburg, to wit; In Obedience (the return of the execution of the
privy Examination of MARY ANN LEWIS); Given under our hands & seals this sixth day of
December 1788                              WILLIAM  HARVEY
Truly Recorded Teste  JNO: CHEW  JR. Cl.        BENJA: DAY


pp.     THIS INDENTURE made the thirteenth day of March one thousand seven hun-
99-     dred and Eighty nine Between ROGER DIXON and LUCY DIXON his Mother of Town
100     of Fredericksburg of one part and GEORGE WEEDON of Fredericksburg of other
        part; Witnesseth that in consideration of the sum of Thirty pounds current
money of Virginia to ROGER DIXON in hand paid by GEORGE WEEDON by these presents
they the said ROGER DIXON and LUCY DIXON his Mother do sell unto GEORGE WEEDON all
that lott or half acre of land lying in Town of Fredericksburg known by number Two
hundred & Fifty nine lying on WATER STREET adjoining the Lot 249 the property of
Colo. PEACHY, and the Lot 260, in the possession of said GEORGE WEEDON and all waters
profits and appurtenances belonging; To have and to hold the land hereby conveyed
with appurtenances unto GEORGE WEEDON his heirs, that the premises now are and so
forever hereafter shall remain and be free and clear of all incumbrances; In Witness
whereof ROGER DIXON and LUCY his Mother have hereunto set their hands and seals the
day and year first above written
Sealed and delivered in the presence of
        JAMES  MADDEN,                      ROGER  DIXON
        JOHN CHEW  JR., PHILIP DIXON         LUCY DIXON
  At a Court of Hustings held for the Town and Corpo: of Fredg. on Fryday the 27th day of
March 1789    This Indenture from ROGER and LUCY DIXON to GEORGE WEEDON Gent. was
proved by three witnesses thereto and ordered to be recorded
Exd. & deld. Col. HUGH MERCER               Test JNO: CHEW C. C. H.


pp.     THIS INDENTURE made this 28 day of March in year of our Lord one thousand
101-    seven hundred and Eighty nine Between DOCTOR ELISHA HALL, CAROLINA his
103     Wife & JOHN LEWIS of Town of Fredericksburg of one part and THOMAS COLSON of
        Town aforesaid of other part; Witnesseth that in consideration of the sum of
Sixty pounds in hand paid, by these presents doth bargain and sell unto THO: COLSON his
heirs a certain lott or half acre of land lying in Town of Fredg., Number 148, laying on
LEWIS STREET and the Lott number 147, and ELISHA HALL, CAROLINA his Wife & JOHN
LEWIS doth warrant and drend all the houses meadows and all other commodities and
appartinances to said lotts belonging; In Witness whereof the parties hereunto sett
their hands and affixed their seals the day and year first above written
Signed Sealed and delivered in presents of          ELISHA  HALL
        (no witnesses shown)                         CAROLIANNA  HALL
  The Commonwealth of Virginia to GEORGE FRENCH AND BENJA: DAY of the Corporation
of Fredericksburg Gent., Greeting (the Commission for the privy Examination of CAROLINNA
the Wife of ELISHA HALL); Witness JOHN CHEW JR., Clerk of our said Court this 24 day of
April 1789 in the 13th year of the Commonwealth          JNO: CHEW  JR.
  In Obedience to the within Commission, we the Subscribers (the return of the Execution of
the privy Examination of CAROLINNA HALL). Certified under our hands & seals this 24th day

of April 1789                          GEORGE  FRENCH
                                       BENJA: DAY

At a Court of Hustings held for the Town and Corporation of Fredericksburg April 24th
1789   This Indenture was acknowledged by the said ELISHA HALL & together with the
Commission annexed and Certificate of the Execution thereof endorsed, were ordered to
be recorded
Exd. & Deld. Capt. G. LEWIS               Teste  JNO: CHEW Cl.


pp.       KNOW ALL MEN by these presents that I ROGER DIXON of Town of Fredericks-
103-      burg in consideration of the sum of Nineteen pounds lawfull money of Virginia
105       to me in hand paid by JOSEPH CHRISTY, Merchant, in the Town aforesaid, by
          these presents do bargain sell and confirm unto said JOSEPH and his heirs all
that parcel of land lying in County aforesaid a part of which said land being within the
Town of Fredericksburg and part adjoining to the said Town, and measuring about one
acre more or less and known by the description following; Beginning at the South West
corner of said Town, thence runing along the back and Western line of the Town North
twenty seven degrees West ten poles, being the length of the South West corner lot in
said Town and number one hundred and eighty nine, thence North sixty three degrees
East eight poles being the whole width of the said Lot, thence South twenty seven degrees East ten poles to the lowest and Southern line of said Town, thence North sixty
three degrees EAst again four poles being the width of and runing across the lowest
and Southern end of said Street, thence North twenty seven degrees West ten poles up
the said Street one boundary of the lot number one hundred and ninety in said Town,
thence North sixty three degrees East five poles, thence South twenty seven degrees
East ten poles, thence in the same straight line one pole fifteen links to one of the
boundary lines of the Meadow ground purchased by said JOSEPH from the Trustees of
the FREDERICKSBURG ACADEMY, thence along the said boundary line of said Meadow
ground South sixty three degrees West seventeen poles and a half to one of the corners
of the said Meadow ground, thence North twenty seven degrees West one pole fifteen
links to the begining, the whole including the whole of Lot number one hundred and
eighty nine a part of the lot nubmer one hundred and ninety and along and ground
lying between the said lots and said boundary line of said Meadow ground a plot of
which is hereunto annexed (Plot on page 105); and all passages common pastures stone
meadow and all other profits; In Witness whereof the said ROGER have hereunto put my
hand and seal this twenty third day of October in year of our Lord one thousand seven
hundred and eighty eight
Teste W. L. STONE,                              ROGER  DIXON
     R. B. CHEW, WILLIAM SMITH
At a Court of Hustings held for Town and Corporation of Fredg., the 24th April 1789
This Indenture for Lotts from ROGER DIXON to JOSEPH CHRISTY was proved by three witnesses thereto and ordered to be recorded
Examined & delivered JOSEPH CHRISTY        Teste  JNO: CHEW Cl.


pp.       THIS INDENTURE made this seventh day of March 1789 Between ROGER DIXON of
105-      one part and DAVID COYLE of other part;; Witnesseth that ROGER DIXON in con-
106       sideration of the sum of One hundred and seventy pounds to him in hand paid by
          DAVID COYLE by these presents doth bargain & sell unto DAVID COYLE all that
parcel of ground situate in Town of Fredericksburg being a part of lot number sixteen
sixteen thus 16.16  measuring thirty four feet front on CAROLINE STREET and runing
the whole width of the lot back begining at the distance of four feet from said ROGER
DIXONs House lately purchased by said DIXON of said COYLE and runing with said Street

Northward thirty four feet; To have and to hold said parcel of ground with all buildings In Witness whereof the parties aforesaid have set their hands and seals the day & year above written

Teste JAMES WALKER, MARIA HUME,        ROGER DIXON
      PHILIP DIXON, WILLIAM REAT        DAVID COYLE

 At a Court of Hustings held for the Town & Corporation of Fredericksburg April 24th 1789   This Indenture was proved by three witnesses thereto and ordered to be recorded

Exd. & deld. DAV:D COYLE        Teste   JNO: CHEW JR. Cl.


pp.     THIS INDENTURE Tripartite made the Twenty fifth day of March in the year of
106-   our Lord 1780 Between HENRY FITZHUGH of STAFFORD, Gentleman, of the 1st part
109    ROBERT WELLFORD of Town of Fredericksburg of 2d. part and BENJAMIN HYDE of
       Town aforesaid of 3d. part, Witnesseth that HENRY FITZHUGH in consideration of the Rents & Covenants in this Indenture contained on part of ROBT: WELLFORD to be paid and performed by these presents doth bargain & sell unto ROBERT WELLFORD his heirs a certain parcel of land lying in Town of Fredericksburg on CAROLINE STREET & being part of lott number one hundred & seventy seven bounded begining at the lower corner of said lott on CAROLINE STREET and runing up said Street fifty five feet, thence one hundred & thirty two feet back on PITT STREET, thence fifty five feet parallel to CAROLINE STREET, thence parallel to PITT STREET one hundred & thirty two feet to the begining; the said ROBERT WELFORD to leave an alley on the upper Corner on CAROLINE STREET three & a half feet wide & extending 28 feet back; To have and to hold the said parcel of land with the appurtenances unto ROBERT WELLFORD his heirs paying for the same on the first day of January next ensuing & on the first day of January yearly unto HENRY FITZHUGH his heirs the annual rent of Seventeen pounds Five shillings good & lawfull money of Virginia issuing out of the demised premises; And if the parcel of land lay unimproved the space of one year after the rent become due and ROBERT WELLFORD should neglrect or refuse to pay the aforesaid rent it shall then be lawfull for HENRY FITZHUGH his heirs the same to repossess; And ROBERT WELLFORD his heirs doth covenant to pay and discharge all kind of Taxes or charges laid upon the land; And whereas the aforementioned BENJAMIN HYDE had heretofore contracted with HENRY FITZHUGH for the parcel of land on which he hath since built part of a large dwelling house but before a conveyance was duly executed and recorded said BENJAMIN HYDE assigned all right of the parcel of land to ROBERT WELLFORD. This Indenture therefore further witnesseth that BENJAMIN HYDE in consideration of the sum of Three hundred & seven pounds good & lawfull money of Virginia to him in hand paid, doth bargain sell & confirm unto ROBERT WELLFORD his heirs all said BENJAMIN HYDE's right title & demand both in Law & Equity in the abovementioned parcel of land; In Witness whereof the parties concerned have hereunto set their hands & seals the day month and year first above written

Signed sealed & delivered in presents of
     RICHARD  GARNER,        HENRY FITZHUGH
     JAMES WALKER, LARKIN STANARD,   R. WELLFORD
     G. FOX, WILLIAM WIATT,       B. HYDE
     ELISHA DICKERSON

 At a Court of Hustings held for the Town and Corporation of Fredericksburg April 24. 1789   This Indenture was proved by three witnesses thereto and ordered to be recorded     Exd. & Deld. R. W.      Teste JNO: CHEW C. C. H.

pp.         THIS INDENTURE made this twenty third day of February in year of our Lord
110-        one thousand seven hundred and eighty nine Betweeen JOHN CALLENDER of the
111         Corporation of Fredericksburg and HAPSY CALLENDER his Wife of one part and
            RICHARD GARNER of said Corporation of other part; Witnesseth that in consi-
deration of the sum of Twenty seven pounds in hand paid by RICHARD GARNER, by
these presents JOHN CALLENDER and HAPSY CALLENDER his wife do bargain and sell
unto RICHARD GARNER and his heirs all that parcell of half lot of land lying in
Fredericksburg being one half of Lott No. 103, begining at the corner of said Lott on
HAWKE STREET, thence runing up PRINCESS ANN STREET to Lot No. (105) thence Westerly half the said lott parrelel with PRINCESS ANN STREET to HAWKE STREET and from
thence to the begining, together with the appurtenances thereon; To have and to hold
the said parcel of land unto RICHARD GARNER his heirs free and clear from all other
gifts sales dowers and incumbrances whatsoever; In Witness whereof JOHN CALLENDER
and HAPSY CALLENDER his Wife have hereunto set their hands and seals the day and
year first above written
Signed sealed and delivered in presents of
        JOHN FERNEYHOUGH,                          JOHN  CALLENDER
        VALENTINE  GARLAND,                        HAPSEY  CALLENDER
        BENJAMIN  BERRY
  At a Court of Hustings held for the Town and Corporation of Fredericksburg April 24th
1789     This Indenture was acknowledged by the said JOHN CALLENDER and ordered to
be recorded


pp.         THIS INDENTURE made the 12th day of December one thousand seven hundred
112-        & Eighty eight Between PHILIP EVANS of Town of Fredericksburg of one part &
113         VALENTINE GARLAND of the same place of other part. Witnesseth that PHILIP
            EVANS in consideration of the rents and covenants herein after menmtioned on
part of VALENTINE GARLAND to be paid and performed hath demised and to farm let
unto VALENTINE GARLAND his heirs one fourth part of a certain part of a lott of land in
Town of Fredericksburg and numbered (141), together with all profits commodities and
appurtenances belonging; To have and to hold unto VALENTINE GARLAND his heirs
from the 15th day of March last for the term of Twenty years paying PHILIP EVANS his
heirs during the term on the 15th of March in each year the sum or yearly rent of Four
pounds specie and VALENTINE GARLAND doth agree he will build or cause to be built
one house twenty feet long and sixteen feet wide with a good Brick Chimney at one end
having a Fire Place to be finished in a workman like manner and will at the expiration
of twenty years which shall happen to be in the year of our Lord One thousand Eight
hundred and Eight deliverup to PHILIP EVANS his heirs the hereby demised premises;
And PHILIP EVANS and VALENTINE GARLAND do bind themselves their heirs in penal
sum of Three hundred pounds specie for their true performance of the above covenant. In Witness whereof the said parties to these presents have hereunto sett their
hands and seals the day and year first afore written
Sealed and Delivered in presence of
        RICHARD  GARNER,                           PHILIP  EVANS
        JOHN CALLENDER, CHARLES URQUHART          VALENTINE  GARLAND
  At a Court of Hustings held for the Town and Corporation of Fredericksburg April 24th
1789     This Deed of Lease from PHILIP EVANS to VALENTINE GARLAND was proved by
three of the witnesses thereto and ordered to be recorded

pp.     THIS INDENTURE made the Twenty second day of September one thousand seven
114-    hundred and Eighty eight Between JAMES MERCER, MANN PAGE, WILLIAM
117     FITZHUGH, CHARLES CARTER, ALEXANDER SPOTSWOOD, GEORGE WEEDON, JOHN
        DAWSON, LAWRENCE BROOKE, JAMES MONROE and THOMAS FITZHUGH Esquires, a
major part of the present Trustees of FREDERICKSBURG ACADEMY of the one part and
JOSEPH CHRISTY of Town of Fredericksburg, Merchant of other part; Whereas the
Commonwealth of Virginia was on the fifth day of May 1783 possessed of a certain tract
of land situate in County of Spotsylvania and adjoining the Town of Fredericksburg and
bounded Beginning at a Stump of a large red Oak in the line of LEWIS WILLIS, South
West of the PROFESSORS STONE HOUSE & runing with said WILLIS line N. 28 East 61 poles
to the back line of Fredericksburg, thence with the Town Line South 27 degrees East to a
Stake, thence North 63 degrees East seventeen poles & an half to a Stake standing twenty feet below DIXONS GRANARY upon the ROAD leading out of Town, thence with the
ROAD South 19 degrees West about 43 poles five poles North of the Mill Race of the
Commonwealth had some time before then purchased of a certain Mr. RICHARD BROOKE
who had before that purchased the same of the REVEREND JOHN DIXON of County of
GLOUCESTER, Devisee and Trustee of ROGER DIXON, late of Town of Fredericksburg deceased, at a Publick Sale thereof made by JOHN DIXON and the Attornies in part of JOHN
HARFORD of City of BRISTOL, Merchant, to whom the said parcel of land together with a
greater tract whereof this was a part was put in Mortgage for a sum of money far above
the value of the whole upon condition and with a Proviso in the said Deed of Mortgage
expressed of redeeming the same by or before a certain day therein mentioned, which
was then past in the lifetime of said ROGER DIXON whereon the said Commonwealth
executed a GUN FACTORY and other Buildings to a considerable value, And also whereas
the General Assembly of Virginia being inclined to convert the said GUN FACTORY
Lands and Buildings into an ACADEMY for the Education of Youth did on the Fifth day of
May 1783 by their Act intitled An Act to vest the Gun Factory and Publick Lands at
Fredericksburg in Trustees for the purpose of an ACADEMY West the said tract of land
before described in certain Trustees thirteen in number and in the said Act named and
their Successors in fee and forever without proviso any saving of right or title whatsoever thereby authorising the Trustees or a major part of them to make any Order Rule
or Regulation that by them might be thought necessary for vesting the same into an
ACADEMY with power to appoint other Trustees in the place of such who might die or
resign upon condition that if the Trustess should neglect or fail to erect the same into
an ACADEMY within five years from the passing of that Act then the same was to be
void and the Commonwealth was in that event to be gain revested in their former right
and title in said land and Buildings; And also whereas said Trustees having established
an ACADEMY as required and applied to the General Assembly of Virginia and obtained
one other Act entitled An Act to impower the Trustees of the FREDERICKSBURG ACADE-
MY to dispose of certain lands, by which Act made and passed the Trustees of said ACA-
DEMY or a major part of them were authorised to sell certain sunken grounds part of
the first described lands or such part thereof as to them should seem best and to the
advantage of the ACADEMY. And also Whereas at a meeting of said Trustees on the ninth
day of July 1788 last consisting of nine members, it was unanimously ordered that a
certain part of the first described tract of land as laid off by JAMES TUTT, Surveyor, and
containing Five acres and one quarter & seven square perches including the said sunken lands should be sold by way of Publick auction to the higher Bidder upon Credit;
And lastly whereas at a Publick Sale made pursuant to the said Resolve, JOSEPH CHRISTY
became the purchaser of the said parcel of land for five acres and one quarter & seven
square perches for the sum of One hundred & one pound Ten shillings being the
highest price bid for the same, NOW THIS INDENTURE WITNESSETH that the aforemen-

tioned Trustess being a major part present do bargain and sell unto JOSEPH CHRISTY his heirs all that tract of land according to the bounds following, to wit, Beginning at a Stone on the North side of the Mill at two poles to the North thereof at the edge of the ROAD leading from the Town of Fredericksburg and running with one of the larger tracts North seventy three degrees West twenty nine poles and a half to a Stone in the last mentioned line, thence North forty degrees & one quarter East forty poles & an half suposed to be the back line of Town of Fredericksburg, thence with the Town Line on the Corner of the Town Line continued South twenty seven degrees East eight poles and three quarters, thence North sixty three degrees East seventeen poles and an half to a Stake on the said Road Side twenty five feet below the GRANARY and from then running in a right line along the said Road to the beginning; In Witness whereof the Trustees have hereunto set their hands and affixed their seals the day afore written

Sealed and Delivered in presence of                    J. MERCER
        ROBERT PATTON,                                 M. PAGE
        SAMUEL SELDON                                  W. FITZHUGH
        JOHN LEWIS                                     CHS. CARTER
                                                       ALEXR. SPOTSWOOD
Reacknowledged the 2d day of May 1789                  G. WEEDON
GEORGE FRENCH              J. MERCER                    J. DAWSON
MARTIN MIMS               M. PAGE                       LAWRENCE BROOKE
G. HEISKELL              WM. FITZHUGH                   THOS: FITZHUGH
        CHS. CARTER, J. DAWSON, LAW. BROOKE,
        THOS: FITZHUGH

 At a Court of Hustings held for Town and Corporation of Fredericksburg on Fryday the 26th day of June 1789        This Indenture was proved by the oaths of GEORGE FRENCH MARTIN MIMMS and GODLOVE HEISKELL as to the acknowledgment of JAMES MERCER. MANN PAGE, WM. FITZHUGH, CHARLES CARTER, GEORGE WEEDON, JOHN DAWSON, LAWRENCE BROOKE AND THOMAS FITZHUGH and ordered to be recorded
Examined and Delivered JOS: CHRISTY        Teste JNO: CHEW Cl.


pp.      TO ALL TO WHOM these presents may come, Know ye that I ELISHA HALL of
118-     Town of Frederickburg in consideration of the sum of Five shillings good &
119      lawfull money of Virginia to me in hand paid have bargained and sold unto
         CHARLES URQUHART of Fredericksburg two Lotts of ground lying in Town of
Fredericksby Numbers 142 & 144; adjoining the lots at present occupied by NEIL McCOULL & PHILIP EVANS, with all houses improvements and appurtenances thereunto belonging; according to the true intent and meaning of the present writing, that is to say that ELISHA HALL may redeem the same & take in this present conveyance by paying the sum of One hundred and fifty seven pounds 14/9 Vg. Cr. on or before the first day of February one thousand seven hundred & ninety, In Witness whereof I have hereunto set my hand and seal this thirty first day of January one thousand seven hundred and Eighty nine
Signed Sealed and Delivered in presents of
        ROBERT GALLOWAY,                                ELISHA HALL
        ALEXANDER ROAN, JAMES WATSON
 N. B. This instrument of writing is to bear Interest from its date until satisfied as witness my hand & seal the day & date above written
        ROBERT GALLOWAY,                                ELISHA HALL
        ALEXANDER ROAN, JAMES WATSON
 At a Court of Hustings held for the Town and Corporation of Fredericksburg June 26th 1789   This Deed of Mortgage from ELISHA HALL to CHARLES URQUHART was acknow-

ledged by the said ELISHA HALL & ordered to be recorded
Exd. & delivered                              Teste          JNO: CHEW JR. Cl C.


pp.       THIS INDENTURE made the twenty ninth day of April in year of our Lord one
119-      thousand seven hundred & Eighty nine Between LAWRENCE BATTAILE of County
120       of CAROLINE and State of Virginia of one part and GEORGE FRENCH of the Town of
          Fredericksburg of other part. Witnesseth that LAWRENCE BATTAILE in consider-
ation of the sum of Forty pounds current money to him in hand paid by GEORGE FRENCH
by these presents doth bargain and sell unto GEORGE FRENCH and his heirs a certain lott
of ground lying in Town of Fredericksburg number 238 and bounded by PRINCESS ANN
STREET and PRUSSIA STREET and Lotts number 237 & 247; Together with all houses gardens and appurtenances thereunto belonging; To have and to hold the said lott of
ground with the appurtenances unto GEORGE FRENCH & his heirs and LAWRENCE BAT-
TAILE and his heirs shall warrant and forever defend by these presents; In Witness
whereof said LAWRENCE BATTAILE hath hereunto set his hand and affixed his seal the
day and year first above mentioned
Signed sealed & delivered in the presents of
       JOHN MILLER, JO: LEGG,                          LAU: BATTAILE
       KEMP  HURST,  JOHN  SANDERS
Received the within consideration money in full 29th April 1789
Test JOHN MILLER                               LAWRENCE BATTAILE
  At a Court of Hustings held for the Town and Corporation of Fredericksburg June 26th
1789    This Indenture was proved by three witnesses thereto and ordered to be
recorded.       Examined & deld. G. FRENCH          Teste  JNO: CHEW Cl.


pp.       THIS INDENTURE made the twenty sixth day of June Anno Domini one thousand
120-      seven hundred and Eighty nine Between WILLIAM ROBINSON and JOHN ROBIN-
122       SON, Acting Executors of MICHAEL ROBINSON late of Town of Fredericksburg, of
          one part and WILLIAM McWILLIAMS of the Town aforesaid of other part;
Whereas MICHAL ROBINSON by his last Will and Testament in writing duly made and
executed on the Sixth day of January in year of our Lord one thousand seven hundred
and Eighty four and recorded in the Court of Hustings of Fredericksburg on the Sixteenth day of February in said year after having made sundry specific devises directs
that all the rest or remainder of his Estate real and personal not before particularly
bequeathed should be sold by his Executors for the purposes in his said Will mentioned
and appointed his Sons, MICHAEL ROBINSON, WILLIAM ROBINSON, JOHN ROBINSON &
BENJAMIN ROBINSON, Executors of his said Will, but MICHAEL and BENJAMIN refusing to
qualify, WILLIAM & JOHN only proved the said Will and took upon themselves the execution thereof; Now This Indenture witnesseth that WILLIAM ROBINSON and JOHN
ROBINSON by virtue of said Power and Authority in and by the said Will granted and in
consideration of the sum of Five hundred pounds to them in hand paid by WILLIAM
McWILLIAMS, do bargain and sell unto WILLIAM McWILLIAMS his heirs all that parcel
of ground containing about one half an acre situate and being on PRINCE EDWARD
STREET in Town of Fredericksburg being the whole of lott No. 134 which was purchased
by MICHAEL ROBINSON in his life time together with lot No. 133 of JAMES DUNCANSON as
by a Deed Indented and acknowledged by said JAMES DUNCANSON and MARY his Wife
and recorded at the Court held for Spotsylvania County on the twenty first day of
November Anno Domini one thousand seven hundred and seventy one, bounded begining at the corner of AMELIA STREET and the said PRINCE EDWARD STREET and extending to the lott number 136, comprehending the whole of lott No. 134, and also all
houses profits and hereditaments to the premises belonging; To have and to hold the

parcel of ground with the appurtenances unto WILLIAM McWILLIAMS his heirs, And
WILLIAM ROBINSON and JOHN ROBINSON for themselves and their heirs the premises
against them and their heirs respectively and also against the claim of the heirs and
the several Children of the said MICHAEL ROBINSON deceased, will warrent and for ever
defend.  In Witness whereof the said WILLIAM and JOHN ROBINSON, Executors as aforementioned, have hereunto set their hands & seals the day and year first above written
Sealed and delivered in the presents of                    WILLIAM  ROBINSON
        (no witnesses shown)                               JOHN  ROBINSON
  At a Court of Hustings held for the Town and Corporation of Fredericksburg on Friday
the 26th of June 1789          This Indenture for Lotts from WILLIAM and JOHN ROBIN-
SON, Executors of MICHAEL ROBINSON, to WILLIAM McWILLIAMS, was acknowledged by
the said WILLIAM & JOHN ROBINSON and ordered to be recorded
Exd. & deld. Col. McWILLIAMS                    Teste   JNO: CHEW C. C. H.


pp.        THIS INDENTURE made this Twenty third day of May in year of our Lord Christ
122-       one thousand seven hundred and Eighty nine Between WILLIAM SMITH, late
125        Postmaster of the Town of Fredericksburg and ANN SMITH his Wife of one part
           and EBENEZER HAZARD, Postmaster General of the United State of North America
of the other part; Witnesseth that WILLIAM SMITH and ANN his Wife in consideration of
the sum of Five hundred and seven pounds, Nine shillings and five pence 5/8 the current money of Virginia in hand paid by these presents do bargain and sell unto EBENE-
ZER HAZARD his heirs all that Lott of ground being part of Lott No. 72 containing Sixty
one and a half feet front on CAROLINE STREET, thence down the said lot adjoining Lot
No. 71 one hundred and thirty two feet, thence up the said Lot sixty one and a half feet
paralel to CAROLINE STREET, thence one hundred and thirty two feet to the begining,
(on this Lot is a Convenient Wherehouse 40 by 20 feet in good repair with a good tiller
under the whole on CAROLINE STREET, also the lot of ground No. 71 containing half an
acre adjoining) the lot No. 72 both which lots lye and are in Fredericksburg; To have
and to hold the above premises with appurtenances unto EBENEZER HAZARD his heirs,
Provided Always that if WILLIAM SMITH his heirs do well and truly pay said EBENEZER
HAZARD or his certain Attorney the full sum of Five hundred and seventy pounds nine
shillings and five pence 5/8 current money of Virginia before the first day of July
which shall be in year one thousand seven hundred and eighty nine with lawful
interest from the eleventh day of November in year of our Lord Christ one thousand
seven hundred and Eighty eight these presents shall cease determine and be void; In
Witness whereof said WILLIAM SMITH and his Wife have hereunto set their hands and
affixed their seals the day and year first above written
Signed sealed and delivered in presents of
        BARTHOLOMEW FULLER,                          WILLIAM  SMITH
        WILLIAM WIATT, GEORGE  TOD                   ANN SMITH
  At a Court of Hustings held for the Town and Corporation of Fredericksburg the 26th
June 1789           This Deed of Mortgage from WILLIAM SMITH to EBENEZER HAZARD
was proved by the oath of three witnesses thereto and ordered to be recorded
Exd. and deld. Mr. WM. WIATT. (Commission Recd. 133.) Teste JNO: CHEW JR., Cl.


pp.        KNOW ALL MEN by these presents that I WILLIAM SMITH, late Postmaster of
125-       Town and Corporation of Fredericksburg am held and firmly bound unto EBENE-
126        ZER HAZARD, Postmaster General of North America, in the just and full sum of
           One hundred and fourteen pounds Eighteen shillings and eleven pence farthing
current money of Virginia to whom payment shall be made I bind myself my heirs
firmly by these presents; Sealed with my seal and dated this 23rd day of May 1789.

The Condition of the above obligation is that whereas WILLIAM SMITH and ANN SMITH his Wife by their Mortgage bearing even date with these presents sold to EBENEZER HAZARD two certain lotts in the Town of Fredericksburg for the condition of the sum of Five hundred and seven pounds nine shillings and four pence 5/8th current money, Now if WILLIAM SMITH his heirs truly pay EBENEZER HAZARD the full sum aforesaid with lawfull interest thereon, Then the above obligation to be void or else to remain in full force power and virtue in Law
Signed sealed and delivered in presents of
      BARTHOLOMEW FULLER,                    WILLIAM SMITH
      WILLIAM WIATT, G. TOD
  At a Court of Hustings held for the Town and Corporation of Fredericksburg the 26th June 1789      This Bond was proved by three witnesses thereto and ordered to be recorded
Exd. & deld. WM. WIATT                    Teste JNO: CHEW JR. Cl.


pp.      THIS INDENTURE made the first day of May in year of our Lord one thousand
126-     seven hundred and Eighty nine Between CHARLES YATES of Corporation of
127      Fredericksburg of one part and GUSTAVUS B. WALLACE also of the Corporation of
      Fredericksburg of other part; Witnesseth that CHARLES YATES in consideration
of the sum of Fifty five pounds current money by GUSTAVUS B. WALLACE to him in
hand paid, by these presents doth bargain and sell unto GUSTAVUS B. WALLACE his
heirs all that or half acre of ground situate in that part of the Borough or Corporation
of Fredericksburg in that addition made thereto by Colonel FIELDING LEWIS numbered
128 situated on PRINCE EDWARD and WILLIAM STREETs, and in the square described by
the numbers 125, 126, 127 & 128, Together with all houses stables gardens profits and
appurtenances to the same belonging; To have and to hold the lott or half acre of land
with the appurtenances unto GUSTAVUS B. WALLACE his heirs and CHARLES YATES for
himself his heirs doth covenant that GUSTAVUS B. WALLACE his heirs shall occupy the
land without the lawfull lett or distrubance of said CHARLES YATES; In Witness whereof
CHARLES YATES hath hereunto set his hand and seal the day and year above written
                      CHARLES YATES
Received of GUSTAVUS WALLACE Fifty five pounds current money being the consideration within mentioned, Witness my hand this first day of May 1789
                      CHARLES YATES
At a Court of Hustings held for the Town and Corporation of Fredericksburg June 26th
1789    This Indenture was acknowledged by CHARLES YATES and ordered to be recorded
Examd. & Delivd. Colo. G. B. WALLACE          Teste   JNO: CHEW C. C. H.


p.       TO ALL PEOPLE to whom these presents may come, ROGER DIXON of Town of
128      Fredericksburg sendeth Greeting. Whereas ROGER DIXON is seized in fee of a
      certain parcel of Ground being in Town of Fredericksburg on CAROLINE STREET
being part of Lot No. 16.16, about 20 feet being on said Street and running to the corner
of said lot, also another part of the said Lot begining at the distance of thirty feet from
the aforesaid parcel of Ground and running 24 feet front on the said Street, and the
whole depth of said lot with all appurtenances houses &c. now in possession of ROGER
DIXON; Now Know ye that ROGER DIXON being about to absent himself from the State of
Virginia to give full assurances to his Creditors that they not apprehend any loss by
said departure doth by these presents impower JOHN DIXON of County of HAMSHIRE and
State of Virginia to Lease or demise the same to such persons and for such term of years
and under such yearly rents as he shall think fit or otherwise to sell and dispose thereof, hereby ratifying and confirming all such Leases Deeds Sales and other conveyances

which shall at any time hereafter be made concerning the premises; In Witness
whereof I hereunto set my hand and seal this 11th day of April in year of our Lord 1789
Signed Sealed and delivered in presents of

    JAMES LERMOTT,                                    ROGER DIXON
    GEO: SOMMERVILLE, JOHN DONALSON

At a Court of Hustings held for Town & Corporaltion of Fredericksburg June 26th 1789
This Power of Attorney from ROGER DIXON to JOHN DIXON was proved by the oath of one
of the witnesses and ordered to be recorded

                Teste          JNO: CHEW C. C. H.


pp.      THIS INDENTURE made the twenty six day of June in year of our Lord one thou-
129-     sand seven hundred and Eighty nine and in the thirteenth year of the Indepen-
130      dence of the United States of America Between JOHN DIXON, Attorney in fact for
         ROGER DIXON and LUCY DIXON, both of Town of Fredericksburg, of one part and
WILLIAM REAT, Merchant, in Fredericksburg of other part; Witnesseth that JOHN
DIXON in consideration of sum of Sixty six pounds current money of Virginia in hand
paid by WILLIAM REAT, by these presents do bargain sell and confirm unto WILLIAM
REAT his heirs all that parcel of land in Town of Fredericksburg lying on CAROLINE
STREET being part of the corner Lot No. 248 in place of the said Town adjoining to lot No.
16.16; Begining at PRUSIA STREET from thence running up CAROLINE STREET twenty
four feet eight inches, thence running in a straight line at right angles with CAROLINE
STREET the whole depth of the lot, one hundred & thirty two feet; from thence another
straight line towards PRUSSIA STREET from thence to the begining; Together with all
houses improvements and appurtenances belonging; To have and to hold the parcel of
land unto WILLIAM REAT his heirs, And JOHN DIXON Attorney in fact for ROGER DIXON
and LUCY DIXON for themselves their heirs the parcel of land to WILLIAM REAT his
heirs shall warrant and forever defend by these presents; In Witness whereof the said
parties have to these presents interchangeably set their hands and seals the day and
year first above written
Sealed and Delivered in the presents of

    JOHN HARDIA,                                    JOHN DIXON for
    ROBT. THROCKMORTON                              ROGER DIXON
    JOHN COAKLEY                                    LUCY DIXON

At a Court of Hustings held for the Town and Corporation of Fredericksburg June 26th
1789;   This Indenture was proved by the oath of three witnesses and ordered to be
recorded


pp.      THIS INDENTURE made the eighteenth of June in year of our Lord one thousand
131-     seven hundred and Eighty nine and in the thirteenth year of the Independence
132      of the United States of America Between JOHN DIXON, Attorney in fact for ROGER
         DIXON of the County of HAMPSHIRE, ROGER DIXON and LUCY DIXON, both of the
Town of Fredericksburg of one part and JOHN COAKLEY, Mercht., of other part; Witnesseth that JOHN DIXON, ROGER DIXON and LUCY DIXON for the sum of one hundred and
Eighteen pounds current money of Virginia to JOHN DIXON in hand paid by JOHN
COAKLEY, by these presents do bargain sell and confirm unto JOHN COAKLEY his heirs
all that parcel of land in Town of Fredericksburg being on CAROLINE STREET begining
at the upper corner of WILLIAM JACKSON's Lease from ROGER DIXON, from thence
runing up said Street twenty eight feet to the lower corner of DAVID COYLEYs lot which
he purchased of ROGER DIXON four feet of which twenty eight is left for a passage between JOHN COAKLEY and the said COYLEY, thence runing in a straight line at right
angles with the said Street the whole depth of Lot No. 16.16. of which this is a part, one

hundred and thirty two feet from then another straight line runing parallel with
CAROLINE STREET,then running up to the begining, Together with all houses improvements thereon belonging and all estate right title and demand of JOHN DIXON, ROGER
DIXON and LUCY DIXON to the said premises; and JOHN DIXON, ROGER DIXON & LUCY DIXON
and their heirs against every person to JOHN COAKLEY his heirs will warrant and for
ever defend by these presents; In Witness whereof the said parties, ROGER DIXON by his
Attorney, have to these presents interchangeably set their hands and seals the day and
year first above written
Sealed and Delivered in presents of
    JOHN  HARDIA,                           JOHN  DIXON  for
    ROBT. THROCKMORTON            ROGER  DIXON
    WILLIAM  REAT                        LUCY  DIXON
  At a Court of Hustings held for the Town & Corporation of Fredericksburg June 26th
1789   This Indenture was proved by three witnesses and ordered to be recorded
Deld. J. COAKLEY             Teste   JNO: CHEW, C. C. H.

pp.     The Commonwealth of Virginia to GEORGE FRENCH, BENJA: DAY and WILLIAM
133-   HARVEY of the Corpo. of Fredericksburg Gent., Greeting: (The Commission for the
134    privy examination of ANN, the Wife of WILLIAM SMITH, for Deed unto EBENEZER HAZARD
       dated 23d. day of May last); Witness JOHN CHEW JUNIOR Clerk of our said Court this
29th day of July 1789 and the 14th year of the Commonwealth
(Deed recorded in (122).              JNO: CHEW JR.
  Corporation of Fredericksburg, to wit
  In Obedience to the within Commission (the return of the execution of the privy Examination
of ANN SMITH). Certifyed under our hands & seals this 29th day of July 1789
                                GEORGE  FRENCH
  Truly recorded JNO: CHEW JR.       WILLIAM  HARVEY

pp.     THIS INDENTURE made this Eight day of August in year of our Lord one thou-
134-   sand seven hundred and Eighty nine Between HUGH THOMPSON of WILMINGTON
136    in the State of DELAWARE of one part and THOMAS COCHRAN of Fredericksburg
       of other part; Witnesseth that HUGH THOMSON in consideration of the sum of
three hundred pounds specie by THOMAS COCHRAN to said HUGH THOMPSON in hand paid
by these presents doth bargain sell and confirm unto THOMAS COCHRAN his heirs the
said HUGH THOMPSONs undivided moiety of a lot of Ground in Town of Fredericksburg
late known by the name and being part of the LONG ORDINARY LOTT and lying part of
Lot number forty three and is adjoining on the South side by WILLIAM SMITH's ground
and containing Thirty one feet in the front on CAROLINE STREET, extending with such
breadth one hundred and thirty two feet Westward where it is adjoined by the COURT
HOUSE LOTT and which Lot was the undivided property of said HUGH THOMPSON and
THOMAS COCHRAN, Together with all gardens and trees and claim an demand of said
HUGH THOMPSON to the same; To have and to hold the said Lott with apurtenances unto
THOMAS COCHRAN his heirs and HUGH THOMPSON for himself his heirs will warrent and
defend the said lot against all persons; In Witness whereof HUGH THOMPSON have here-
unto set his hand and seal at Fredericksburg the day and year first above written
Sealed and Delivered in presents of us
    JOSEPH CHRISTY, G. HIESKILL,           HUGH  THOMSON
    WILLIAM HERNDON, WILLIAM SMITH
  At a Court of Hustings held for Town & Corporation of Fredericksburg August 28th 1789
This Indenture was proved by three witnesses thereto and ordered to be recorded
Examined and delivered Mr. THOS: COCHRAN      Teste JNO: CHEW Cl.

pp.        THIS INDENTURE made the twenty first day of July one thousand seven hundred
137-    and Eighty nine Between EDWARD CARTER of County of ALBEMARLE and SARAH
138     his Wife of one part and his Son, CHARLES CARTER, of the Corporation of
        Fredericksburg of the other part; Witnesseth that in consideration of the sum of
Five hundred pounds current money of Virginia in hand paid by CHARLES CARTER, by
these presents EDWARD CARTER and SARAH his Wife do bargain and sell unto CHARLES
CARTER and his heirs all those four lots of ground lying in Corporation of Fredericksburg No. 85, 86, 97, 98; and bounded, beginning at the upper corner of Lott No. 85 on
CAROLINE STREET thence running up said Street to FAUQUIER STREET, thence running
Westwardly along FAUQUIER STREET across PRINCIS ANN STREET to CHARLES STREET,
thence down CHARLES STREET to the corner of Lott No. 96; thence paralel with FAU-
QUIER STREET to the begining; Together with all houses and all other appurtenances
thereto; To have and to hold the land hereby granted unto CHARLES CARTER his heirs
free and clear of and from all incumbrances whatsoever; In Witness whereof the said
parties have hereunto affixed their hands & seals the day and year above written
Signed Sealed and delivered in presence of
        JOHN LEGG,                                    EDWARD  CARTER
        JAMES HEATH, JOHN BENSON
  At a Court of Hustings held for the Town and Corporation of Fredericksburg the 23d. of
October 1789   This Indenture was proved by the oath of three witnesses thereto and
ordered to be recorded


pp.        THIS INDENTURE made this 24th day of March in year of our Lord one thousand
139-    seven hundred and eighty nine Between SUSANNAH and JAMES HEATH of the
141     Town of Fredericksburg on one part and ELISHA HALL of said Town of other part
        Witnesseth that SUSANNAH and JAMES HEATH in consideration of the Rents and
Covenants in this Indenture contained on the part of ELISHA HALL to be paid and performed by these presents doth bargain and sell unto ELISHA HALL his heirs a certain
parcell of ground in Town of Fredericksburg part of the lott No. .20 in the part of said
Town beginning at the corner of MAJOR FORSYTHs Lott and extending from said corner
twenty one feet on CAROLINE STREET, from thence a right line one hundred feet from
the Street and bounded on the left by the Lot No. 18 belonging to MAJR. FORSYTH, on the
right by the remaining part of Lott No. 20, and on the back part by the said Lott 20; Together with all water courses profits commodities or hereditaments whatsover, To have
and to hold the parcel of land unto ELISHA HALL his heirs paying for the same on the
Twenty fourth day of March next ensuing and yearly unto SUSANNAH and JAMES
HEATH his heirs the rent of Ten pounds ten shillings specie current money of Virginia
at the rate of Four shillings and six pence Sterling per Dollar, issuing out of said premises, and ELISHA HALL his heirs will at all times hereafter pay all manner of Taxes
and Charges laid upon the said premises and save harmless said SUSANNAH and JAMES
HEATH; In Witness whereof the parties concerned have hereunto interchangeably set
their hands and seals the day month and year above written
Signed sealed and delivered in the presence of
        JOHN HARDIA,                              SUSANNAH HEATH
        GUST. B. WALLACE, THOMAS COCHRAN     JAMES HEATH
  At a Court of Hustings held for the Town and Corporation of Fredericksburg the 23d of
October  1789  This Deed of Lease from SUSANNAH and JAMES HEATH to ELISHA HALL
was acknowledged by the said JAMES and ordered to be certified;  And at a Court held for
said CorpoL the 23d. July 1790; This Deed of Lease was proved by the oaths of three witnesses and ordered to be recorded

pp.     THIS INDENTURE made the first day of April in year of our Lord Christ one
142-    thousand seven hundred and Eighty nine Between SUSANNAH HEATH and JAMES
143     HEATH of Corporation of Fredericksburg and County of Spotsylvania of one part
     and JOHN MAY of the Corporation and County aforesaid of other part; Witnesseth
that SUSANNAH HEATH and JAMES HEATH in consideration of the Rents and Covenants
in this Indenture contained on part of JOHN MAY to be paid and performed, by these
presents do bargain and sell unto JOHN MAY his heirs one part of a lott of ground
situate in Town of Fredericksburg, Lott No. 20, begining twenty one feet from the lower
corner of the said Lott on CAROLINE STREET, thence running up the said Street twenty
one feet, thence runing back one hundred feet, thence runing down the said lott
paralel to CAROLINE STREET twenty one feet and from thence to the begining; To have
and to hold the said part of a lott with the appurtenances unto JOHN MAY his heirs
paying for the same on the first day of April which shall be in the year one thousand
seven hundred and ninety and every year thereafter unto SUSANNAH HEATH and
JAMES HEATH his heirs the sum of Ten pounds Ten shillings current money of Virginia
issuing out of the said hereby bargained premises, to be discharged in Gold at the rate
of Five shillings and four pence a penny weight or Silver at Six shillings and eight
pence the ounce unto SUSANNAH HEATH her heirs on the day appointed for payment,
In Witness whereof SUSANNAH HEATH & JAMES HEATH have hereunto interchangeably
set our hands and affixed our seals the day and year first above written
Sealed & Delivered in presence of
     W.L.STONE,                SUSANNAH HEATH
     JOSEPH CHRISTY, WM. FRENCH     JAMES HEATH
  At a Court of Hustings held for the Town & Corporation of Fredericksburg October 23d
1789   This Deed of Lease was acknowledged by JAMES HEATH and proved by three wit-
nesses as to SUSANNAH and ordered to be recorded
Examined & Deld. W. MAY          Teste JNO: CHEW Cl.

pp.     THIS INDENTURE made this twenty eight day of October Anno Domini one thou-
144-    sand seven hundred and Eighty nine Between JOHN BROWNLOW of Town of
145     Fredericksburg of the first part and WILLIAM LOVEL and ROBERT WALKER all of
     said Town, Merchants, of other part. Witnesseth whereas JOHN BROWNLOW
stands justly indebted to said WILLIAM LOVEL and ROBERT WALKER in the full sum of
Five hundred and Forty pounds Sterling money of Great Britain and desirous to make
the most full provision for payment of said debt and is about to draw one or more Bills
of Exchange in favor of & payable to said WILLIAM LOVEL and ROBERT WALKER or their
or either of their Order directed to JOHN BERARD, Merchant at L'Orient in the Kingdom
of FRANCE, Now the said JOHN in consideration of the performance of the Trusts and
confidences hereinafter contained and the sum of Five shillings in hand paid by WIL-
LIAM LOVEL and ROBERT WALKER by these presents doth bargain and sell unto WIL-
LIAM LOVEL and ROBERT WALKER their heirs all that certain lott of land lying in Town
of Fredericksburg number No. 4, known at this time by the name of the STAGE OFFICE
and also all houses commodities and advantages belonging; To have and to hold the
premises with appurtenances unto WILLIAM LOVEL and ROBERT WALKER their heirs
upon this special condition, nevertheless, that if said Bills of Exhange should not be
honoured and paid but shall come back protested that then WILLIAM LOVEL and ROBERT
WALKER or the Survivor of them their heirs shall sell at publick sale the said lott and
premises sufficient to discharge such sums of money as shall be due on the said Bills of
Exchange together with all reasonable charges for making such sale; In Witness
whereof the parties hereto have set their hands and seals the day and year written

Sealed and Delivered in presents of
  CHARLES  URQUART,    JOHN  BROWNLOW
  ALEXANDER  ROANE    WILLIAM  LOVELL
  JOHN  SANDERS,  KEMP  HURST  ROBERT  WALKER
 At a Court of Hustings held for Town and Corporation of Fredericksburg on Fryday the
27. Novr. 1789   This Deed of Trust from JOHN BROWNLOW to ROBERT WALKER and
WILLIAM LOVELL was proved by three witnesses and ordered to be recorded
Exd. & deld. W. LOVELL    Teste  JNO: CHEW Cl.


pp.  THIS INDENTURE made the twenty first day of May Anno Domini one thousand
146- seven hundred and Eighty nine Between WILLIAM McWILLIAMS and DOROTHEA
149  his Wife of Town and Corporation of Fredericksburg of one part and ROBERT
   GALLOWAY of said Town of other part; Witnesseth that WILLIAM McWILLIAMS
and DOROTHA his Wife in consideration of the rents and covenants herein after contained on part of ROBERT GALLOWAY to be paid and performed by these presents do bargain and sell unto ROBERT GALLOWAY his heirs all that parcel of ground situated and
adjoining the parcel of ground conveyed or sold by said WILLIAM McWILLIAMS to
JAMES PETTIGREWs on the Main Street of the aforesaid Town, extending on the said
Main Street twenty nine feet and from thence back to the Warehous commonly called
ROYSTONs, one hundred feet making an oblong of one hundred feet by twenty nine; To
have and to hold the parcel of ground unto ROBERT GALLOWAY his heirs paying therefore every year on his first day of January the full sum of Seventeen pounds Eight
Shillings of good and lawfull money in Gold or Silver coin at the rate of Six shillings
per dollar without any deduction for Taxes or Charges imposed on said premises by Act
of Assembly or otherwise; And ROBERT GALLOWAY his heirs will at their own proper
costs in all things set up and finish before the first day of January one thousand seven
hundred and ninety one good and substantial House of Brick or well framed of Wood,
two stories high each story of the courses on customary height and divide the same into
roomes and finish them in a good and substantial manner, Provided always that if
ROBERT GALLOWAY his heirs do not before the first day of January one thousand seven
hundred and ninety set up and finish a House of the description aforesaid then this
present grant shall be void; And WILLIAM McWILLIAMS and DOROTHEA his Wife will
warrant and forever defend by these presents; In Witness whereof the above parties to
these presents have hereunto set their hands and seals the day and year above written
Sealed and Delivered in the presence of
  THOMAS COLSON    WILLIAM McWILLIAMS
  ELISHA HALL,  WILLIAM WIATT  DOROTHA B. McWILLIAMS
 The Commonwealth of Virginia to GEORGE FRENCH,  BENJAMIN DAY and JAMES SOMER-
VILLE of Town and Corporation of Frederickburg Gent. Greeting; (the Commission for the
privy Examination of DOROTHA, the Wife of WILLIAM McWILLIAMS); Witness JOHN CHEW clerk
of our said Court this 30th day of November one thousand seven hundred and Eighty
nine and in the 14th year of the Commonwealth
 Corporation of Fredericksburg, to wit, In Obedience to the within Commission to us
directed (the return of the Execution of the privy Examination of DOROTHEA McWILLIAMS); Certified under our hands and seals this fourth day of December 1789
       GEORGE  FRENCH
       BENJ: DAY
 At a Court of Hustings held for the Town and Corporation of Frederickburg on Fryday
the 27th day of November 1789  This Indenture was proved by the oaths of three
witnesses thereto and together with the Commission annexed and Certificate of the
Execution thereo Indorsed were ordered to be recorded

Exd. & deld. ROBT. GALLOWAY                    Teste JNO: CHEW Cl.

pp.      THIS INDENTURE made the third day of December Anno Domini one thousand
150-     seven hundred and Eighty nine Between WILLIAM McWILLIAMS and DOROTHEA
152      his Wife of Town of Fredericksburg of one part and WILLIAM DRUMMOND of said
         Town of other part; Witnesseth that WILLIAM McWILLIAMS and DOROTHEA his
Wife in consideration of the Rents and Covenants herein after contained on part of
WILLIAM DRUMMOND to be paid and performed, by these presents do bargain and sell
unto WILLIAM DRUMMOND his heirs all that parcel of ground lying between the piece
of ground conveyed and sold by WILLIAM McWILLIAMS to ROBERT GALLOWAY and
WILLIAM TAYLOR on the Main Street forty feet and from thence running back to the
Warehouse commonly called ROYSTONs one hundred feet making an oblong one
hundred by forty feet; To have and to hold the parcel of ground unto WILLIAM DRUM-
MOND his heirs paying yearly on the first day of January the full sum of Twenty four
pounds of good and lawfull money without deduction for the Taxes or Charges imposed
on said premises by Act of Assembly or otherwise; And WILLIAM DRUMMOND his heirs
shall at their own proper costs in all things set up and finish before the first day of
January Anno Domini one thousand seven hundred and ninety one good and substantial House of Brick or well framed of wood two stories high each story of the common or
customary height in a good and workman like manner; In Witness whereof the said
parties to these presents have hereunto set their hands and seals the day and year first
above written
Sealed and Delivered in the presents of
        ROBERT GALLOWAY,   JAMES PETTIGREW,          WILLIAM McWILLIAMS
        GEORGE FRENCH, BENJ: DAY                      DORATHEA McWILLIAMS
                                                      WM. DRUMMOND
    The Commonwealth of Virginia to GEORGE FRENCH & JAMES SOMERVEILL, Gentlemen
Justices of the Town and Corporation of Fredericksburg Greeting; (the Commission for the
privy Examination of DOROTHEA, the Wife of WILLIAM McWILLIAMS); Witness JOHN CHEW Clerk
of our said Court this 4th day of December 1789 in the 14th year of the Commonwealth
    Corporation of Fredericksburg Sct. In Obedience to the within Commission to us
directed (the return of the Execution of the privy Examination of DOROTHEA McWILLIAMS);
Given under our hands and seals this 25th day of November 1789
                                JAMES SOMERVILLE
                                GEO: FRENCH
    At a Court of Hustings held for the Town and Corporation of Fredericksburg the 25th
day of December 1789        This Indenture was proved by three witnesses and together with the Commission annexed and Certificate of the Execution thereof indorsed
were ordered to be recorded
Exd. & deld. WM. DRUMMOND            Teste   JNO: CHEW Cl Cur

pp.      THIS INDENTURE made the Second day of July Anno Domini one thousand seven
153-     hundred and Eighty nine Between ABRAHAM MAURY of County of CULPEPPER of
154      one part and THOMAS POSEY, Executor in Wright of his Wife of GEORGE THORNTON
         deceased, of other part; Whereas certain Bonds and Accounts the property of
said GEORGE THORNTONs Estate were put into the hands of said ABRAHAM MAURY by said
THOMAS POSEY to collect and there now remains in the hands of said ABRAHAM MAURY
the sum of Two hundred and forty pounds Virginia currency or thereabouts, of the
money collected and received on the said Bonds & Accounts which said ABRAHAM hath
not accounted for and discharged and ABRAHAM MAURY is desirous of making provision for the paiment of all such sums of money as has been by him received on account

of said Estate, And whereas ABRAHAM MAURY hath by a certain Deed indented bearing date the fourteenth day of December 1789 assigned over to FRANCIS THORNTON, THOMAS POSEY, JAMES LEWIS & JOHN THORNTON certain lands rights slaves goods chattles and Credits, (as by a schedule to the Indenture annexed will more fully appear) the said ABRAHAM MAURY is intitled to receive the reversion and remainder of certain property now in the possession of his Mother, MARY MAURY, to be occupied by him after the death of his said Mother, MARY MAURY, Now This Indenture Witnesseth that in consideration of receiving and paying all such sums as may be due from ABRAHAM MAURY to the Estate of GEORGE THORNTON and the sum of Five shillings in hand paid by THOMAS POSEY by these presents doth bargain sell and confirm unto THOMAS POSEY every part of the Estate and Interest which ABRAHAM MAURY may have in the residue of said property in the said Schedule mentioned after debts in said Deed are discharged; and the Reversion of said ABRAHAM may have in any property of his Mother, MARY MAURY, In Witness whereof the above parties to these presents have hereunto set their hands and seals the day and year first above written

Sealed and Delivered in presence of

    FONTAINE MAURY,                        ABRAHAM MAURY

    JOHN T. BROOKE, THOMAS GOODWIN      THOMAS POSEY

(No recording follows this Deed.)


pp.      THIS INDENTURE made the thirty first day of December in year of our Lord one

155-    thousand seven hundred and Eighty nine Between ELISHA HALL and CAROLI-
       ANNA his Wife of Town of Fredericksburg of one part and RICHARD GARNER of same Town of other part; Witnesseth that ELISHA HALL and CAROLIANNA his Wife for sum of one hundred and ten pounds current money to them in hand paid by RICHARD GARNER by these presents doth bargain and sell unto RICHARD GARNER his heirs one lott or half acre of land lying in Town aforesaid number 144, and adjoines the lotts number 142 and 143; and is on the Cross Street called AMELIA STREET , together with all houses improvements and appurtenances thereon belonging; To have and to hold the said lott or half acre of land unto RICHARD GARNER his heirs and ELISHA HALL and CAROLIANNA his Wife doth further covenant with RICHARD GARNER his heirs that they will warrent and defend the said lott against the claims of all persons; In Witness whereof ELISHA HALL and CAROLIANNA his Wife have hereunto set their hands and seals the day and year first above written

Sealed and Delivered in presents off

    GUSTAVUS B. WALLACE,                ELISHA HALL

    CHARLES URQUHART,

    BENJ: STUBBLEFIELD,  BEVERLEY W. STUBBLEFIELD

At a Court of Hustings held for the Town and Corporation of Fredericksburg the 26th day of May 1790       This Indenture was acknowledged by the said ELISHA HALL and ordered to be recorded


p.      (In margin: from page 157). Memo. The said PHILIP EVANS to pay all Taxes due

156    and imposition that the said Lott as a vacant Lott may be subjected to, during the
      time the said JAMES ABBOTT possesses it

Witness HENRY WHITE                    PHILIP EVANS

    WILLIAM LOVELL, THOS: RUTHERFORD     JAMES ABBOTT


p.      THIS INDENTURE made this fourth day of September in year of our Lord one

157    thousand seven hundred and Eighty nine Between PHILIP EVANS of Town of
      Fredericksburg of one part and JAMES ABBOTT of Town aforesaid of other part;

Witnesseth that PHILIP EVANS in consideration of the Rents and Covenants herein
after mentioned on part of said JAMES ABBOTT to be paid and performed hath demised
and to farm let unto JAMES ABBOTT his heirs one lot of land number 168 in Town of
Fredericksburg which PHILIP EVANS purchased of Mr. JOHN LEWIS, Together with all
profits commodities and appurtenances to the same belonging; To have and to hold the
lott of land with appurtenances unto JAMES ABBOTT his heirs paying PHILIP EVANS his
heirs during the term on first day of June in each year the sum of Ten pounds current
money of Virginia (at its present value) and JAMES ABBOTT doth agree to build such
buildings as he may think necessary; In Witness whereof the parties to these presents
have hereunto set their hands and seals the day & year first above mentioned
Sealed & Delivered in the presents of
    HENRY WHITE,                                    PHILIP EVANS
    WILLIAM LOVELL, THOMAS RUTHERFORD
 At a Court of Hustings held for the Town and Corporation of Fredericksburg May 28.
1790,   This Deed of Lease between PHILIP EVANS and JAMES ABBOTT was acknowledged
by the parties and ordered to be recorded
Examined and delivered JAMES ABBOTT        Teste JNO: CHEW, C.C. H.
(See page 156).


pp.    THIS INDENTURE made the first day of January one thousand seven hundred
158-   and Ninety Between HENRY VOWLES of Town of FALMOUTH of one part and
159    WILLIAM WILLSON of Corporation of Fredericksburg of othe part. Witnesseth
       that said VOWLES for the consideration hereafter mentioned do grant let and
lease to said WILSON during the natural life of said WILSON, his Sons, WALTER and
JAMES, or the longest liver of them, all that part of the lotts in Town of Fredericksburg
that said WILSON now occupies known by numbers twenty three and twenty four, to wit
beginning twenty three feet from the North corner of the lot whereon the BRICK
HOUSE now stands and extending towards the South down the streets sixty eight and one
half feet, thence running back towards the River thirty feet making an oblong of Sixty
eight and one half feet by thirty feet; Also thirty feet beginning at the South East
corner of the Square and running towards the River on a line, thence towards
GENERAL WEEDON's TAVERN LOT twenty feet making a second oblong square of thirty by
twenty feet with the liberty of a four feet alley or passage to get into that part; likewise
Sixty two feet beginning at the Southeast corner on the back lot towards the River and
adjoining COLO. JAMES DUNKINSONs Lot and runing up the River with the Street, thence
extending towards the West in a straight line one hundred and twelve feet making a
third oblong of one hundred and twelve by sixty two feet, the Gate House now occupied
by WILSON covering sixteen feet square of ground with the use of the ally or pass way
between the front and back lots which is made use of to pass to his garden, With all the
appurtenances thereunto belonging to said WILSON his heirs during the three lives; to
possess as long as said VOWLES has a legal right to do so and if said VOWLES his heirs
shall not erect or allow to be any division or pealling higher than five feet on that part
of the lotts adjoining the said WILSONs Dwelling and Store Houses and said WILSON will
not sell nor tenant out any premises to any persons but are proved Good Citizens, it is
also agreed that the revenue and Corporation Tax on the Houses not built by said
WILSON shall be deducted out of the Rent. It is likewise agreed that said WILSON his
heirs will pay VOWLES his heirs the annual Rent of Forty five pounds specie at Quality
payments each year if demanded; the contracting parties bind themselves to the other
in the penal sum of Two thousand pounds specie and have hereunto set their hands and
affixed their seals the day and year first above written    HENRY VOWLES
                         WILLIAM WILSON

At a Court of Hustings held for the Town and Corporation of Fredericksburg May 28th 1790    This Deed of Lease from HENRY VOWLES to WILLIAM WILSON was acknowledged by the parties and ordered to be recorded
Examined & deld. WM. WILSON        Teste  JNO: CHEW, C. C. H.


pp.        THIS INDENTURE made this Twenty second day of March in year of our Lord one
160-       thousand seven hundred and Ninety Between JAMES HEATH and SUSANNAH
162        HEATH both of Town of Fredericksburg of one part and HENRY WHITE of same
           Town of other part; Witnesseth that JAMES HEATH and SUSANNAH in considera-
tion of the Rents and Covenants in this Indenture contained to be paid and performed
by HENRY WHITE by these presents do bargain sell unto HENRY WHITE his heirs a part
of a lot of ground lying in Town of Fredericksburg, Lot No. 20, beginning seventy one
and a half feet from the upper corner of said Lot on CAROLINE and GEORGE STREETs
thence running down CAROLINE STREET twenty five and a half feet, thence back and
adjoining WILLIAM REATs lot one hundred 20 feet, thence running up the said lot
paralel to CAROLINE STREET twenty five and a half feet and from thence to the beginning; And JAMES HEATH and SUSANNAH HEATH for themselves their heirs give for the
benefit of said premises an Alley twelve feet wide extending from GEORGE STREET to the
lowest corner of the above sold premises; To have and to hold to him said HENRY WHITE
his heirs paying for the same on the second day of March each year unto JAMES HEATH
and SUSANNAH HEATH the Rent of Fourteen pounds and Six pence current money of
Virginia issuing out of the said demised premises; And HENRY WHITE his heirs shall pay
and discharge all kind and manner of Taxes or Charges laid or imposed upon the premises; In Witness whereof the said parties have hereunto interchangeably set their
hands and seals the day month and year above written
Signed Sealed & Delivered in presents of
        JOSEPH CHRISTY,                      JAMES HEATH
        WILLIAM SMOCK,                       SUSANNAH HEATH
        THOMAS COCKRAN                       HENRY WHITE
  At a Court of Hustings held for the Town & Corporation of Fredericksburg the 28th May
1790    This Deed of Lease was proved by three witnesses thereto and ordered to be
recorded
Exd. & deld. H. WHITE               Teste   JNO: CHEW, C. C. H.


p.        KNOW ALL MEN by these presents that I GEORGE BAYN of Spotsylvania County
163       for the causes hereafter mentioned & for the sum of Five shillings to me in hand
          paid by HENRY MITCHELL of the Borough of Fredericksburg by these presents do
sell unto HENRY MITCHELL his heirs all my estate and personal vizt. four Negroes
named Clarke, Molly and her Child, Dick, & Cuss, three horses, twenty five head of cattle
six feath beds & the furniture of my House; To have and to hold said premises in Trust
for the sole use and behoof of my Wife, JEAN BAYN & her Children being thereto moved
by the love and regard I bear to them; In Witness whereof I have hereunto set my
hand & seal at Frederickburg this Fourth day of June in year of our Lord one thousand
seven hundred and ninety
Signed sealed and Delivered in presents of
        WILLIAM his mark X  JENKINS,                 GEORGE BAYN
        JOHN CHEVIS
(No recording follows this Deed).          (Page number 163 repeated)

pp.     THIS INDENTURE made on the twenty fourth day of May in year of our Lord one
163-    thousand seven hundred and ninety Between WILLIAM McWILLIAMS and
165     DORATHA his Wife of Town of Fredericksburg of one part and ROBERT GALLO-
        WAY of same Town of other part; Whereas WILLIAM McWILLIAMS and DORATHA
his Wife by a certain Deed indented bearing date the twenty first day of May Anno
Domini one thousand seven hundred and Eighty nine admitted to record in the Court of
said Corporation; did bargain and sell unto ROBERT GALLOWAY his heirs a certain parcel of land lying in Town of Fredericksburg adjoining a parcel of ground conveyed and
sold by WILLIAM McWILLIAMS to JAMES PETTIGREW on the Main Street of aforesaid
Town, extedning from said PETTIGREW & corner along the said Main Street upwards
twenty nine feet and from thence runing back toward the Warehouse commonly called
ROYSTONs one hundred feet making an oblong figure of one hundred feet by twenty
nine feet upon certain Rents and Covenants in said Deed of Indenture mentioned; by
virtue of which Deed ROBERT GALLOWAY became possessed of the piece of ground; Now
this Indenture witnesseth that WILLIAM McWILLIAMS and DOROTHA his Wife for the
sum of Three hundred and forty eight pounds Currency of Virginia to them paid; by
these presents doth bargain and sell unto ROBERT ALLOWAY his heirs all that parcel of
ground with appurtenances thereto belonging; To have and to hold the parcel of
ground unto ROBERT GALLOWAY his heirs without the interruption and denial of
WILLIAM McWILLIAMS his heirs; In Witness whereof the parties to these presents
have hereunto affixed their hands and seals the day and year first afore written
Signed sealed and delivered in presents of
        DAVID HENDERSON,                     WILLIAM McWILLIAMS
        JAMES PETTIGREW,  JAMES OWINS        DORATHA McWILLIAMS
  At a Court of Hustings held for the Town and Corporation of Fredericksburg June 25th
1790;   This Indenture was proved by three witnesses thereto & ordered to be recorded
Exd. & Deld. R. GALLOWAY            Teste            JNO: CHEW Cl.
  The Commonwealth of Virginia to GEORGE FRENCH,  BENJAMIN DAY and JAMES SOMER-
VILLE of the Corporation of Fredericksburg Gent., Greeting (the Commission for the privy
Examination of DORATHA BRAYNE, Wife of WILLIAM McWILLIAMS); Witness JOHN CHEW Clerk
of our said Court this 13th day of June 1790 in the 14th year of the Commonwealth
  Corporation of Fredericksburg Sct. In Obedience to the within Commission to us
directed (the return of the Execution of the privy Examination of DORATHA BRAYNE McWILLIAMS)
Certifyed under our hands and seals this Second of July 1790
                                           GEORGE  FRENCH
Truly Recorded Teste JNO: CHEW C.C.H.      BENJ: DAY

pp.     THIS INDENTURE made this fifteenth day of February in year of our Lord one
166-    thousand seven hundred and ninety Between JAMES HEATH and SUSANNAH
168     HEATH of Corporation of Fredericksburg of one part and WILLIAM REAT of the
        Corporation aforesaid of other part; Witnesseth that JAMES HEATH and SUSAN-
NAH HEATH in consideration of the Rents and Covenants in this Indenture contained on
part of WILLIAM REAT to be paid and performed by these presents do bargain & sell
unto WILLIAM REAT his heirs part of a lot of ground lying in Town of Fredericksburg,
lot No. Twenty, begining ninety seven feet from the upper corner of said Lot on
CAROLINE and GEORGE STREETs, thence running down CAROLINE STREET twenty six feet,
from thence running back and joining JOHN MAYs Lot one hundred and twenty feet,
from thence running up said lot paralel to CAROLINE STREET twenty six feet and from
thence to the beginning, and the Benefit of an Alley twelve feet wide extending from
GEORGE STREET to the lowest corner of the above sold premises; To have and to hold unto
WILLIAM REAT paying for the same on the fifteenth day of February next ensuing and

every year unto JAMES HEATH and SUSANNAH HEATH their heirs the Rent of Fourteen
pounds Six shillings current money of Virginia issuing out of the said demised premises
In Witness whereof the parties concerned have hereunto interchangeably set their
hands and seals the day month and year above written
Signed Sealed and Delivered in presents of

|  |  |
|---|---|
| THOMAS COCKRAN | SUSANNA HEATH |
| HENRY WHITE, | JAMES HEATH |
| THOMAS BARWISE | WILLIAM REAT |

At a Court of Hustigns held for the Corpo: of Fredericksburg the 23d. of July 1790
This Indenture of Lease was proved by the oath of three witnesses thereto and ordered
to be recorded
Exd. and Delivered WM. REAT          Teste  JNO: CHEW, C. C. H.

pp.        THIS INDENTURE made this 16th day of July in year of our Lord one thousand
169-       seven hundred and ninety Between SUSANNAH HEATH and JAMES HEATH of
171        Town of Fredericksburg of one part and THOMAS BARWISE of the same Town of
           other part; Witnesseth that said SUSANNA and JAMES  HEATH in consideration of
the Rents and Covenants in this Indenture contained to be paid and performed by THO-
MAS BARWISE by these presents do bargain and sell unto THOMAS BARWISE his heirs a
tract of land in Town of Fredericksburg being part of Lott No. 20, bounded beginning at
the corner of the parcel of ground lately purchased by DOCTOR ELISHA HALL of said
SUSANNA and JAMES HEATH where it corners on Major FORSYTH's Lott No. 18; running
thence back binding on said FORSYTHs lott thirty two feet, thence a Northwesterly
course forty two feet parallel with CAROLINE STREET, thence by a line parallel with the
first line thirty two feet and thence to the beginning, making an oblong figure of
Forty two feet by thirty two feet, Together with all appurtenances thereunto belonging;
To have and to hold unto THOMAS BARWISE during the term of Ninety nine years renewable at the will of THOMAS BARWISE his heirs and paying for the same on the Sixteenth day of July next ensuing and yearly during the term unto SUSANNAH and JAMES
HEATH their assigns the Rent of Two pounds Two shillings Specie current money of
Virginia at the rate of Four and Six pence Sterling per Dollar issuing out of said premises; THOMAS BARWISE his heirs will at all times hereafter pay and discharge all kinds
and manner of Taxes or Charges laid or imposed upon the said premises; In Witness
whereof the parties hereto have set their hands and affixed their seals the day and year
first above written
Signed Sealed & Delivered in presents of

|  |  |
|---|---|
| G. HEISKELL, | SUSANNA HEATH |
| HENRY WHITE, | JAMES HEATH |
| THOMAS COCKRAN | THOMAS BARWISE |

At a Court of Hustings held in Town of Fredericksburg 23d. day of July 1790
This Indenture of Lease was proved by three witnesses thereto and ordered to be
recorded
Examined and deld. THOMAS BARWISE          Teste  JNO: CHEW, C. C. H.

pp.        THIS INDENTURE made this Twenty second day of March in year of our Lord one
172-       thousand seven hundred and ninety Between JAMES HEATH and SUSANNA
174        HEATH both of Town of Fredericksburg of one part and HENRY WHITE of same
           Town of other part; Witnesseth that JAMES HEATH and SUSANNA HEATH in con-
sideration of the Rents and Covenants in this Indenture contained to be paid and performed by HENRY WHITE by these presents doth bargain and sell unto HENRY WHITE his
heirs a part of a lot of ground lying in Town of Fredericksburg Lot No. 20, beginning

seventy one and a half feet from the upper corner of said lott on CAROLINE and GEORGE
STREETs, thence running down CAROLINE STREET twenty five and a half feet, thence
back and joining WILLIAM REAT's Lot one hundred and twenty feet, thence running up
the said Lot paralel to CAROLINE STREET twenty five and a half feet and from thence to
the beginning, And JAMES HEATH and SUSANNAH HEATH for themselves their heirs do
by these presents grant the use and benefit of the said premises an Alley twelve feet
wide extending from GEORGE STREET to the lowest corner of the above sold premises; To
have and to hold the parcel of land unto HENRY WHITE his heirs, paying for the same
on the twenty second day of March next ensuing and yearly the Rent of Fourteen
pounds and six pence current money of Virginia issuing out of said premises; said
HENRY WHITE his heirs shall at all times hereafter pay and discharge all kinds and
manner of Taxes and Charges laid or imposed upon the said premises; In Witness whereof the parties concerned have hereunto interchangeably set their hands and seals the
day month and year above written
Signed Sealed and Delivered in presents of
          THOMAS BARWISE,                    SUSANNAH HEATH
          G. HIESKILL,                       JAMES HEATH
          THOMAS COCHRAN                      HENRY WHITE
   At a Court held for the Town and Corporation of Fredericksburg on Fryday the 23rd day
of July 1790   This Indenture was proved by the oath of THOMAS BARWISE, GODLOVE
HIESKILL and THOMAS COCHRAN the witnesses thereto and ordered to be recorded
Exd. & deld. H. WHITE                Teste   JNO: CHEW, C. C. H.


pp.        THIS INDENTURE made this fifth day of July Anno Domini one thousand seven
175-       hundred and ninety Between BENJAMIN ROBINSON and MARGT. his Wife of one
177        part and JOHN LEGG of other part, Whereas BENJAMIN ROBINSON is indebted to
           and hath good right and lawfull authority to grant and assign a certain parcel
of ground during the term of the natural lives of JOHN DOLTON and WALTER DOLTON, his
Son, late of Town of Fredericksburg, which parcel of land situate on CAROLINE STREET
in said Town being part of the Lot No. (blank); Beginning on CAROLINE STREET at the
corner of a piece of ground now the property of DAVID SIMONS, from thence running
along the said Street twenty feet, from thence back from the said Street one hundred
and thirty two feet, from thence at right angles with the last line twenty feet and from
thence one hundred and thirty two feet to the begining, making an area or oblong one
hundred and thirty two feet by twenty feet; NOW THIS INDENTURE Witnesseth that BEN-
JAMIN ROBINSON and MARGT. BRUCE his Wife for sum of Twenty pounds to them in
hand paid by JOHN LEGG, by these presents do bargain sell and set over unto JOHN LEGG
his heirs the parcel of ground above mentioned; To have and to hold the piece of
ground unto JOHN LEGG his heirs during the residue of said term of two lives above
mentioned which is yet to come, JOHN LEGG paying yearly the annual Rent of Forty
Shillings to BENJAMIN ROBINSON his heirs from the 22 day of November in the present
year without the denial of said BENJAMIN and MARGT. BRUCE his Wife their heirs and
also of the Executors of the Last Will and Testament of MICHAEL ROBINSON deceased,
Father of said BENJAMIN, and will warrant & forver defend by these presents; In Witness whereof the parties thereto have interchangeably set their hands and seals the
day and year above written
Sealed and Delivered in presents of
          WILLIAM SMITH,                     BENJAMIN ROBINSON
          JOS: CHRISTY, HY: L. GASKINS       MARGARET B. ROBINSON
                                             JNO: LEGG

At a Court of Hustings held for the Town & Corporation of Fredericksburg July 23rd 1790   This Indenture was proved by three of the witnesses thereto and ordered to be recorded
Examined & deld. JOHN LEGG          Teste          JNO: CHEW C. C. H.

pp.       THIS INDENTURE made this Nineteenth day of July in year of our Lord one
178-      thousand seven hundred and Ninety Between ELISHA HALL and CAROLINE his
181       Wife of Town of Fredericksburg of one part and THOMAS BARWISE of same Town
          of other part; Whereas SUSANNA HEATH and JAMES HEATH of said Town did by
their Deed indented bearing date the twenty fourth day of March one thousand seven
hundred and Eighty nine in consideration of the Rents and Covenants in the said Indenture contained did bargain and sell unto ELISHA HALL a tract of ground in said
Town part of lot No. 20, beginning at the corner of MAJOR FORSYTHs Lott and extending
from thence in a right line one hundred feet from the Street and bounded on the left
by Lott No. 18 belonging to MAJOR FORSYTH, on the right by the remaining part of Lott
No. 20, and on the back part by said Lott No. 20, Together with all profits commodites and
hereditaments; To have and to hold the parcel of land to ELISHA HALL his heirs for term
of Ninety nine years renewable forever; paying for the same on the twenty fourth day
of March every year unto JAMES HEATH and SUSANNAH HEATH their heirs the Rent of
Ten pounds Ten shillings specie current money of Virginia at the rate of Four shillings
and six pence Sterling, And ELISHA HALL his heirs will at all times hereafter pay and
discharge all kind and manner of Taxes or Charges laid upon the said premises; To
which said Indenture said SUSANNA HEATH and JAMES HEATH did affix their hands and
seals and whereas THOMAS BARWISE hath purchased the said lot of ground of the said
ELISHA HALL for the sum of Three hundred and twenty pounds current money of Virginia; Now This Indenture Witnesseth that for the sum of Three hundred and twenty
pounds to ELISHA HALL in hand paid by the said THOMAS, said ELISHA HEATH and CARO-
LINE his Wife hath bargained sold and set over unto THOMAS BARWISE and assigns the
said Indenture and Lease  In Witness whereof ELISHA HALL and CAROLINE his Wife
hath hereunto set their hands & affixed their seals the day and year above written
Signed Sealed and Delivered in presence of
          THOS: COCKRAN,                              ELISHA HALL
          JAMES POTTINGER, DW. BACKHOUSE              C. HALL
   At a Court of Hustings held for Town and Corporation of Fredericksburg 23rd. July 1790
This Indenture was proved by the oath of three of the witnesses thereto and ordered to
be recorded     (Commission recorded folio 294).
Examined and deld. THOS: BARWISE          Teste  JNO: CHEW

pp.       THIS INDENTURE TRIPARTITE made the fifteenth day of February in year of our
181-      Lord one thousand seven hundred and Eighty nine Between WILLIAM PEACHY
182       of County of RICHMOND of the first part;  LeROY PEACHY of same County of
          second part; and WINIFRED ARMISTEAD and her Daughters, ELIZABETH BURGES
ARMISTEAD and ALICE PEACHY ARMISTEAD of the third part; Witnesseth that WILLIAM
PEACHY as well for the natural love and Effection which he bares to his Daughter,
WINIFRED ARMISTEAD, and her Daughters, ELIZABETH BURGESS and ALICE PEACHY
ARMISTEAD af for the sum of Five shillings in hand paid the said WILLIAM PEACHY by
LeROY PEACHY, by these presents doth give and confirm unto LeROY PEACHY the lot of
land in City of Fredericksburg number Two hundred and forty nine which WILLIAM
PEACHY encouraged HENRY ARMISTEAD deceased, the late Husband of his said Daugh-
ter, WINIFRED ARMISTEAD, to improve and build on for the benefit of said HENRY
during his life and afterwards for the benefit of his Wife & Daughters by a promise to

secure it to his said Wife and Daughters by Will or Deed after his death In Trust and for
the several purposes following, that is to say, the said lott of land No. 249 with all appurtenances to the use of said WINIFRED ARMISTEAD during the term of her natural
life and after her decease for the use of ELIZABETH BURGES ARMISTEAD and ALICE
PEACHY ARMISTEAD, the Daughters of said HENRY and WINIFRED ARMISTEAD, and their
heirs; To have and to hold said lott No. 249 unto WINIFRED ARMISTEAD and her Daughters according to the aforesaid limitation; In Witness whereof WILLIAM PEACHY hath
hereunto set his hand and seal the day and year above written
Signed sealed & delivered in presents of
    M. PAGE,  WILLIAM LEWIS,     ) acknowledged this 11th day of May 1790
    JAMES LEWIS, JUNR.         )      before JOHN RICHARDS
    JOHN MINOR JR.           )     BEVERLEY CHEW,  WM. C. WILLIS
At a Court of Hustings held for Town & Corporation of Fredericksburg the 23rd July
1790    This Indenture was proved by the oath of one witness thereto and ordered to be
certified

pp.     KNOW ALL MEN by these presents that I JOHN DAWSON of City of RICHMOND in
183-    consideration of JOS: JONES becomes Security for me in a Replevy Bond for the
184     sum of One hundred and twelve pounds 10/, at the suit of CHARLES SAFFRARY,
      assignee of HAYMON and MOFFAT against me as Bail for NATH: TWINING, And in
order to secure and indemnify him from any loss or damage he may sustain on account
thereof, also to secure and make good unto JOSEPH JONES any sum of money I now owe
him or he may be made answerable for on my Account to Messrs. HUNTER and BANKS
and COMPANY, have bargained and sold unto JOSEPH JONES his heirs the following
slaves in his possession, to wit, Joffery and his Wife, Parcilla, with her two Children
Kitty and Abner; To have and to hold the said slaves with their future increase to
JOSEPH JONES his heirs; In Witness whereof I have hereunto set my hand and seal this
the 20th day of June 1790
Witness Attest CHARLES CARTER,                J. DAWSON
  Acknowledged on the 23 July 1790 before us ROBERT MERCER,
      R. BROOKE,  JNO: CHEW
At a Court of Hustings held for Town & Corporation of Fredericksburg the 23d July 1790
This Deed of Trust was proved by the oath of ROBERT MERCER, ROBERT BROOKE & JOHN
CHEW three of the witnesses thereto and ordered to be recorded
Deld. Mr. JONES                Teste   JNO: CHEW, C. C. H. F.

pp.     THIS INDENTURE made this first day of April in year of our Lord one thousand
184-    seven hundred and Ninety Between JOHN COAKLEY and MARY his Wife of one
187     part and WILLIAM GLASSELL of other part; Witnesseth that JOHN COAKLEY for
      sum of Two hundred and twenty pounds to him in hand paid by WILLIAM GLAS-
SELL, by these presents have bargained and sold unto WILLIAM GLASSELL all that parcel of land in Town of Fredericksburg lying on CAROLINE STREET and bounded, Beginning at the upper corner of the land Leased by WILLIAM JACKSON and running thence
up said CAROLINE STREET twenty eight feet to the lower corner of the Lott purchased by
DAVID COYLEY of ROGER DIXON (reserving a Right of Way of four feet between the lott
herein sold and that purchased by DAVID COYLEY), running thence by a straight line at
right angles with CAROLINE STREET the whole depth of Lott No. 16 of which this is a
part, one hundred and thirty feet from thence by a right line parralel with CAROLINE
STREET one hundred and thirty two feet and then by a right line to the beginning; Together with all the lands hereditaments and appurtenances thereunto belonging; To
have and to hold the said Lott unto WILLIAM GLASSELL his heirs and JOHN COAKLEY and

MARY his Wife for themselves their heirs unto WILLIAM GLASSELL his heirs will warrent and forever defend by these presents; In Witness whereof JOHN COAKLEY and MARY his Wife have hereunto set their hands and affixed their seals the day and year first above written
Signed sealed and delivered in presents of                    JOHN  COAKLEY
         (no witnesses shown)                                 MARY  COAKLEY
  The Commonwealth of Virginia to GEORGE WEEDON and GEORGE FRENCH of the Corporation of Fredericksburg Gent., Greeting; (the Commission for the privy Examination of MARY, the Wife of JOHN COAKLEY), Witness JOHN CHEW Clerk of our said Court this 26th day of August 1790 in the 15th year of the Commonwealth
  In Obedience to the within Commission to us directed (the return of the Execution of the privy Examination of MARY COAKLEY); Given under our hands this 26th day of August 1790 in the fifteenth year of the Commonwealth        GEORGE  WEEDON
                                                              GEORGE  FRENCH

  At a Court of Hustings held for Town of Fredericksburg 27th day of August 1790
This Indenture for Land from JOHN COAKLEY and MARY his Wife to WILLIAM GLASSELL was acknowledged by said COAKLEY and together with the Commission annexed and Certificate of execution thereof by the said MARY indorsed ordered to be recorded
Exd. & deld. WM. GLASSELL                      Teste   JNO: CHEW C. C. H.


pp.        THIS INDENTURE made the Seventh day of December in year of our Lord one
187-       thousand seven hundred and Eighty nine Between THOMAS BROWN and SARAH
191        his Wife of Town of Fredericksburg of one part and ZACHARIAH LUCAS of said
           Town of other part; Witnesseth that for the sum of one hundred and thirteen
pounds current money of Virginia to paid to THOMAS BROWN by these presents do bargain and sell unto ZACHARIAH LUCAS his heirs part of a lot of ground lying in said Town number 74, beginning at the upper corner of said lot on CAROLINE STREET, thence running 132 feet on FAQUIER STREET to the beginning; Together with all houses and appurtenances belonging; To have and to hold the premises unto ZACHARIAH LUCAS his heirs and THOMAS BROWN and SARAH his Wife will warrent and forever defend against the claim of all persons; In Witness whereof THOMAS BROWN and SARAH his Wife have herunto interchangeably set their hands and affixed their seals the day and year first above written
Sealed & Delivered in presents of
         WILLIAM WIATT,                                THOMAS  BROWN
         WILLIAM  BERRY G. T. TODD                     SARAH her mark × BROWN
  The Commonwealth of Virginia to BENJA: DAY,  GEORGE FRENCH and WILLIAM HARVEY Gent. Greeting; (the Commission for the privy Examination of SARAH, Wife of THOMAS BROWN), Witness JOHN CHEW Clerk of our said Court the 24th day of August 1790 and in the 15th year of the Commonwealth                   JNO: CHEW
  In Obedience to the within Commission to us directed (the return of the execution of the privy Examination of SARAH BROWN); Given under our hands and seals this 25th August 1790                                          GEORGE  FRENCH
                                                       WILLIAM  HARVEY
  At a Court of Hustings for Town of Fredericksburg the 27th day of August 1790
This Indenture for Land from THOMAS BROWN to ZACHARY LUCAS was proved by three witnesses thereto and together with the Commission annexed and Certificate of the Execution thereof Indorsed, were ordered to be recorded
Exd. & deld. Z. LUCAS                          Teste JNO: CHEW C. C. H. F.

pp.  THIS INDENTURE made this thirtieth day of April in year of our Lord one thou-
191-  sand seven hundred and Ninety Between JOHN BENSON and ELEANOR his Wife of
196  Town of Fredericksburg of the first part, ROBERT WELLFORD of Town of
Fredericksburg of second part; and JOHN WHITAKER WILLIS Gent. of County of
Spotsylvania of the third part. Whereas JOHN BAGGOTT by his last Will and Testament in
writing duly proved and recorded in County Court of Spotsylvania devised to his Daughter, the said ELENOR, one lott and houses (in Town of Fredericksburg) at the River side
which lott was formerly conveyed by FIELDING LEWIS and BETTY his Wife unto JOHN
BAGGOTT by Indenture duly recorded in said County Court and described as all that lott
of ground at the upper end of SOPHIA STREET and No. one hundred and seventy nine
and the said BENSON having intermarried with the said ELENOR, they have agreed to sell
the same to ROBERT WELLFORD: Now this Indenture witnesseth that JOHN BENSON and
ELENOR his Wife for sum of One hundred and fifty pounds current money of Virginia to
them in hand paid by ROBERT WELLFORD by these presents do bargain and sell unto
ROBERT WELLFORD his heirs all the aforementioned lott of ground No. 170; Together
with all houses gardens and Improvements to said lot belonging; To have and to hold Lot
No. 179 with all appurtenances to ROBERT WELLFORD his heirs free and discharged from
all former bargains sales mortgages quit rents taxes & Incumbrances; And whereas the
aforementioned JOHN WHITAKER WILLIS had heretofore contract with JOHN BENSON
and ELINOR his Eife the the lot of ground but before a conveyance was duly made and
recorded for the same, JOHN WHITAKER WILLIS for the consideration herein mentioned
sold all his right in the lot of land; This Indenture therefore further witnesseth that
JOHN W. WILLIS for the sum of Ten Guinea to him in hand paid doth sell to ROBERT
WELLFORD his heirs all said JOHN W. WILLIS's right title and demand both in Law and
Equity in Lot 179; In Witness whereof JOHN BENSON and ELENOR his Wife and JOHN W.
WILLIS have hereunto set their hands and affixed their seals the day month and year
afore written
Sealed and Delivered in presents of
       F. THORNTON, W. L. STONE,                    JOHN BENSON
       WILLIAM WIATT, JOSEPH FANT,                  ELENOR BENSON
       ABNER  VERNON                                JOHN  WHITAKER  WILLIS
  The Commonwealth of Virginia to CHARLES MORTIMER, BENJ: DAY, GEORGE FRENCH,
GEORGE WEEDON and WILLIAM HARVEY Gentlemen of the Corporation of Frederickburg
Greeting; (the Commission for the privy Examination of ELENOR, Wife of JOHN BENSON). Witness
JOHN CHEW Clerk of our said Court this 1st day of May 1790 and in the 14th year of the
Commonwealth                                    JNO: CHEW
  By virtue of the above Commission, we the Subscribers (the return of the Execution of the
privy Examination of ELENOR BENSON); all which we certify from under our hands and
seals as we are within commanded this 1st day of May one thousand seven hundred and
Ninety                                          GEORGE  FRENCH
                                                WM.  HARVEY

  At a Court of Hustings held for the Corpo: of Fredericksburg the 27th August 1790
This Indenture for land was proved by the oath of two witnesses thereto and ordered to
be certified; At a Court continued and held for said Corporation the 28th August 1790;
This Indenture was further proved by the Oath of Wm. L. STONE a witness thereto and
together with the Commission annexed and the Certificate of Execution thereof indorsed
were ordered to be recorded
Examined and Delivered ROBERT  WELLFORD         Teste  JNO: CHEW  C. C. H.

pp.        THIS INDENTURE made this the thirteenth day of July in year of our Lord one
196-       thousand seven hundred and Ninety Between THOMAS POSEY of County of
199        Spotsylvania of one part and JAMES DUNCANSON of Town of Fredericksburg of
           other part; Whereas ROBERT BROOKE Esquire by Deed indented bearing date the
first day of January Anno Domini one thousand seven hundred and eighty six did
demise and to farm let that parcel of ground lying in Town of Fredericksburg between
the lots of JOHN WELCH and MARKET HOUSE LOT containing Fifty five feet front upon
CAROLINE STREET & extending one hundred and thirty two feet back making an oblong
figure fifty five feet by one hundred and thirty two feet, being the third of a Lott formerly sold by the Trustees of SAINT GEORGEs PARISH; To have and to hold the same the
term of thirteen years from the date of said Deed; And Whereas JAMES DUNCANSON hath
obtained a Judgment against ABRAHAM MAURY and the said THOMAS POSEY for the sum
of Five hundred and two pounds, Eighteen shillings and ten pence with lawfull interest
thereon from the fifteenth day of October in year one thousand seven hundred and
Eighty six till paid, and Two hundred and sixty three pounds of Crop Tobacco and Sixteen
Shillings and Six pence which has not been paid or discharged; Now This Indenture
Witnesseth that THOMAS POSEY for the better securing the payment of the sums aforesaid and for Five shillings to him in hand paid by JAMES DUNCANSON, by these presents
doth bargain and sell unto JAMES DUNCANSON his term yet to come in the parcel of
ground before mentioned with all appurtenances except the BLACKSMITHs SHOP, To
have and to hold the said parcel of land except the Shop to JAMES DUNCANSON and
assigns untill the term of Thirteen years shall be fully complete upon Trust to pay and
satisfy out of the Rents and profits thereof the aforesaid sum with interest and costs of
suit aforesaid; and after said Debt interest and costs be fully paid then in Trust for the
use of THOMAS POSEY; In Witness whereof the parties hereto have set their hands and
affixed their seals the day and year first above written
Signed sealed and delivered in presents of
     JAMES DYKES,                                          THOMAS POSEY
     THOMAS GOODWIN, EDWARD HACKLEY                        JAMES DUNCANSON
  At a Court of Hustings for Town of Fredericksburg August 27th 1790
This Indenture between THOMAS POSEY and JAMES DUNCANSON was proved by three
witnesses thereto and ordered to be recorded
Examined & deld. Mr. DUNCANSON             Teste   JNO: CHEW, Cl Cur

pp.        THIS INDENTURE made this fourth day of August Anno Domini one thousand
200-       seven hundred and Ninety Between WILLIAM McWILLIAMS and DORATHA his
203        Wife of Town of Fredericksburg of one part and WILLIAM DRUMMOND of said
           Town of other part; Witnesseth that WILLIAM McWILLIAMS and DOROTHA his
Wife for sum of Four hundred and eighty pounds to them in hand paid by WILLIAM
DRUMMOND, by these presents do bargain and sell unto WILLIAM DRUMMOND his heirs
all that parcel of ground lying in the Town aforesaid and bounded Beginning thirty
feet from the lower corner of ROYSTONs WAREHOUSE LOT from CAROLINE STREET, thence
up CAROLINE STREET forty feet, thence at right angles with said Street one hundred
feet, then at right angles with last mentioned line forty feet, then again at right angles
to the begining, making an oblong figure or area of one hundred feet by forty feet,
And all Houses gardens commodities and hereditaments belonging; To have and to hold
the parcel of ground unto WILLIAM DRUMMOND his heirs, And WILLIAM McWILLIAMS
and DOROTHA his Wife gainst all persons will warrent and forever defend by these presents; In Witness whereof the said parties have hereunto affixed their hands and seals
the day and year first above mentioned

Signed Sealed & Delivered in presents of
    WILLIAM  HARVEY,                    WILLIAM McWILLIAMS
    GEORGE FRENCH, JOHN PROUDFIT    DOROTHA B. McWILLIAMS
  The Commonwealth of Virginia to GEORGE FRENCH,  CHARLES MORTIMER and WILLIAM
HARVEY of Town and Corporation of Fredg., Gent. Greeting; (the Commission for the privy
Examination of DOROTHA, Wife of WILLIAM McWILLIAMS), Witness JOHN CHEW Clerk of our
said Court the (blank) day of August 1790 in the 14 year of the Commonwealth
  Corporation of Fredericksburg, to wit:  In Obedience to a Commission directed to us (the
return of the Execution of the privy Examination of DOROTHA McWILLIAMS);
                             WILLIAM  HARVEY
                             GEORGE  FRENCH

  At a Court held for the Town & Corpo: of Fredericksburg the 27th day of August 1790
This Indenture from WILLIAM McWILLIAMS to WILLIAM DRUMMOND was proved by
three witnesses thereto and together with a Commission annexed and Certificate of Execution thereof endorsed, were ordered to be recorded
Examined & Deld. WM. DRUMMOND        Teste   JNO: CHEW Cl.

pp.      THIS INDENTURE made this the Second day of August Anno Domini one thou-
204-    sand seven hundred and Ninety Between WILLIAM McWILLIAMS and DOROTHA
207     his Wife of Town of Fredericksburg of one part and JOHN PROUDFIT of the said
       Town of other part;  Witnesseth that WILLIAM McWILLIAMS and DOROTHA his
Wife for sum of Three hundred pounds to them in hand paid by JOHN PROUDFIT, by
these presents do bargain and sell unto JOHN PROUDFIT his heirs a parcel of ground
lying in said Town on the Main Street called CAROLINE STREET between the lot of
ground the property of JOHN LEGG and that piece now holden by WILLIAM DRUMMOND
and is bounded; Beginning at the lower corner of the lotts in which ROYSTONs WARE-
HOUSE stands on the Main Street, thence up said Steet and along it thirty feet, thence at
right angles with said Street one hundred feet towards the WAREHOUSE, thence at right
angles with the last line thirty feet to the lower line of said lots and from thence along
the said lower line untill it intersects the Street at the beginning; including an oblong
or area of one hundred feet by thirty; To have and to hold the parcel of ground unto
JOHN PROUDFIT his heirs and WILLIAM McWILLIAMS and DOROTHA his Wife for them
selves their heirs do covenant with JOHN PROUDFIT his heirs that at all times have hold
and enjoy the parcel of ground without interruption or denial of said McWILLIAMS and
DOROTHA his Wife;  In Witness whereof the parties have hereunto affixed their hands
and seals the day and year first above written
Signed Sealed and Delivered in presents of
    WILLIAM  HARVEY,                WILLIAM  McWILLIAMS
    GEORGE FRENCH, WILLIAM DRUMMOND    DOROTHA B. McWILLIAMS
  The Commonwealth of Virginia to GEORGE FRENCH & WILLIAM HARVEY Gent., Greeting
(the Commission for the privy Examination of DOROTHA, the Wife of WILLIAM McWILLIAMS), Wit-
ness JOHN CHEW, Clerk of our said Court the (blank) of August 1790 in the 15th year of
the Commonwealth                    JNO: CHEW
  Corporation of Fredericksburg; In Obedience to a Commission to us directed from the
Worshipfull Court of Hustings (the return of the execution of the privy examination of
DOROTHA McWILLIAMS);              WM.  HARVEY
                             GEORGE  FRENCH

  At a Court of Hustings contd. & held for the Town and Corporation of Fredericksburg
August 28th 1790    This Indenture was proved by the oath of GEORGE FRENCH a witness thereto, and the same being proved by the oath of WILLIAM HARVEY & WILLIAM

DRUMMOND, two other witnesses thereto, And together with the Commission annexed, and Certificate of the Execution thereof indorsed are ordered to be recorded
Exd. & Deld. J. P.                          Teste   JNO: CHEW, C. C. H.


pp.       THIS INDENTURE made the twelvth day of May Anno Domini one thousand
207-      seven hundred and Ninety Betweeen WILLIAM LOTSPEICH and MAGDELEN his
212       Wife of the Town of Fredericksburg of one part and JOHN PROUDFIT of said Town
          of other part; Witnesseth that WILLIAM LOTSPEICH hath this day bargained and
sold JOHN PROUDFIT his heirs part of a lott of ground in aforesaid Town being the upper
moiety of Lott Number Five and bounded by WILLIAMS STREET on the North West,
SOPHIA STREET on the South West and extending along SOPHIA STREET as far as lott
number twenty three being opposite the same and on South East by one other part of
lott number Five belonging to ARRELL of ALEXANDRIA, and on the North West by the
River RAPPAHANNOCK containing one quarter of an acre be the same more or less with
the appurtenances free and clear from WILLIAM LOTSPEICH and MAGDELIN his Wife
their heirs; which moiety of ground WILLIAM LOTSPEICH hath for sum of Forty pounds
current money of Virginia bargained and sold unto JOHN PROUDFIT his heirs; In Witness whereof WILLIAM LOTSPEICH and MAGDELIN his Wife hve hereunto set their
hands and seals the day & year above written
Signed sealed and delivered in the presents of
         WM. GLASSELL, H. VOWLES              WM. LOTSPEICH
         JOHN DAY, WILLIAM TAYLOR             MAGDALIN LOTSPEICH
   The Commonwealth of Virginia to DANIEL TRIPLET,  HENRY VOWLES & ALEXANDER
MORSON of County of STAFFORD, Gent., Greeting (the Commission for the privy Examination of
MAGDALIN, Wife of WILLIAM LOTSPEICH); Witness JOHN CHEW Clerk of our said Court the
29th day of July 1790 in the 15 year of the Commonwealth
   STAFFORD County to wit: In Compliance with the within Dedimus to us directed (the
return of the Execution of the privy Examination of MAGDALIN LOTSPEICH); Given under our
hands and seals this 27th August 1790                    H. VOWLES
                                                ALEXANDER  MORSON
   At a Court continued and held for the Town and Corporation of Fredericksburg August
28th 1790       This Indenture was proved by the oath of HENRY VOWLES & WILLIAM
TAYLOR, two of the witnesses thereto and ordered to be certified; At a Court of Hustings
held for the Town and Corporation of Fredericksburg March 25th 1791; This Indenture
was further proved by the the oath of WILLIAM GLASSELL another witness thereto and
together with the Commission annexed & Certificate of the Execution thereof indorsed,
was ordered to be recorded
Exd. & deld. J. P.                          Teste         JNO: CHEW, C. C. H.


pp.       The Commonwealth of Virginia to BENJA: DAY and GEORGE FRENCH of the Cor-
212-      Corporation of Fredericksburg Gent., Greeting (the Commission for the privy Exami-
213       nation of JANE, the Wife of PHILIP LIPSCOMB for land sold WILLIAM STANARD by Deed
          bearing date 17th day of December 1788); Witness JOHN CHEW, Clerk of our said Court
this 6th day of November 1790 in the 15th year of the Commonwealth
   Corporation of Fredericksburg Sct. In Obedience to the within Commission (the return
of the execution of the privy examination of JANE LIPSCOMB); Certifyed under our hands and
seals this 17th day of November 1790             BENJN: DAY
                                                 GEORGE  FRENCH

Truly Recorded  (Deed in folio 95)
Exd. & Deld. W. L.                          Teste  JNO: CHEW C. C. H.

pp.  THIS INDENTURE made the Sixteenth day of October 1790 Between JOHN LEWIS
214-  Esquire of County of Spotsylvania and MARY ANNE his Wife of one part and
218   ROBERT WELLFORD of Town of Fredericksburg of other part; Witnesseth that said
JNO: LEWIS and MARY ANNE his Wife for the sum of Fifteen pounds to them in
hand paid by ROBERT WELLFORD said JNO: LEWIS and MARY ANNE his Wife do bargain
and sell unto ROBERT WELLFORD his heirs a certain piece or parcell of land bounded by
RAPPAHANNOCK RIVER and lying between the said River and Lott 179 at the upper end
of SOPHIA STREET formerly conveyed by FIELDING LEWIS Esqr. and BETTY his Wife unto
JNO: BAGGOTT); To have and to hold the parcel of land together with all water courses
and improvements and all appurtenances to said parcel of land belonging; the said JNO:
LEWIS and MARY ANNE his Wife for themselves their heirs doth covenant and grant
with ROBERT WELLFORD his heirs that ROBERT WELLFORD his heirs may at any time
hereafter hold occupy and enjoy the said parcel of land without any interruption of
JNO: LEWIS and MARY ANNE his Wife their heirs and will warrant and forever defend
by these presents; In Witness whereof the said JNO: LEWIS and MARY ANN his Wife
have hereunto set their hands and affixed their seals the day and year first above
written
Sealed and Delivered in presents of
     ELIEZER  CALLENDER,                        JNO: LEWIS
     WM. YATES, SAM: STEVENS                    MARY A. LEWIS
  The Commonwealth of Virginia to CHARLES MORTIMER, BENJAMIN DAY, GEORGE
FRENCH, GEORGE WEEDON and WILLIAM HARVEY Gent. of the Town of Fredericksburg
Greeting: (the Commission for the privy Examination of MARY ANNE, the Wife of JOHN LEWIS);
Witness JOHN CHEW Clerk of our said Court this 17th day of October  1790 and in the 15th
year of the Commonwealth              JNO: CHEW
  By virtue of the above Commission, we the Subscribers this day (the return of the Execu-
tion of the privy Examination of MARY ANNE LEWIS); all which we certify under our hands
and seals this 11th day of January one thousand seven hundred and ninety one
                              WILLIAM  HARVEY
                              GEO: FRENCH
  At a Court of Hustings held for the Corporation of Frederickburg 28th Jany: 1791
This Indenture for Land from JOHN LEWIS and MARY ANN his Wife to ROBERT WELL-
FORD was proved by three witnesses thereto and together with the Commission annexed
and Certificate of the execution thereof endorsed, were ordered to be recorded
Exd. & deld. R. WELLFORD                     Teste JNO: CHEW, C. C. H.


pp.  KNOW ALL MEN by these presents that I THOMAS MIDDLETON of Town of
218-  Frederickburg having adjusted closed and finally settled all my Accounts all
220   well with Mr. THOMAS SOUTHCOMB of LONDON, Merchant, with all those whose
transactions with me in consideration of the sum of One hundred and thirty
pounds Sixteen shillings and Ten pence to me paid by CHARLES CROUGHTON as Attorney
in fact for said THOMAS SOUTHCOMB in fault for all demand against him for any Sallery
wages, services and expences incurred concerning his business do by these presents
release and quit said THOMAS SOUTHCOMB from and of any claim I might have against
him on account of any business transacted for or with him and also for the consideration aforesaid as well as other good causes me thereunto moving I do by these presents
under assign and set over under the said THOMAS SOUTHCOMB all my right title claim
and interest in and to all Bonds, Bill, Notes, Goods, Chattles and Credits whatsoever
which have come to my hand whilst engaged in business with said THOMAS SOUTHCOMB
do authorise the aforesaid CHARLES CROUGHTON in my name to take any lawfull means

to effect such end as I myself could or might do for the proper use and benefit of THO-
MAS SOUTHCOMB, In Witness whereof, I have hereunto set my hand and seal this second
day of July Anno Domini one thousand seven hundred and Ninety
Sealed and Delivered in presents
     R. BROOKE,                                    THOMAS MIDDLETON
     R. S. HACKLEY, JERE. MORTON
  At a Court of Hustings held for the Town of Fredericksburg the 25th March 1791
This Release from THOMAS MIDDLETON to THOMAS SOUTHCOMB was acknowledged by the
said MIDDLETON & ordered to be recorded


pp.     KNOW ALL MEN by these presents that I CHARLES CROUHTON as Attorney in fact
220-    for THOMAS SOUTHCOMB of LONDON, Merchant, in consideration of a Release and
221     assignment this day entered into & executed by THOMAS MIDDLETON to THOMAS
       SOUTHCOMB and for divers other good causes and considerations me thereunto
especially moving by these presents do for THOMAS SOUTHCOMB his heirs release and
forever quit claim under the said THOMAS MIDDLETON all dues demands and claims of
him the said THOMAS SOUTHCOMB against said THOMAS MIDDLETON on all and every
account whatsoever originating in North America from the beginning of the world to
the date of these presents which are to be considered and held as a full and compleat
discharge for the same; In Witness whereof I have hereunto set my hand and seal this
Second day of July Anno Domini one thousand seven hundred and ninety
Signed and Delivered in presents of
     R. BROOKE,                                    CHS. CROUGHTON
     JERE. MORTON, RICHARD S. HACKLEY
  At a Court of Hustings held for the Town of Fredericksburg on Fryday the 25th day of
March 1791;   This Release and Indemnity from CHARLES CROUGHTON, Attorney in fact
for THOMAS SOUTHCOMB, was acknowledged by the said CHARLES and ordered to be
recorded
Exd. & Deld. T. MIDDLETON                Teste    JNO: CHEW, C. C. H.


pp.     THIS INDENTURE made this thirteenth day of January in year of our Lord one
222-    thousand seven hundred and Ninety one Between WILLIAM LOVELL and JANETT
223     his Wife of Town of Fredericksburg and County of Spotsylvania of one part and
       ROBERT WALKER of Town and County aforesaid of other part; Witnesseth that
WILLIAM LOVELL and JANETT his Wife for sum of Six hundred and thirty six pounds
specie by said ROBERT WALKER to said WILLIAM LOVELL and JANETT his Wife in hand
paid by these presents do bargain and sell unto ROBERT WALKER his heirs part of the
lott or parcell of ground on the Main Street in the Town aforesaid being numbered 37;
and at present occupied by said ROBERT WALKER, Beginning at the lower corner of said
lott and adjoining the Main Street and runing up the said Street Fifty five feet, from
thence in a straight line back half way through the said lott one hundred and thirty
two feet, thence in a direct line fifty five feet to the Cross Street between the said
WILLIAM LOVELLs and WILLIAM HERNDONs Lotts, thence down the said Cross Street to
the Main Street a beginning, it being the same that WILLIAM LOVELL purchased of
WILLIAM JACKSON Gentleman, Together with all houses stables gardens profits commodities and appurtenances to the same belonging; To have and to hold to ROBERT
WALKER his heirs and WILLIAM LOVELL and JANETT his Wife for themselves and their
heirs do agree with ROBERT WALKER that they will warrent and forever defend the said
granted part of a lott and premises unto ROBERT WALKER against the claim of every
person whatsover; In Witness whereof WILLIAM LOVELL and JANETT his Wife have

hereunto set their hands and seals the day and year first above written
Sealed and Delivered in presents off

|  |  |
|---|---|
| JONATHAN HARRIS, | WILLIAM LOVELL |
| JAMES BLAIR, DAVID HENDERSON, | JANETT LOVELL |
| G. HEISKILL, ANTHONY BUCK | |

At a Court of Hustings held for the Town and Corporation of Fredericksburg 25th March 1791    This Indenture for Land from WILLIAM LOVELL to ROBERT WALKER was proved by three witnesses thereto and ordered to be recorded

pp. 226-227    The Commonwealth of Virginia to WILLIAM HARVEY, CHARLES URQUHART and BENJ: DAY Gent., Justices of Corporation of Fredericksburg, Greeting (the Commission for the privy Examination of CAROLIANNA, Wife of ELISHA HALL, for Deed bearing date 31st day of December 1789 for half acre of land sold to RICHARD GARNER); Witness JOHN CHEW Clerk of our said Court this 1st day of April 1791 in the 15th year of the Commonwealth                    JNO: CHEW

 Corporation of Fredericksburg, to wit;
 In Obedience to the within Commission, we the Subscribers two of the Commissioners therein named (the return of the Execution of the privy Examination of CAROLIANNA HALL); Given under our hands and seals this 27th of May 1791
                    WILLIAM  HARVEY
                    CHARLES  URQUHART

(No further notations or recording shown)

pp. 228-232    THIS INDENTURE made this Twenty fifth day of February Anno Domini one thousand seven hundred and Ninety one Between RICHARD GARNER and ANN RITTA his Wife of Town of Fredericksburg and County of Spotsylvania of one part and GUSTAVUS BROWN WALLACE of the Town and County aforesaid of other part; Witnesseth that RICHARD GARNER and ANN RITTA his Wife for the sum of Two hundred pounds to them in hand paid by GUSTAVUS BROWN WALLACE, do by these presents bargain and sell unto GUSTAVUS BROWN WALLACE his heirs all one certain lott or half acre of ground situate in Town of Fredericksburg marked in the plan by the number 144; adjoining the lotts numbered 142 & 143; and lying on the Cross Street called and known by the name of AMELIA STREET, Together with all houses out houses stables gardens commodities and improvements thereon or thereunto belonging; To have and to hold all the lott and half acre of ground and appurtenances unto GUSTAVUS BROWN WALLACE his heirs; And RICHARD GARNER and ANN RITTA his Wife for themselves their heirs further covenant and grant to and with GUSTAVUS BROWN WALLACE his heirs shall at all times hereafter quietly have hold occupy and enjoy the said Lott or half acre of land with all the appurtenances by these presents conveyed without the let trouble denial or interruption of them the said RICHARD GARNER and ANN RITTA his Wife or of any other persons; In Witness whereof RICHARD GARNER & ANN RITTA his Wife have hereunto set their hands and affixed their seal the day and year first above written
Sealed and delivered in presents of

|  |  |
|---|---|
| BEVERLEY CHEW, GEO: T. TOD, | RICHD: GARNER |
| JNO: CHEW | ANNA RITTA GARNER |

 The Commonwealth of Virginia to BENJ: DAY, CHARLES MORTIMER and WILLIAM HARVEY Gent., of the Corporation of Fredericksburg Greeting; (the Commission for the privy Examination of ANN RITTA, Wife of RICHARD GARNER); Witness JOHN CHEW, Clerk of our said Court the 8th day of April 1791, in the 15th year of the Commonwealth

Fredericksburg to wit:

In Obedience to the within Commission to us directed we the subscribers have this day privately examined ANN RITTA, Wife of the within named RICHD. GARNER; (the return of the execution of the privy Examination ANN RITTA GARNER); Given under our hands this 21st day of April 1791                                    BENJ: DAY
                                                            WM. HARVEY

At a Court of Hustings held for the Town & Corporation of Fredericksburg on the 27th day of May 1791        This Indenture for lotts from RICHARD GARNER to GUSTAVUS B. WALLACE was proved by the oath of three witnesses thereto & together with the Commission annexed & Certificate of the Execution thereof indorsed, were ordered to be recorded

Examd. & deld. GUST. B. WALLACE                Teste JNO: CHEW, C. C. H.


pp.        KNOW ALL MEN by these presents that I HENRY WHITE of Town of Fredericks-
233-     burg and County of Spotsylvania in consideration of Five shillings to me in
235      hand paid as well as for other good causes and considerations me hereunto
            moving, by these presents do for me my heirs release and forever quit claim
unto JAMES BROWN SENR. of the Town and County aforesaid and to his heirs all the
estate right title & demand of me the said HENRY WHITE of in or to one certain part of a
lot of land lying in Town of Fredericksburg containing Fifty seven feet front on CARO-
LINE STREET and extending the full breadth back to the next parallel Street, now in the
possession of said JAMES BROWN SENR. (which tenement WILLIAM JACKSON Gent. by his
certain Indenture bearing date the sixteenth day of June in year of our Lord one thousand seven hundred and Eighty eight did demise grant and to farm let unto said JAMES
BROWN SENR. and HENRY WHITE, their heirs from the first day of December last past
during the term of twenty one years paying unto WILLIAM JACKSON his heirs the yearly rent or sum of Twenty pounds during the term; To have and to hold said part of a lot
of land with its appurtenances unto JAMES BROWN SENR. his heirs during the rest of
the said time of twenty one years yet to come and unexpired under the yearly rent of
Twenty one pounds payable to said WILLIAM JACKSON his heirs and HENRY WHITE his
heirs unto JAMES BROWN SENR. his heirs shall warrant and forever defend; In Witness
whereof I have hereunto set my hand and seal the Twenty seventh day of May in the
year of our Lord one thousand seven hundred and Ninety one
Signed Sealed & Delivered in presents of
        W. W. HENING,                                    HENRY WHITE
        JOHN HARDIA,  EDWD. HERNDON
(No recording shown, the remainder of the page is blank)


pp.        KNOW ALL MEN by these presents that I JAMES MERCER of Town of Fredericks-
236-     burg in County of Spotsylvania in the Commonwealth of Virginia (being one of
237      the United States of America), one of the Judges of the Court of Appeals for the
            said Commonwealth, for diverse causes and considerations me thereunto moving
by these presents do make and appoint WILLIAM BYNHAM Esquire at present of the
County of ESSEX in the Commonwealth aforementioned, Doctor of Physic, and JAMES
MAURY, late of said Commonwealth Esquire, at present a Merchant residing in LIVER-
POOL in the Kingdom of Great Brittain my true & lawfull Attorney and Attornies jointly
and severally for me and in my name as heir at Law, devisee or Administrator of my
Brother, GEORGE MERCER, formerly Lieutenant Governor of NO. CAROLINA, and late of
LONDON deced., to ask demand sue for recover and receive all debts duties or demands
due or owing to me either in my own right or as Heir at Law, Devisee or Administrator

of my Brother, GEORGE MERCER; from every person now residing in the Kingdom of
Great Brittain, and to that end to prosecute for recovery of any such debts or for the
recovery of any last Will and Testament Charter, Deed or other Instrument in writing,
and also all books of Accounts whether the same be in the form of a Ledger, Journal or
waste book lately kept by the said GEORGE MERCER deced., in his own hand writing or by
any other person for his use, and also all printed books, Household furniture, Plate or
Jewels to said GEORGE MERCER belonging at or before his death; hereby granting my
Attornies full power to arbitrate by private submission or rule of Court as fully and
amply as I myself cou'd do were I personally present, hereby ratifying and confirming
all my Attornies or either of them shall do in the premises as fully and amply as if the
same was done by myself; In Witness whereof I have hereunto set my hand and affixed
my seal this 18th day of July in the year of our Lord 1791
Sealed and Delivered in presence of
    G: WEEDON,                                        JS. MERCER
    JNO: CHEW
  At a Court of Hustings held for the Corporation of Fredericksburg on Fryday the 22nd
day of July 1791     The Honble. JAMES MERCER this day in his proper person and in
open Court acknowledged the foregoing Letter of Attorney to be his act and deed which
was ordered to be recorded

pp.    THIS INDENTURE made this 30th day of November in year of our Lord one thou-
238-    sand seven hundred and Ninety Between JOHN FRAZOR, Son and heir at Law of
240    ANDREW FRAZOR deceased, of one part and ELISHA DICKERSON of the Town and
    Corporation of Fredericksburg of the other part; Witnesseth that JOHN FRAZOR
for sum of Fifty five pounds current money of Virginia to him in hand paid, by these
presents doth bargain sell and confirm unto ELISHA DICKERSON his heirs all that lott or
half acre of land in Town of Fredericksburg described by the number 227; And is the
same lott or half acre of land which ANDREW FRAZER in his life time purchased of
ROGER DIXON as by Deed bearing date the seventh day of September 1761 and duly recorded in the County of Spotsylvania will more fully appear; which said lott or half acre
of land is bounded; Beginning at the corner of the said Lott No.227 on the Cross Street,
thence along the Cross Street eight pole, thence a paralel course with the Main Street
Ten pole, thence a paralel course with the Cross Stree eight pole, thence along the back
Street ten pole to the beginning; being at present occupy'd by PATRICK FRITCH, together with all rights members and appurtenances to said lott or half acre of land belonging; To have and to hold the said lott of land with the appurtenances unto ELISHA
DICKERSON his heirs and JOHN FRAZER and his heirs the lawfull claim of all manner of
persons whatsoever shall and will warrent and forever defend by these presents; In
Witness whereof the said JOHN FRAZOR hath hereunto set his hand and affixed his seal
the day and year first above written
Sealed & Delivered in presents of
    BEVERLEY CHEW,                                   JNO: FRAZOR
    WILLIAM W. WILLIS, JOHN HARDIA
  At a Court of Hustings held for the Town & Corpo: of Fredericksburg the 22nd July 1791
This Indenture was proved by three witnesses thereto and ordered to be recorded
Exd. & deld. WM. TAYLOR                              Teste  JNO: CHEW, C. C. H.

pp.    THIS INDENTURE Witnesseth that JOHN ARMSTRONG hath put himself by these
241-    presents with the Consent of his Mother, MARY ARMSTRONG, doth voluntarily
242    and of his own free will and accord put himself Apprentice to JOHN LAWRENCE
    of the Corporation of Fredericksburg & State of Virginia to learn his art trade

and Mistery and after the manner of an Apprentice to serve the said JOHN LAWRENCE
his heirs from the day of the date hereof during the full term of Five years and five
months next ensuing And the said Master shall use the utmost of his Endeavour to teach
or cause to be taught and instructed the said Apprentice in the trade and mistery of a
Taylor, during which time his sd. Master is to give him sufficient schooling to enable
him to carry on his Business, & sd. Apprentices is to have at the expiration a full suit of
cloths besides his common wearing apparell and for the true performance of all the
covenants and agreements aforesaid the parties bind themselves each unto the other
firmly by these presents;  In Witness whereof the said parties interchangeably have
set their hands and seals hereunto dated the twenty second day of July in the year of
our Lord 1791
Sealed & delivered in presents of              JNO: his mark X  ARMSTRONG
        (no witnesses shown)                   MARY her mark X ARMSTRONG
                                               JNO: LAWRENCE
  At a Court of Hustings held for the Corporation of Fredericksburg the 22nd day of July
1791   This Indenture of Apprenticeship was acknowledged by the parties and ordered
to be recorded
Examined and delivered JOHN LAWRENCE   Teste   JNO: CHEW, C. C. H.


pp.      THIS INDENTURE of Apprenticeship made this first day of January Seventeen
243-     hundred and Ninety one Between JOHN FREDERICK, STEPHEN SPOONER, CORBIN
244      TANSILL of the Corporation of Fredericksburg of one part and WILLIAM PEAR-
         SON of the Corporation of Fredericksburg on the other part; Witnesseth that
JOHN FREDERICK, STEPHEN SPOONER, CORBIN TANSILL (being of age) doth voluntarily
and of his own free will and accord put himself Apprentice to WILLIAM PEARSON to
learn his art trade and mistery and after the manner of an Apprentice with him to
dwell and serve for the term of Four years commencing this Inst., and ending the first
day of January one thousand seven hundred and Ninety five during which term they
shall behave as good and faithfull Apprentice ought to do and WILLIAM PEARSON on his
part doth promise to teach or cause to be taught to his Apprentices the trade and
mistery of Hat Making which he now proffesseth and at the expiration of the time of
service to pay him such dues as the Law in that case provide;  In Witness whereof the
parties have set their hands & affixed their seals the day and year above written
Signed sealed & acknowledged in presents of
        JNO: LAWRENCE,                          JNO. & S. & C. TANSILL
        GEO: W. B. SPOONER                       W. PEARSON
  At a Court of Hustings held for the Town and Corporation of Fredericksburg the 22nd
day of July 1791        This Indenture of Apprenticeship was acknowledged by the parties thereto and ordered to be recorded
Examd. & deld. Mr. PEARSON           Teste   JNO: CHEW, C. C. H.


pp.      THIS INDENTURE Witnesseth that WILLIS SWETMAN hath put himself and by
245-     these presents with the assent of the Court of Hustings for the Corpo. of
246      Fredericksburg doth voluntarily and of his own free will and accord put him-
         self Apprentice to GEORGE NORWOOD of the Corpo. of Fredericksburg to learn his
art trade and mistery and after the manner of an Apprentice to serve the said GEORGE
NORWOOD from the day of the date hereof during the full term of four years & ten
months next ensuing; and in all things behave himself as a faithfull Apprentice ought
to do during the said term; And the said Master shall use the utmost of his indeavour to
teach or cause to be taught and instructed the said Apprentice in the art and mistery of

a Shoe Maker in which time the said Master is to give him sufficient Schooling to
enable him to carry on his business, said Apprentice is to have at the expiration a full
suit of cloths besides his common wearing apparell and for the true performance of all
the covenants and agreemtns aforesaid the said parties bind themselve each unto the
other firmly by these presents; In Witness whereof the said parties have interchangeably set their hands and seals hereunto dated the 22d. day of July in the year of our
Lord one thousand seven hundred and Ninety one

Sealed and Delivered in presence of            WILLIS his mark  X  SWEATMAN
        (no witnesses shown)                   GEORGE  NORWOOD

  At a Court of Hustings held for the Town & Corporation of Fredericksburg the 22nd
July 1791         This Indenture of Apprenticeship was acknowledged by the parties and
ordered to be recorded
Exd. and deld. Mr. NORWOOD                      Teste  JNO: CHEW C. C. H.


pp.       TO ALL TO WHOM these presents shall come, I JOHN LEWIS of the County of
247-      Spotsylvania send Greeting. Whereas I the said JOHN LEWIS together with MARY
250       ANNA my Wife by our Deed in Writing this day executed wherein it is ex-
          pressed to be made between me the said JOHN LEWIS and MARY ANNE my Wife of
the one part and Mr. JACOB KUHN of Fredericksburg, Merchant, of the other part, I did
for sum of five pounds current money of Virginia therein mentioned grant bargain
sell and confirm unto JACOB KUHN and his heirs one tract of land containing three
hunered and eighty acres lying and being in County of GREENBRIAR on BIG CLEER
CREEK joining the land of GEORGE CLENDENAN and WILLIAM McCLUNG inclding sd. land
known by FLINUS POINT and bounded, Beginning on the South side of BIG CLEARE
CREEK at a white Oak and Spanish Oak corner of CLENDENNEN & McCLUNG and with their
line struck North seventy seven degrees West two hundred and eighty five pole, crossing CLEAR CREEK to four large white Oaks on a Flatt and leaving said line North fifteen
degrees West seventy four pole to four white Oaks on the point of a Ridge and North
forty nine degrees East thirty eight pole to two white Oaks and North seventy seven
degrees East one hundred and eighty poles to a red Oak by a Gut, North forty three
degrees East one hundred and thirty nine poles to two white Oaks on a Flatt, and North
twenty five degrees West eight two poles to a large white and Hickory and South seventy four degrees East one hundred and forty poles crossing the Creek to a white Oak and
South twenty degrees East three hundred and forty four pole to the beginning; with its
appurtenances thereunto belonging; in which said Deed I did bind myself my heirs to
said JACOB KUHN and his heirs to warrent and defend the said lands generally as by said
Deed more fully appear and since I cannot travel to the Court of said County of GREEN-
BRIAR in order to acknowledge said Deed before the Court of sd. County in order to
admit the same to Record in that Court, Now Know ye that I JNO: LEWIS in consideration
of the foregoing premises and being desirous that the said Deed should be recored in
the County Court of GREENBRIAR so as to forever assure the said lands therein mentioned to said JACOB KUHN his heirs, I JNO: LEWIS doth hereby nominate and appoint my
trusty and faithfull Friend, THOMAS EDGAR Esqr. of LEWISBURG in GREENBRIAR County
my lawfull Attorney in fact to go before the Court of said County at such time as shall be
agreeable to Law and then and there in the presents of said Court to acknowledge for
me and in my name the said Deed hereto annexed to be my act and deed and that the
same was sealed and delivered by me to said JACOB KUHN for the purposes therein
declared; In Witness whereof I have hereunto subscribed my name and affixed my seal
this Sixth day of June  1791

Signed & Delivered in presents of
    JNO: BU(?)                              JNO; LEWIS
    GEO: C. SMOOT,   JOHN UNDERWOOD
  At a Court of Hustings held for the Town and Corporation of Fredericksburg the 22nd
July 1791        This Power of Attorney from JOHN LEWIS to THOMAS EDGAR Esqr., was
acknowledged by the said LEWIS and ordered to be recorded
Exd. & Deld. Mr. KUHN                    Teste        JNO: CHEW C. C. H.


pp.        THIS INDENTURE made the 21st day of July in year of our Lord one thousand
250-       seven hundred and Ninety one Between Messrs. SMITH, YOUNG and HYDE, late
252        of Town of Fredericksburg and State of Virginia of one part and RICAHRD GAR-
       NER of Town and State aforesaid of other part; Witnesseth that said SMITH,
YOUNG and HYDE for the sum of one hundred and fifteen pounds current money of Virginia to them in  hand paid by RICHARD GARNER by these presents doth bargain sell
release and confirm unto RICHD. GARNER & to his heirs the estate right title and
demand whatsoever either in Law or Equity which said SMITH, YOUNG and HYDE now
have or may hereafter claim in a certain lott of ground lying in Town of Fredericksburg and number (65) bounded by LEWIS and SOPHIA STREETs, it being the same lott of
ground purchased by said SMITH, YOUNG and HYDE of JOHN LEWIS and MARY ANNE his
Wife as by a Deed duly proved and recorded in the Court of Hustings for the Corporation
of Fredericksburg reference being thereunto had will more fully appear; Together
with all buildings improvements allys rights and appurtenances thereunto belonging;
To have and to hold the hereby bargained and sold premises with the appurtenances
unto RICHD. GARNER his heirs, and said SMITH, YOUNG and HYDE & their heirs will
warrant and forever defend by these presents; In Witness whereof the said SMITH,
YOUNG & HYDE have hereunto set their hands & affixed their seals the day and year
first above written
Signed Sealed & Acknowledged in the presents of
    JNO: RICHARDS,                          SMITH, YOUNG & HYDE
    BEVERLEY CHEW, GEORGE T. TOD
(No recording shown)


pp.        THIS INDENTURE made the 21st day of July in the year of our Lord one thousand
253-       seven hundred and Ninety one Between RICHARD GARNER and ANN his Wife of
255        of Town of Fredericksburg and State of Virginia of one part and JOHN LEWIS of
       County of Spotsylvania and State of Virginia of other part; Witnesseth that
RICHD. GARNER and ANN his Wife for sum of One hundred pounds current money of
Virginia to them in hand paid by JOHN LEWIS, by these presents hath bargained and
sold unto JOHN LEWIS and to his heirs all the Estate right title and demand either in Law
or Equity which RICHD. GARNER and ANN his Wife now have or may hereafter claim in
a certain lott of ground lying in Town of Fredericksburg No. 65, bounded by LEWIS and
SOPHIA STREETs, it being the same lott of ground purchased by SMITH, YOUNG and HYDE
of the aforesaid JNO: LEWIS and MARY his Wife as by Deed proved and recorded in the
Court of Hustings for the Corporation of Fredericksburg; Together with all buildings
improvements rights and appurtenances thereunto belonging; To have and to hold the
said hereby bargained and sold premises unto JNO: LEWIS his heirs; In Witness whereof
RICHD. GARNER and ANN his Wife have hereunto set their hands and seals the day and
year above written
Signed sealed and delivered in presents of
    JNO: RICHARDS,                          RICHD. GARNER
    BEVERLEY CHEW, GEO: T. TOD

(No recording shown)

pp.     THIS INDENTURE made this Eighth day of Aught one thousand seven hundred
256-   and Ninety one Between JOHN FURNEHOUGH and MARGARETT his Wife of one
257     part and HUMPHREY McAUSLAND of the other part.  Whereas JOHN FURNEHOUGH
hath become bound with one WILLIAM THOMPSON in a Twelve month Replevy
Bond payable to a certain JOHN JOUETT but for the benefit of BOYD & KERR, Merchants
of RICHMOND, and of one GEORGE RICE on which an execution has been issued and
levied on the goods and chattles of the said FURNEHOUGH which execution excluding
Sherrifs Commission amounts to One hundred and sixty nine pounds Five shillings &
three pence; for the satisfying and paying which execution said FURNEHOUGH hath
agreed to convey to said HUMPHREY McAUSLAND the lott and appurtenances herein
after mentioned in Trust for the purpose of selling the same after having advertised it
for three months in the VIRGINIA GAZETTE and VIRGINIA HERALD for ready money and
out of the sale thereof to pay off and discharge the said execution; Now This Indenture
Witnesseth that JOHN FURNEHOUGH and MARGARET his Wife in consideration of the
premises and also of the sum of Five shillings to him in hand paid by HUMPHREY
McAUSLAND do bargain and sell aunto HUMPHREY McAUSLAND all that lott of ground
situate in Town of Fredericksburg known by the number Sixty Eight containing by
survey Seventy six square poles and is bounded, Northwardly by HAWKE STREET, Easterly by RAPPAHANNOCK RIVER, Southerly by lott number Sixty Seven and Westerly by
SOPHIA STREET, together with all houses profits and appurtenances to the same belonging; To have and to hold the said premises unto HUMPHREY McAUSLAND his heirs
In Trust nevertheless for the purpose of selling the same to the best bidder for ready
money, And JOHN FURNEHOUGH and MARGARETT his Wife for themselves their heirs to
said HUMPHREY McAUSLAND his heirs against every person will warrant and defend;
In Witness whereof the said parties have hereunto set their hands and affixed their
seals the day and year first above written
Signed Sealed and Delivered in presence of
      ADAM DARBY,               JOHN  FERNEYHOUGH
      ZEPHA: NOOE,              PEGGY  FERNEYHOUGH
      PHILIP LIPSCOMB          H. McAUSLAND
  At a Court of Hustings held for the Town and Corporation of Fredericksburg 26th
August 1791   This Deed of Trust from JOHN FERNEYHOUGH to HUMPHREY McAUSLAND
was proved by the oath of three witnesses thereto and ordered to be recorded
Exd. & deld. A. DARBY             Teste   JNO: CHEW, C. C. H.


pp.     THIS INDENTURE made the seventh day of April in the year of our Lord one
257-   thousand seven hundred and Ninety one Between THOMAS TOWLES Esqr., late
260     High Sheriff of the County of Spotsylvania of one part and WILLIAM HARVEY
of the Corporation of Fredericksburg of other part; Witnesseth that whereas in
pursuance of a part in the Revenue Act lands are made subject to the Taxes due thereon
and charges attending the sale &c., And Whereas ANTHONY WALKE of County of PRIN-
CESS ANN in the Commonwealth aforesaid, held and possessed a lott or part of a lott of
ground laying in the Corporation of Fredericksburg known by the number 268 and
being so seized stood indebted to said High Sheriff the sum of Two pounds Sixteen shillings for Taxes due on said part of a lott for the years 1784, 1785, 1786, 1787 and 1788; as
per account annexed; Now this Indenture witnesseth that he the said High Sheriff
being constrained to have recourse to the said Revenue Act for want of the said sum of
money due for Taxes on said part of lott of ANTHONY WALKE did give notice in the

VIRGINIA GAZETTE according to Law that so much of said part of lott would be sold at publick auction as would pay the said Taxes and charges accruing by means of said sale and afterwards, to wit, on the twenty fifth day of April in year 1790, the High Sheriff proceeded on the premises to sell by way of publick auction as would make good the sd. deficiency when WM. HARVEY consented to pay the Taxes due on sd part of a Lott of said ANTHONY WALKE for that part of lott contained in the following boundaries; Begining at the upper corner of said lott or part of lott on WATER STREET, thence running down WATER STREET twenty feet, thence Eastwardly to the RIVER RAPPAHANNOCK, thence up said River twenty feet to the upper end, thence Westwardly to the begining at the upper Corner on WATER STREET which boundaries then and there consented to be sold by the High Sheriff as should include the same since which the High Sheriff in confor- mity to the terms of his sale has caus'd the piece of ground to be surveyed by THOMAS MILLER, sworn Geographer for Fredericksburg, agreeable to his plan and Certificate of the same hereunto annexed and THOMAS TOWLES late High Sheriff hath by his author- ity as late High Sheriff sold under the sanction and by the authority aforesaid part of the Revenue Act unto WILLIAM HARVEY & his heirs all that lott of ground contained in the above boundaries and annexed survey and certificate aforesaid; with the appurte- nances thereto belonging; To have and to hold the lott of ground with the appurte- nances by the sanction and authority aforesaid unto WILLIAM HARVEY his heirs.  In Witness whereof THOMAS TOWLES, late High Sheriff aforesaid, hath hereunto set his hand and seal the day and year first above written
Signed Sealed & Delivered in presence of
     JNO: RICHARDS,  WILL: WINSLOW,                    THOMAS TOWLES
     JAMES SLATER,  THOS: MILLER

| ANTHONY WALKE (Princess Ann  To Spots. Sheriff | Dr. |
|---|---|
| Certificate Tax on a lott for 1784 | Ł... 6..0 |
| Ditto & specie half Tax for 1785 | 10..6 |
| Ditto & ditto whole Tax 1786 | 15..0 |
| Revenue Tax for 1787 | 9..0 |
| Do. 1788 | 6..0 |
|  | 2..6..6 |
| Charges advertising 1/; Comrs. fee 6/ | 7 |
|  | 2..13..6 |
| Sheriff Comm. | 2..6 |
|  | 2..16.. |

Errors Excepted  JNO: HERNDON, D. Shf.
 At a Court of Hustings held for the Town and Corporation of Fredericksburg the 26th August 1791   This Indenture for Land from THOMAS TOWLES, late Sheriff of Spotsyl- vania County to WILLIAM HARVEY was proved by the oaths of two witnesses thereto and ordered to be certified;  At a Court of Hustings held for Corpo: afsd., 22nd March  1793. This Indenture was fully proved by the oath of JOHN RICHARDS another of the witnesses thereto & ordered to be recorded
Examined & deld. Mr. HARVEY                    Teste   JNO: CHEW C. C. H.


pp.          THIS INDENTURE made the first day of January in year of our Lord one thou-
260-        sand seven hundred and Ninety one Between PHILIP EVANS of Town of
261          Fredericksburg and County of Spotsylvania of one part and JOHN  BINGIE of the
             Town and County aforesaid of other part; Witnesseth that PHILIP EVENS in consideration of the Rents and covenants hereinafter mentioned on part of JOHN BINGIE to be paid and performed, said PHILIP EVANS hath demised and to farm lett unto

JNO: BINGIE his heirs one certain tenement of land number One hundred and four in
the Town of Fredericksburg which PHILIP EVANS purchased of JOHN LEWIS, Together
with all profits commodities and appurtenances to the same belonging; To have and to
hold the lott of land with the appurtenances unto JOHN BINGIE his heirs from the first
of January paying PHILIP EVANS his heirs the sum of Ten pounds current money of
Virginia (at its present value) and JOHN BINGIE doth agree in consideration of the premises to build or cause to be built such buildings on the lott as he may think necessary;
In Witness whereof the parties to these presents have hereunto set their hands and this
day and year first above mentioned
Sealed and delivered in the presence of
    JAMES SMITH,                       PHILIP EVANS
    RT. GRAY                           JOHN BINGIE
  At a Court of Hustings held for the Corpo: of Fredericksburg the 26th day of August
1791    This Deed of Lease from PHILIP EVANS to JOHN BINGIE was acknowledged by the
parties and ordered to be recorded

pp.      KNOW ALL MEN by these presents that we HENRY FLETCHER of WHITEHAVEN in
262-   County of CUMBERLAND and RICHARD FLETCHER, late of the same place but now
266    of LIVERPOOL in the County of PALATINE of LANCESTER, both in the Kingdom of
       Great Britain, Merchants, surviving partners in trade of the Mercantile House
carried on by them and JOHN SUNDERLAND, late of Fredericksburg in the State of Virginia in North America, Merchant, deceased, under the name of FLETCHERS & SUNDER-
LAND & also surviving Partners in Trade of the Mercantile House carried by them &
JOHN GIBSON, late of WHITEHAVEN aforesaid, Merchant deceased, under the name or
firm of FLETCHERS and GIBSON, by these presents do nominate and appoint and in our
place and stead put and depute CHARLES YATES of Fredericksburg aforesaid and THO-
MAS SIMPSON of the same place, Merchants, our true and lawful Attornies for us and in
our names to enter into & take possession of alll the Warehouses, Stores, Storehouses,
wares, goods, merchandizes, books of account, effects and things whatsoever belonging to us under the name or firm of FLETCHERS & SUNDERLAND, FLETCHERS &
GIBSON or any other account whatsoever, and after possession so had to sell and dispose
of all the goods wares and things in publick open sale or by private contract for the
most money and best price or prices that can or may be had for the same and to receive
all sums of money to arise from such sale or other dispostion thereof, and also to sue for
recover and receive of every person whom it may concern every sum of money both
principal and Interest that shall now be due owing or belonging to us agreeing further to ratify allow and confirm all our said attornies shall lawfully do or cause to be
done in and about the premises by virtue of these presents; In Witness whereof we
have herunto set our hands and seals the third day of March in the year of our Lord
one thousand seven hundred and ninety one
Sealed & Delivered by the above named HENRY
  FLETCHER (being first duly stamped in the
  presence of JOSEPH STEEL,              HENRY FLETCHER
         WM. MOORE                 RICHD. FLETCHER
Sealed and delivered by the said RICHARD FLETCHER
  in presence of JOSA: LACE, J. TAYLOR JUNR.
  This is the letter of Attorney mentioned and referred unto by JOSEPH STEEL Gent. in
his affidavit sworn before me this day, I hereunto annexed      JOHN THOMPSON
                                  Bailiff of the Borough of COCKERMOUTH
                                  3rd March 1791

This is the paper writing or Power of Attorney referred unto by JOHN TAYLOR, Gentleman, in his affidavit hereto annexed, sworn before me this seventh day of March 1791
                    J. SPARLING, Mayor of LIVERPOOL

JOSEPH STEEL of COCKERMOUTH in County of CUMBERLAND and Kingdom of England Gentleman maketh oath and saith that he knows HENRY FLETCHER of WHITE-HAVEN in County of CUMBERLAND aforesaid, Merchant, and that he was present and did see HENRY FLETCHER duly sign and seal and as his act and deed deliver the Letter of Attorney hereunto annexed                          JOSEPH STEEL

The above named JOSEPH STEEL who is a person well known & worthy of good credit was duly and solemnly sworn upon the Evangelists of Almighty God to the truth of the affidavit above before me, JOHN THOMPSON, Esquire, Bailiff and Chief Magistrate of the Borough of COCKERMOUTH in County of CUMBERLAND this third day of March one thousand seven hundred and ninety one                  JOHN THOMPSON
                    Bailiff of the Borough of COCKERMOUTH

JOHN TAYLOR the Younger of LIVERPOOL in County of PALATINE of LANCASTER and Kingdom of Great Britain Gentleman maketh oath and saith he did see RICHARD FLETCHER duly sign and as his act and deed deliver the said paper writing or Power of Attorney hereunto annexed and that the names JOSA: LACE and J. TAYLOR JUNR. set as witnesses to the execution of the said Power of Attorney are of the several hand writing of JOSHUA LACE of LIVERPOOL aforesaid, Notary Publick and of him this deponent
                              J. TAYLOR JUNR.

Sworn at LIVERPOOL aforesaid the seventh day of March in year of our Lord one thousand seven hundred and ninety one before JOHN SPARLING, Mayor of LIVERPOOL

To all to whom these presents shall come, I JOHN SPARLING Esquire, Mayor of the Borough and Corporation of LIVERPOOL in the County PALATINE of LANCASTER do hereby certify that JOHN TAYLOR the Younger of LIVERPOOL Gentleman did solemnly depose to be true the several matters contained in the above affidavit

In Faith and Testimony whereof I the said Mayor have cuase the Seal of the Office of Mayoralty of the Borough and Corporation of LIVERPOOL to be hereunto put and affixed, Dated the seventh day of March in the year of our Lord one thosuand seven hundred and ninety one
Witness JOHN COLQUITT Town Clerk of Liverpool

At a Court of Hustings held for the Town and Corporation of Frederickburg on Fryday August the 26th 1791          This Letter of Attorney from HENRY FLETCHER and RICHARD FLETCHER to CHARLES YATES and THOMAS SIMPSON, together with the affidavit of JOSEPH STEEL and a Certificate of JOHN THOMPSON, Bailiff of the Borough of COCKERMOUTH hereto annexed, and also the affidavit of JOHN TAYLOR JUNR. and Certificate of JOHN SPARLING, Mayor of the Borough and Corporation of LIVERPOOL also hereto annexed are on motion of said THOMAS SIMPSON ordered to be recorded
Exd. & deld. T. SIMPSON                    Teste JNO: CHEW C. C. H.

pp.        KNOW ALL MEN by these presents that we the Honourable GEORGE WEBBE
267-       DANIELL of the ISLAND of NEVIS Esquire, and JOHN ARTHURTON JUNIOR late of
269        the ISLAND of SAINT BARTHOLOMEW but at present residing in the said ISLAND
           of NEVIS Esquire, Merchants and Copartners, by these presents do revoke and
make void all and every Letter, Power of Attorney by us heretofore given unto JAMES REID of ISLAND of NEVIS, Merchant, or unto JAMES ALLASON and JOHN HUNTER now or late of the Town of NORFOLK in the Province or State of Virginia Esquires, Merchants and Copartners, substitutes of him the said JAMES REID for such uses and purposes as in such letters or power of Attorney are therein particularly mentioned And do hereby in

consequence of our revoking such Letter of Power of Attorney by these presents nominate and appoint JAMES SMITH, late of Fredericksburg, in the State of Virginia but at
present residing in said ISLAND of NEVIS, Gentleman our lawful Attorney to ask demand
recover and receive from all persons residing in said Province or State of Virginia or
in any other Province or State belonging or subject to the United States of America, all
such debts sums of money as now are or hereafter shall be owing or payable to us in
the United States of America, and particularly for that purpose to state settle and finally
to adjust all reckonings & accounts now open and depending between us and Capt. JOHN
COOKE, now or late of said Town of NORFOLK, and upon refusal to bring suit for the
recovery thereof; In Witness whereof we have hereunto set our respective hands and
seals this seventh day of September one thousand seven hundred and ninety one
Sealed and delivered in the presence of
    THOMS: PERCIVAL                      GEORGE  WEBBE  DANIELL
                                         JOHN  ARTHURTON JR.

  At a Court of Hustings held for the Town land Corporation of Fredericksburg the 28th
day of October 1791   This Letter of Attorney from the Honble. GEORGE WEBBE DANIEL
Esqr. and JOHN ARTHURTON JR., Esqr. to JAMES SMITH, Gent., was proved by the oath of
the witness thereto and ordered to be recorded
Examined and deld. JAS. SMITH           Teste   JNO: CHEW, C. C. H.

pp.     THIS INDENTURE made the Twentieth day of October in year of our Lord one
270-   thousand seven hundred & ninety one Between ROBERT WALKER of Town of
272    Fredericksburg and County of Spotsylvania of one part and WILLIAM PEARSON
      of the Town and County aforesaid of other part; Witnesseth that ROBERT WAL-
KER for the sum of Two hundred & seventy pounds specie by said WILLIAM PEARSON to
said ROBERT WALKER in hand paid, by these presents do bargain sell & confirm unto
WILLIAM PEARSON his heirs part of the lott of ground on the Main Street in the Town
of Fredericksburg being numbered 37; and at present occupied by GEORGE NORWOOD and
adjoining the house at present occupied by Mr. JOHN MORTIMER, beginning at the Corner of said MORTIMER's House and running down the Main Street thirty two feet, from
thence in a straight line back half way through the said Lott or one hundred and thirty
two feet, thence in a direct line thirty two feet to the corner of said MORTIMERs Fence,
thence down the said Fence to the corner of said MORTIMERs House or begining, it
being part of the lott that said ROBERT WALKER purchased of WILLIAM LOVELL, Together with all houses thereon and appurtenances to the same belonging; To have and to
hold the said part of a lott of ground with the appurtenances to said WILLIAM PEARSON
his heirs, and ROBERT WALKER for himself & his heirs will warrant and forever defend
the granted part of a lott unto WILLIAM PEARSON his heirs against the claim of every
person claiming under said ROBERT WALKER; In Witness whereof ROBERT WALKER
have hereunto set his hand and seal the day and year first above written
Sealed and Deliver in the presence of
    THOMAS MOFFATT,                       ROBERT  WALKER
    ANTHY: BUCK,  JNO: ANDERSON
  At a Court of Hustings held for the Town and Corporation of Fredericksburg the 28th
October 1791   This Indenture was proved by the oaths of THOMAS MOFFATT & JOHN
ANDERSON, two of the witnesses thereto & ordered to be Certified
  At a Court continued and held for the Town & Corpo: aforesaid the 24th March 1792
This Indendure was further proved by the oath of ANTHONY BUCK a witness thereto and
ordered to be recorded
Examd. & deld. WM. PEARSON          Teste  JNO: CHEW, C. C. H.

pp.     THIS INDENTURE made the twenty third day of April in year of our Lord one
272-    thousand seven hundred & ninety one Between WILLIAM HARVEY and FRANCES
277     his Wife of Town of Fredericksburg of one part and CHARLES CROUGHTON of the
      same Town of other part; Witnesseth that WILLIAM HARVEY and FRANCES his
Wife for sum of Nine hundred pounds current money by these presents doth bargain
and sell unto CHARLES CROUGHTON his heirs their part of the Lotts number thirty three
& thirty four situate in Town of Fredericksburg and bounded, beginning on CARROLINE
STREET at the corner of Lott number Thirty three where it joins the lott number thirty
five, the Corner to the STORE of SPOONERs, and running thence sixty five feet two
inches more or less along CARROLINE STREET to the corner of the STORE now occupied
by JAMES SOMERVILLE and formerly called & known by ye name of READS STORE,
thence at right angles by a straight line parallel to WOLFE STREET till it intersects or
runs to PRINCIS ANN STREET to the lott number Thirty six, thence with lotts thirty six
and thirty five to the begining, Together with the Mansion or Dwelling House and all
out houses structures and buildings thereon erected and built standing & being; and all
priviledges profits and appurtenances to the same belonging; To have and to hold the
parcel of land unto CHARLES CROUGHTON his heirs; that the premises now are and forever hereafter shall remain free and clear of and from all other gifts, sales, dower
right and title of dower, and all other charges suffered by WILLIAM HARVEY and
FRANCES his Wife or any other person claiming under them; and WILLIAM HARVEY
and FRANCES his Wife and their heirs against all persons unto CHARLES CROUGHTON his
heirs shall warrant and forever defend by these presents; In Witness whereof the
parties to these presents have hereunto interchangeably set their hands and seals the
day and year first above written
Sign'd Seal'd and Delivered in the presence off
     ROBT. B. CHEW,                        WILLIAM  HARVEY
     CHARLES VOWLES, ZEPH: TURNER         FRANCES  HARVEY
The Commonwealth of Virginia to BENJAMIN DAY & CHAS. URQUHART, JAS: SOMER-
VILLE, CHARLES MORTIMER Esqrs., Gent. of the Corporation of Fredericksburg Greeting
Whereas (the Commission for the privy Examination of FRANCES, the Wife of WILLIAM HARVEY);
Witness JOHN CHEW Clerk of our said Court the 25th day of April 1791 in the 15th year of
the Commonwealth                        JNO: CHEW
Agreeable to the within Commission to us directed, (the return of the Execution of the privy
Examination of FRANCES HARVEY); Certified under our hands & seals this twenty fifth day
of April in Fredericksburg in the year of our Lord one thousand seven hundred and
ninety one                         CHARLES  URQUHART
                                 JAMES  SOMERVILLE
At a Court of Hustings held for the Town and Corporation of Fredericksburg the 28th
October 1791        This Indenture was acknowledged by the within named WILLIAM
HARVEY and together with the Commission annexed & the Certificate of the Execution
thereof indorsed, were ordered to be recorded
Exd. & deld. CHAS. CROUGHTON         Teste   JNO: CHEW, C. C. H.

pp.     THIS INDENTURE Witnesseth that RICHARD MILLS, the Son of MILLY WEST of
277-    the Corporation of Fredericksburg hath put himself and by these presents with
278     the consent of his Mother doth voluntarily and of his own free will and accord
      put himself Apprentice to COLLIN MILNE of the Corporation, aforesaid, Barber,
to learn his art and myster and after the manner of an Apprentice to serve Nine years
and nine months from the day of the date hereof during which term in all things behave himself as a faithful Apprentice ought to do and the said Master shall use the ut-

mose of his Endeavour to teach or cause to be taught and instructed the said Apprentice
in the Trade and Mistery of Barberising and procure and provide for him fitting for an
Apprentice during the said Term, the said Master doth agree to give him sufficient
Schooling in learning said Apprentice to read & write and at the expiration of which
time to have a new suit of cloaths. And for the true performance of all the covenants
and agreements aforesaid the said parties bind themselves ech unto the other firmly by
these presents; In Witness whereof the said parties have interchangeably set their
hands and seals hereunto dated the 25th day of November in the year of our Lord one
thousand seven hundred and Ninety one
Sealed and Delivered in the presence of us          RICHARD his mark X  MILLS
        (No witnesses shown)                        COLLEN MILNE
                                                    MILLY her mark X  WEST

(No recording shown)


p.        TO ALL WHOM these presents shall come, Know ye that I WILLIAM SLAUGHTER
279       of the County of BERKELEY in consideration of the natural live and affection
          which I bear to my Daughter, MARY NOOE, Wife of ZEPHANIAH NOOE, and also for
the sum of Five shillings to me in hand paid by said MARY NOOE and by BAZEL NOOE, a
party to these presents, by these presents do bargain and sell unto the said (blank) Six
Negroe slaves now in possession of said ZEPHANIAH NOOE to wit, Rachell, Esther, Eve,
Milly, James and Frank, together with all and each of their increase; To have and to
hold the said slaves and their increase to said BAZEL NOOE and his heirs forever, In
Trust nevertheless to and for the seperate and particular use of said MARY NOOE & her
heirs and for not other Trust or purpose whatsoever; And said BAZEL NOOE doth covenant for himself his heirs with WILLIAM SLAUGHTER that he and they will at all times
well and truly perform and fulfill the Trust before declared and that he will at all times
hold the said slaves to the use of said MARY NOOE and her heirs forever; In Witness
whereof the parties hereunto have set their hands and affixed their seals in the year of
our Lord one thousand seven hundred and Ninety one April the 19th
Signed and sealed in the presence of
        RICHD. KENNY,                               WILLIAM SLAUGHTER
        JOHN CRUTCHFIELD,  JOHN FERNEHOUGH
(No recording shown)


pp.       THIS INDENTURE made the twenty fifth day of November in year of our Lord
280-      one thousand seven hundred and Ninety one Between PHILIP ROOTS of the
281       DISTRICT of KENTUCKY of one part and GEORGE WEEDON of County of Spotsyl-
          vania & Town of Fredericksburg of other part; Witnesseth that for the sum of
Ninety pounds current money of Virginia to PHILIP ROOTS in hand paid by GEORGE
WEEDON, by these presents doth bargain sell and confirm unto GEORGE WEEDON & his
heirs those two lotts of ground lying in Town of Fredericksburg known by the numbers 230 and 231, and lie contiguous to each other on the Back Street called PRINCESS
ANN STREET and the Lott No. 231 being also on DIXON STREET, and all the Estate right
title and demand of said PHILIP ROOTS to said premises; To have and to hold the lotts
hereby conveyed with appurtenances unto GEORGE WEEDON his heirs, And PHILIP
ROOTS for himself and his heirs the bargained and sold premises with the appurtenances unto GEORGE WEEDON his heirs against every person shall warrant and forever
defend by these presents; In Witness whereof PHILIP ROOTS have hereunto set my have
and seal the day and year above written
Signed sealed and delivered in the presence of
        (no witnesses shown)                        PHILIP ROOTES

At a Court of Hustings held for the Town of Fredericksburg the 25th November 1791
This Indenture for Land from PHILIP ROOTES to GEO: WEEDON was acknowledged by the
said PHILIP & ordered to be recorded
Examined & Deld. JOHN MERCER, one of
the Exrs. of GENL. WEEDON                    Teste  JNO: CHEW, C. C. H.


pp.      This Indenture made this 22nd. day of November in year of our Lord one thou-
281-     sand seven hundred and Ninety one Between JOHN LEWIS of County of Spotsyl-
282      vania and MARY ANN his Wife of one part and JOHN FURNEHOUGH of Town of
         Fredericksburg of other part; Witnesseth that JOHN LEWIS and MARY ANN his
Wife for the sum of One hundred and Ten pounds current money of Virginia by said
JOHN FERNEYHOUGH to JOHN LEWIS in hand paid, by these presents doth bargain and
sell unto JOHN FERNEYHOUGH his heirs all those two lotts or half acres of ground lying
in Town of Fredericksburg known by the numbers 69 & 70, and are bounded by PITT
STREET,  SOPHIA STREET and HAWKE STREET, Together with all the appurtenances there-
unto belonging and all estate right and demand of said JOHN LEWIS and MARY ANN his
Wife their heirs in the same; To have and to hold the two lotts or half acres of ground
and premises with the appurtenances unto JOHN FERNEYHOUGH hs heirs and JOHN
LEWIS and MARY ANN his Wife will warrant and forever defend the title of said Lotts
Number 69 & 70 against the claims of every person whatsoever; In Witness whereof
JOHN LEWIS and MARY ANN his Wife have hereunto set their hands and affixed their
seals the day and year first afore written
Sealed and Delivered in presence off
         GO: LEWIS,                                    JOHN LEWIS
         ALEXR. DUNCAN,                                MARY  ANNE LEWIS
         JOSEPH  WALKER
The Commonwealth of Virginia to CHAS. MORTIMER & GEORGE WEEDON Gent. of the
Corporation of Fredericksburg Greeting, Whereas (the Commission for the privy examination
of MARY ANNE, Wife of JOHN LEWIS); Witness JOHN CHEW Clerk of our said Court the 28th
day of Jany. 1792 in the 16th year of the Commonwealth
  Agreeable to the Commission to us directed, we have this day (the return of the execution
of the privy examination of MARY ANNE LEWIS); Certified under our hands & seals May 6th
1792                                         CHAS. MORTIMER
                                             G. WEEDON

(No recording shown)


pp.      THIS INDENTURE made this 24th day of November in the 16th year of the
283-     Commonwealth and in the year of our Lord one thousand seven hundred and
284      Ninety one Between ELISHA HALL and CAROLIANNA his Wife of the Town and
         Corporation of Fredericksburg of one part and GUSTAVUS BROWN WALLACE of
the same Town & Corporation of other part; Witnesseth that for the sum of Fifty pounds
current money to them in hand paid by these presents do bargain and sell unto GUSTA-
VUS BROWN WALLACE his heirs one certain lott or half acre of land lying in the Town
and Corporation of Fredericksburg and described by the number One hundred and forty
two and is the back Lott on the West side of WILLIAM STREET and adjoins the Lott
number one hundred and forty four; now in possession of RICHARD GARNER, and the
Lott belonging to PHILIP EVANS; To have and to hold the said Lott or half acre of land
and all appurtenances thereunto belonging unto GUSTAVUS BROWN WALLACE his heirs
And ELISHA HALL and CAROLIANNA his Wife for themselves their heirs do further
promise and agree with GUSTAVUS BROWN WALLACE his heirs that they will forever

warrent and defend the said lot or half acre of land to GUSTAVUS BROWN WALLACE
against all persons claiming any right title or demand to the same; In Witness whereof
ELISHA HALL and CAROLIANNA his Wife have hereunto set their hands and affixed
their seals the day month and year first above written
Signed Sealed and Acknowledged in the presence off
    JNO: CHEW,   RICHD. GARNER,          ELISHA HALL
    GEO: T. TOD,  BEVERLEY CHEW
(No recording shown)


pp.      THIS INDENTURE made this 5th day of December in year of our Lord one thou-
285-   sand seven hundred and Ninety one Between PHILIP ROOTES of the DISTRICT of
286     KENTUCKY of one part and JAMES FURGASON of County of Spotsylvania & Town
       of Fredericksburg of other part; Witnesseth that PHILIP ROOTES for the sum of
Twenty pounds current money of Virginia to him in hand paid by JAMES FURGASON, by
these presents doth bargain sell and confirm unto JAMES FURGASON his heirs one lott
of ground lying Town of Fredericksburg known by the No. 211, and lies on PRINCESS
AUGUSTA STREET & PRINCESS ELIZABETH STREET, together with all houses ways profits
and appurtenances to the premises belonging; To have and to hold the lott hereby conveyed unto JAMES FURGASON his heirs and PHILIP ROOTES & his heirs shall warrant and
forever defend by these presents; In Witness whereof PHILIP ROOTES hath hereunto
set his hand & seal the day and year first above written
Signed Sealed and Delivered in the presence of
    GUST. B. WALLACE,            PHILIP ROOTES
    ELISHA DICKERSON, RICHARD PEACOCK
January 31st 1792, Received of JAMES FURGASON Twenty pounds being the whole
amount of the within mentioned consideration money     JNO: DIXON
 At a Court of Hustings held for the Town of Fredericksburg being 24 day of February
1792   This Indenture for Lott from PHILIP ROOTES to JAMES FARGUSON was proved by
three witnesses thereto and ordered to be recorded


pp.      THIS INDENTURE TRIPARTITE made this twenty fifth day of January in the year
286-   of our Lord one thousand seven hundred and Ninety two Between MARGARET
290     BAGGOTT, Widow, Late Wife of JOHN BAGGOTT deceased, and JOHN BAGGOTT one of
       the Sons of the said JOHN BAGGOTT deced. and MARY his Wife of Town of
Fredericksburg of one part and JOHN BENSON of the Town aforesaid of other part;
Whereas JOHN BAGGOTT deceased by his last Will and Testament in Writing bearing date
the third day of April in year of our Lord one thousand seven hundred and seventy
three among other things hath devised in manner following, to wit, I give and bequeath unto my wife, MARGARETT BAGGOTT all my Estate real and personal but one Lott
and Houses at the River Side, I give and bequeath to my Daughter, ELINOR BAGGOTT, the
said Lott and Houses, and if said ELINOR BAGGOTT please God should due without Ear of
her body then said Lott and Houses to be the property of my Wife, MARGARETT BAGGOTT,
Also after the death of my Wife, my Estate to be equally divided between my Four Sons,
JOHN BAGGOTT, JAMES BAGGOTT, THOMAS BAGGOTT, GEORGE BAGGOTT, and if any or
either of the four Children should die, their part to be divided among them living; As by
the said Will duly executed and now of Record in the County Court of Spotsylvania more
fully appears; And Whereas JOHN BAGGOTT hath given and confirmed to JOHN BENSON
and his heirs his undivided fourth part of said JOHN BAGGOTT of in and to the Real Estate
devised by JOHN BAGGOTT deced. to said JOHN BAGGOTT after the decease of said MARGA-
RETT BAGGOT as by the said recited part of the Will of JOHN BAGGOTT deced more fully

appears, NOW THIS INDENTURE WITNESSETH that for the sum of One hundred and fifty pounds Virginia Currency in hand paid, by these presents do bargain sell & confirm to JOHN BENSON and to his heirs one fourth part of the Real Estate devised as aforesaid to said MARGARET BAGGOTT by the said JOHN BAGGOTT deceased and the said undivided fourth part of the Reversion Remainder title and demand of said JOHN BAGGOTT in the Real Estate devised as aforesaid to said JOHN BAGGOTT by said JOHN BAGGOTT deceased; To have and to hold the said undivided fourth part of the aforesaid Real Estate devised to the said MARGARETT and the said undivided fourth part of the Reversion Remainder title and demand of JOHN BAGGOTT in the Real Estate devised to him to said JOHN BENSON his heirs, In Witness whereof the parties to this Indenture have hereunto set their hands and affix'd their seals the day month and year first above written
Signed sealed and delivered in the presence of

| | |
|---|---|
| GEORGE BAGGOTT, | MARGARET BAGGOTT |
| ROBERT  BRANHAM, | JOHN BAGGOTT |
| HENRY L. GASKINS | MARY BAGGOTT |

The Commonwealth of Virginia to GEORGE WEEDON, BENJA: DAY and JAS. SOMERVILLE Gent. of the Town and Corporation of Fredericksburg Greeting, Whereas (the Commission for the privy Examination of MARY, the Wife of JOHN BAGGOTT); Witness JOHN CHEW Clerk of our said Court the twenty sixth day of January 1792 in the 16th year of the Commonwealth                                        JNO: CHEW

In Obedience to the annexed Commission to us directed we have privately (the return of the Execution of the privy Examination of MARY BAGGOTT); Certified under our hands and seals this Twenty sixth day of January 1792                       BENJ: DAY
                                                                 G. WEEDON

(No recording shown)


pp.        THIS INDENTURE made this sixth day of July in year of our Lord one thousand
291-       seven hundred and Ninety one Between GEORGE AUGUSTINE WASHINGTON and
293        FRANCES his Wife of County of FAIRFAX of one part and LARKIN SMITH of Coun-
           ty of KING and QUEEN of other part; Witnesseth that GEORGE AUGUSTINE
WASHINGTON and FRANCES his Wife for the sum of Seven hundred pounds Virginia currency, by these presents doth bargain sell release and confirm unto LARKIN SMITH and to his heirs all the estate right title and demand either in Law or Equity which said GEORGE AUGUSTINE WASHINGTON and FRANCES his Wife now have or may hereafter have in two lotts of ground lying in Town of Fredericksburg marked number Eighty seven and Eighty eight as by Deed from WARNER LEWIS to CHARLES WASHINGTON and by Deed from said CHARLES WASHINGTON and MILDRED his Wife to said GEORGE AUGT. WASHINGTON recorded in the County Court of Spotsylvania may more fully appear; Together with all buildings improvements rights and appurtenances thereunto belonging; To have and to hold the hereby bargained and sold premises with the appurtenances unto LARKIN SMITH his heirs and GEORGE AUGUSTINE WASHINGTON and FRANCES his Wife and their heirs against all persons shall warrant and forever defend by these presents; In Witness wherof GEORGE AUGUSTINE WASHINGTON and FRANCES his Wife have hereunto set their hands and seals the day and year above written
Sealed & Delivered in presence of

| | |
|---|---|
| WM. HERBERT, JOHN POTTS JR., | GO: WASHINGTON |
| CHARLES LEE, BUSHROD WASHINGTON, | FRANCES WASHINGTON |

Reacknowledged this 23rd day of Feby. 1792 in presence of us

| | |
|---|---|
| CHAS. CARTER JUNR., B. BALL, | GO: WASHINGTON |
| HOWELL LEWIS, LAWRENCE LEWIS, | |
| GO: LEWIS | |

The Commonwealth of Virginia to WM. HERBERT & JNO. POTTS JUNR., Gent. Greeting;
Whereas (the Commission for the privy Examination of FRANCES, the Wife of GEORGE AUGUSTINE
WASHINGTON); Witness JOHN CHEW, Clerk of our said Court the Sixth day of July in the
fifteenth year of the Commonwealth                JNO: CHEW
   FAIRFAX County, to wit: Pursuant to the within Commision, we went personally to the
within named FRANCES and examined her privately (the return of the Execution of the privy
Examination of FRANCES WASHINGTON); Given under our hands and seals this Sixth day of
July in the year of our Lord one thousand seven hundred and Ninety one
                              WM. HERBERT
                              JOHN POTTS JUNR.
(No recording shown)


p.       The Commonwealth of Virginia to BENJN. DAY, GEORGE FRENCH and GEORGE
294      WEEDON Gent. of Town and Corporation of Fredericksburg Greeting, Whereas
         (the Commission for the privy Examination of CAROLINE, Wife of ELISHA HALL, for sale of
land by Deed bearing date 19th day of July 1790 to THOMAS BARWISE); Witness JOHN CHEW,
Clerk of our said Court this 21st January 1791 in the 15th year of the Commonwealth
  Corpo: of Fredg. Sct.  In Obedience to the annexed Commission to us directed, we (the
return of the Execution of the privy Examination of CAROLINE HALL); Certified under our hands
and seals this twenty seventh day of January 1791      BENJN: DAY
Truly Recorded JNO: CHEW, C. C. H.                     GEO: FRENCH
Exd. & Deld. Mr. BARWISE


pp.      THIS INDENTURE made this sixth day of March one thousand seven hundred
295-     and Ninety two Between JOHN LEGG of the one part and DAVID SIMONS of the
297      other part; Whereas JOHN LEGG is intitled to and hath good right full power and
         lawfull authority to assign a certain parcel of ground with the appurtenances
during the term of the natural lifes of JOHN DALTON and his Son, WALTER DALTON, late
of the Town of Fredericksburg, which parcel of ground situate on CAROLINE STREET is
part of lott No. 49; and bounded Beginning on CAROLINE STREET at the corner of a piece
of ground now the property of DAVID SIMONS, from thence running along the said
Street twenty feet, from thence back from said Street one hundred and thirty two feet
from thence at right angles with the last line twenty feet & from thence one hundred &
thirty two feet to the beginning, making an acre or oblong of one hundred and thirty
two feet by twenty feet, Now This Indenture Witnesseth that JOHN LEGG for sum of fifty
pounds to him paid by DAVID SIMONS by these presents do bargain sell and sett over
unto DAVID SIMONS his heirs the said parcel of ground and all right estate and demand
of said JOHN LEGG in the said premises; To have and to hold the piece of ground with the
appurtenances unto DAVID SIMONS his heirs during the rest of the said term of two
lives above mentioned which is yet to come, said DAVID SIMONS paying yearly the
annual Rent or sum of Forty shillings to JOHN LEGG his heirs to be estimated from the
date hereof; In Witness whereof the parties have hereto interchangeably sett their
hands and seals the day and year above written
          (No witnesses shown)                    JNO: LEGG
                                                  DAVID SIMONS
   At a Court held for the Town and Corporation of Fredericksburg the 23rd of March 1792
This Deed of Lease was acknowledged by the parties and ordered to be recorded


pp.      THIS INDENTURE Witnesseth that Whereas WILLIAM JACKSON in his lifetime by
298-     Indenture of Lease bearing date the 22nd day of October in year of our Lord one
300      thousand seven hundred and Eighty seven did demise grant and to farm lett unto

WILLIAM LOVELL one certain parcel of ground being in Town of Fredericksburg
fronting on CAROLINE STREET Twenty four feet and runing back the same breadth one
hundred and thirty two feet, being part of the lott of ground at that time in the tenure
and occupation of Mr. WILLIAM SMOCK, wherein it was covenanted that WILLIAM
LOVELL should hold the parcel of ground for the term of Sixteen years paying WILLIAM
JACKSON yearly on the first day of January the sum of One shillings current money if
the same should be demanded as will appear by the said Indenture duly recorded in the
Court of Hustings of Fredericksburg; And whereas it having been mutually agreed
between WILLIAM LOVELL and ROBERT BEVERLEY CHEW (now deceased) that for the
sum of One hundred and fifty pounds by ROBERT BEVERLEY CHEW in his lifetime to
WILLIAM LOVELL in hand paid said WILLIAM LOVELL and ROBERT BEVERLEY CHEW
would hold the parcel of ground during the term mentioned as Tenants in Common &
account with each other for the profits that might arise from the said premises by way
of Rent or otherwise, But the agreement between WILLIAM LOVELL and ROBERT
BEVERLEY CHEW never having been carried into effect by any written Instrument,
they solely depending on the Confidence they placed in each otehr for the performance of the agreement, And Whereas ROBERT BEVERLEY CHEW deceased having by his
last Will and Testament devising his moiety & interest to his Brother, JOHN CHEW, to be
held by him in Trust for the use of said JOHN CHEW's two Daughters, POLLY and ELIZA-
BETH, and said WILLIAM LOVELL in consideration of the agreement between him and
ROBERT BEVERLEY CHEW being willing to secure the said JOHN CHEWs. (for the purpose
of the Trust aforesaid) one moiety of the profits that may arise from the said premises,
the said WILLIAM LOVELL by these presents convey unto JOHN CHEW his heirs one
moiety of the aforesaid premises during the term stipulated in as full and ample manner if the agreement had been carried into effect; And further WILLIAM LOVELL doth
agree with JOHN CHEW that he will warrant and defend the title of one moiety of the
aforesaid premises during the term stipulated in the Indenture of Lease from said
WILLIAM JACKSON; In Witness whereof WILLIAM LOVELL hath hereunto set his hand &
seal this the twenty third day of March one thousand seven hundred and ninety two
Sealed and Delivered in the presence of
        (no witnesses shown)                          WILLIAM  LOVELL
   At a Court of Hustings held for the Town and Corporation of Frederickburg the 23rd
day of March  1792    This Indenture was acknowledged by WILLIAM LOVELL and
ordered to be recorded

pp.      THIS INDENTURE TRIPARTITE made this 20th day of October in year of our Lord
300-     one thousand seven hundred and Ninety one Between LARKIN SMITH of County
305      KING & QUEEN and MARY ELEANOR his Wife of the first part; JAMES  GILLIES of
         Town of ALEXANDRIA in the County of FAIRFAX, Doctor of Phisick, and FRANCES
his Wife of the second part and GEORGE FRENCH of the Town of Fredericksburg in the
County of Spotsylvania, Doctor of Phisick, of the third part; Whereas LARKIN SMITH in
consideratin of the sum of Eight hundred pounds to him in hand paid, did sell unto
JAMES GILLIES two lotts or half acres of ground lying in Town of Fredericksburg and
known by the numbers 255 & 265, and JAMES GILLIES before obtaining a Conveyance
from LARKIN SMITH for the said Lotts hath agreed to sell the same to GEORGE FRENCH
herein after expressed; Now This Indenture Witnesseth that JAMES GILLIES and FRAN-
CES his Wife for the sum of Seven hundred & fifty pounds current money of Virginia to
them in hand paid by GEORGE FRENCH, and the said JAMES GILLIES and FRANCES his
Wife with the consent and approbation of LARKIN SMITH & MARY ELEANOR his Wife,
testified by their being parties to and sealing and delivering of these presents, do bar-

sell and confirm unto GEORGE FRENCH his heirs all those two lotts or half acres of
ground above mentioned with the appurtenances thereto belonging; To have and to
hold the two lotts numbered 255 and 265 unto GEORGE FRENCH and heirs, And LARKIN
SMITH and JAMES GILLIES and their heirs further promise they will warrant and
forever defend the title of the conveyed two lotts against the claims of every person, In
Witness whereof LARKING SMITH and MARY ELEANOR his Wife and JAMES GILLIES and
FRANCES his Wife have hereunto set their hands and affixed their seals the day and
year first afore written
Sealed and delivered in presence of
        JNO: CHEW,                          LARKIN  SMITH
        JOS: CHEW,                          MARY  ELEANOR  SMITH
        BEVERLEY  CHEW                      JAMES  GILLIES
                                            FRANCES  GILLIES
   The Commonwealth of Virginia to EDWARD HILL,  CHRIS: HARWOOD and RICHARD
BROOKE Gentlemen of the County of KING and QUEEN, Greeting:  Whereas (the Commission
for the privy Examination of MARY ELEANOR, the Wife of LARKIN SMITH); Witness JOHN CHEW,
Clerk of our said Court at Fredericksburg the 21st day of October 1791 in the 16th year of
the Commonwealth
   KING and QUEEN, Sct.  In obedience to the within Commission to us directed we have
examined (the return of the Execution of the privy Examination of MARY ELEANOR SMITH); Certi-
fied under our hands & seals the 25th day of October  1781
                                            EDWARD  HILL
                                            CHRISR.  HARWOOD
   The Commonwealth of Virginia to WILLIAM HARVEY & JAS: SOMERVILLE Gent., of the
Town and Corporation of Fredericksburg Greeting; Whereas (the Commission for the privy
Examination of FRANCES, the Wife of JAMES GILLIES); Witness JOHN CHEW, Clerk of our said
Court at Fredericksburg the 16th day of November 1691 in the 16th year of the
Commonwealth                                JNO: CHEW
   Corporation of Fredericksburg Sct.  By virute of the within writ to us directed, we
caused the within FRANCES GILLIES to come before us (the return of the Execution of the
privy Examination of FRANCES GILLIES); Given under our hands & seals this 17th day of
November one thousand seven hundred and ninety one
                                            WILLIAM  HARVEY
                                            JAMES  SOMERVILLE
   At a Court of Hustings held for the Town of Fredericksburg the 27th of April 1792
This Indenture was proved by the oaths of two witnesses thereto and ordered to be
certified; And at a Court held for the said Corporation the 22nd June 1792; This Indenture was fully proved by the oath of JOSEPH CHEW, a witness thereto, and together with
the Commissions annexed and Certificates of the Executions thereof endorsed, were
ordered to be recorded
Examd. & deld. GEO: FRENCH                   Teste  JNO: CHEW, C. C. H.


pp.        THIS INDENTURE made the 16th day of November in year of our Lord one thou-
305-    sand seven hundred and ninety one Between JAMES GILLIES and FRANCES his
308     Wife of County of FAIRFAX and Town of ALEXANDRIA of one part and LARKIN
           SMITH of County of KING and QUEEN & State of Virginia of other part; Witnes-
seth that JAMES GILLIES & FRANCES his Wife for sum of Four hundred and sixty seven
pounds to them paid by LARKIN SMITH doth by these presents bargain sell & confirm
unto LARKIN SMITH his heirs all that Lott or piece of ground lying in the Corporation
of Fredericksburg and numberd (43); which the said GILLIES purchased of JOHN ATKIN-

SONs Trustees by Deed recorded in the Honourable the District Court of Fredericksburg bearing date the six day of October one thousand seven hundred & ninety one and at large will more fully appear; Also by Deed recorded in County Court of Spotsylvania the 20th day of March one thousand seven hundred and Seventy one from GEORGE MITCHELL to said JOHN ATKINSON, and bounded Beginning at the lower South East Corner of said Lott on CAROLINE STREET being the upper Corner of a Lott formerly the LONG ORDINARY LOTT, thence with the same Westward one hundred and thirty two feet to the Lotts called the COURT HOUSE LOTTS, thence with the same thirty seven feet and one half, thence in a direction nearly parelel with the first course above mentioned to CAROLINE STREET so as to make the last course upon and along the said Street to the Begining distance of thirty three feet; Together with all houses gardens profitts & hereditaments to the same belonging; To have and to hold the said lott of land sold unto LARKIN SMITH his heirs, And JAMES GILLIES & FRANCES his Wife for themselves their heirs doth promise to and with LARKIN SMITH his heirs that they shall warrant & forever defend by these presents; In Witness whereof the parties have hereunto sett their hands and seals the day & year first above written
Sealed and Delivered in the presence of us
    ROB: B. CHEW; JOHN CHEW JR.,     JAMES GILLIES
    JNO: CHEW, A. PARKER        FRANCES GILLIES
The Commonwealth of Virginia to WILLIAM HARVEY & JAMES SOMERVILLE Gent. of Town of Fredericksburg Greeting; Whereas (the Commission for the privy Examination of FRANCES, the Wife of JAMES GILLIES); Witness JOHN CHEW, Clerk of our said Court (blank) 1791 and in the 16th year of the Commonwealth       JNO: CHEW
Corporation of Fredericksburg Sct. By virtue of the within writ to us directed we have caused the within FRANCES GILLIES to come before us (the return of the Execution of the privy Examination of FRANCES GILLIES); Given under our hands and seals the 17th day of November 1791          WILLIAM HARVEY
                     JAMES SOMERVILLE

Deld. Comm. to this place   (no recording shown)

pp.      THIS INDENTURE made the 28th day of September in year of our Lord one thou-
309-   sand seven hundred and ninety two Between EDWARD SHEPHERD of Town of
310    Fredericksburg of one part and JOHN SHEPHERD (Son of the said EDWARD) of the
       same place of other part; Witnesseth that EDWARD SHEPHERD in consideration
of the sum of Five shillings current money of Virginia to him in hand paid and in consideration of the natural love and affection the said EDWARD SHEPHERD hath and doth bear to his Son, the said JOHN SHEPHERD, doth bargain and sell to JOHN SHEPHERD his heirs all the horses & cattle and also all of his the said EDWARD SHEPHERDs Household and kitchen furniture, to wit, one Cow and two Calves; one Horse and two Goats, two beds and furniture, two bedsteads, one Gun, three Trunks, three tables, one dozen chairs, one nest of wooden ware, four pots, one spaid, one Ax, 1 Case and six Silver tea spoons and one Silver Watch; together with the future increase of the said Cow and Goats; To have and to hold the said Stocks and furniture to JOHN SHEPHERD his heirs and EDWARD SHEPHERD doth promise JOHN SHEPHERD his heirs that he will warrant and forever defend the stock and furniture to him the said JOHN SHEPHERD his heirs free and clear from all claim and demand of all persons; In Witness whereof the said EDWARD SHEPHERD hath hereunto set his hand and affixed his seal the day and year first written
Sealed and delivered in presence of
    B: W: CHEW                    EDWARD SHEPHERD
At a Court of Hustings held for the Town and Corporation of Fredericksburg the 28th

September 1792        This Deed of Gift from EDWARD SHEPHERD to (his Son) JOHN
SHEPHERD was acknowledged by the said EDWARD and ordered to be recorded

pp.       KNOW ALL MEN by these presents that SAMUEL LEGG of FLEET STREET in the
310-      City of LONDON, Upholsterer, by these presents do make and appoint Mr. JOHN
311       LEGG of Fredericksburg in the State of Virginia, Merchant, my true and lawfull
          Attorney for me and in my name to ask demand and receive from all persons
whom it doth concern residing in said State of Virginia or elsewhere in America all the
debts sums of money goods effects Estate and demands due and to grow due to me upon
account or by reason of any matter whatsoever, nothing excepted or reserved, and
upon non payment for me and in my name to sue arrest imprison and prosecute the
same and upon such suit proceed to Judgment and Execution and such persons in prison
to hold untill payment thereof be made and also to perform all lawfull and reasonable
acts and things whatsoever both for obtaining and discharging of the same as shall be
needfull granting my said Attorney absolute power in the premises; In Witness whereof I have hereunto set my hand and seal the Fifteenth day of May in the Thirty second
year of the Reign of our Sovereign Lord George the Third by the grace of God of Great
Britain France and Ireland, King Defender of the faith, and in the year of our Lord one
thousand seven hundred and ninety two
Sealed and delivered (being first duly stampt) in
   the presence of ROBERT WALKER                       SAML. LEGG
   At a Court of Hustings held for the Town and Corporation of Fredericksburg the 28th of
September 1792;       This Power of Attorney was proved by the oath of ROBERT WAL-
KER the witness thereto and ordered to be recorded
Examined & deld. J. LEGG              Teste        JNO: CHEW, C. C. H.


pp.       TO ALL TO WHOM these presents shall come, We ROBERT LILLY and JAMES
312-      FISHER of the Town of Fredericksburg send Greeting; Whereas we the said
313       ROBERT LILLEY and JAMES FISHER together with ANN and MARTHA our Wives by
          our Deed in writing this day done wherein it is expressed to be made between us
the said ROBERT LILLY and ANN my Wife and JAMES FISHER and MARTHA my Wife of
the one part and a certain JACOB KUHN of the Town of Fredericksburg of other part; we
did in consideration of the sum of Five pounds therein mentioned bargain sell & confirm unto JACOB KUHN his heirs one lott or half acre of land No. one  as also seven other
lotts or half acres of land numbered one, two, three, four, five, six and seven commonly called Out Lotts situate in KESILTOWN in County of ROCKINGHAM and State of Virginia
in which said Deed we did bind ourselves our heirs to said JACOB KUHN his heirs to warrant and defend the said lotts of land generally forever; as by the Deed hereto annexed
will more fully appear; And whereas we cannot travell to the Court of said County of
ROCKINGHAM in order to acknowledge the said Deed before the Court of said County in
order to admit the same to Record in that Court, NOW KNOW YE that we the said ROBERT
LILLEY and JAMES FISHER in consideration of the foregoing premises and being de-
sireous that said Deed should be recorded in County Court of ROCKINGHAM, to assure the
said Lotts to JACOB KUHN his heirs, we the said ROBERT LILLY and JAMES FISHER doth
hereby appoint our true and faithfull friend, GEORGE KIESEL of ROCKINGHAM County
our lawfull Attorney in fact hereby requesting and fully impowering our said Attorney
for us before the Court of said County at such times as shall be agreeable to Law and in
the presence of said Court to acknowledge for us and in our names the same Deed hereto
annexed to be our act and deed; In Witness whereof we have hereunto set our hands and
seals the seventeenth day of September one thousand seven hundred and ninety two
(1792).

Sealed and delivered in the presence of
     ZACH: LUCAS,                       ROBERT LILLY
     TULLY WHITHURST,              JAMES FISHER
     WILLIAM HARVEY, GEORGE C. SMOOT
(The name JOHN BREDIN erased and GEORGE KEISEL interlined before signed)
 At a Court of Hustings held for the Town and Corporation of Fredericksburg October
26th 1792     This Power of Attorney from ROBERT LILLY and JAMES FISHER to GEORGE
KEISEL was proved by the oaths of ZACHARIAH LUCAS, GEORGE C. SMOOT and TULLY
WHITHURST, three witnesses thereto, and ordered to be recorded
Exd. & deld. JACOB KUHN                Teste JNO: CHEW, C. C. H.

pp.     THIS INDENTURE made this 28th day of April in year of our Lord one thousand
314-    seven hundred and Ninety two Between LARKIN SMITH of County of KING and
317     QUEEEN Esqr. and MARY E. his Wife of one part and GUSTAVUS B. WALLACE of
       the Town of Fredericksburg and County of Spotsylvania Esquire of other part;
Witnesseth that LARKIN SMITH and MARY E. his Wife for sum of Seven hundred pounds
Virginia currency to them in hand paid by GUSTAVUS B. WALLACE, by these presents
doth bargain sell and confirm unto GUSTAVUS B. WALLACE and to his heirs all the Estate
right title and demand either in Law or Equity which said LARKIN SMITH and MARY E.
his Wife now have or may hereafter claim to certains lotts of ground situate in Town of
Fredericksburg and marked number Eighty seven and Eighty eight as by Deed from
GEORGE AUGUSTINE WASHINGTON and FRANCES his Wife to LARKIN SMITH of Record in
the Court of Hustings in the Corporation of Fredericksburg may more fully appear; Together with all buildings improvements and appurtenances thereunto belonging; To
have and to hold the hereby bargained and sold premises with the appurtenances unto
GUSTAVUS B. WALLACE his heirs; and LARKIN SMITH and MARY E. his Wife and their
heirs will warrant and forever defend by these presents; In Witness whereof LARKIN
SMITH and MARY E: his Wife have hereunto set their hands and seals the day month &
year first afore written
Sealed & acknowledged in the presence of
     JNO: CHEW,                      LARKIN SMITH
     JOHN CHEW JR., BEVERLEY CHEW     MARY E. SMITH
 At a Court of Hustings continued and held for the Town & Corporation of Fredericks-
burg the 24th of November 1792    This Indenture was proved by the oaths of two of
the witnesses thereto and ordered to be Certified;
 At a Court held for sd. Corpo: 25th Jany. 1793. This Indenture was fully proved by the
oath of JOHN CHEW a witness thereto & together with the Commission annexed and
Certificate of the execution thereof endorsed were ordered to be recorded
                  Teste JNO: CHEW, C. C. H.
 The Commonwealth of Virginia to FONTAINE MAURY & BENJAMIN DAY of the Town and
Corporation of Fredericksburg Gentlemen, Greeting; Whereas (the Commission for the
privy Examination of MARY E., Wife of LARKIN SMITH); Witness JOHN CHEW, Clerk of our said
Court the 18th day of September 1792, in the 17th year of the Commonwealth
 Corporation of Fredericksburg to wit; Pursuant to the within Commission to us
directed (the return of the Execution of the privy Examination of MARY E. SMITH); Given under
our hands and seals this thirteenth day of October 1792

                                   FONTAINE MAURY
Examined & deld. GUSTAVUS BROWN WALLACE     BENJN: DAY

pp.      THIS INDENTURE made the Sixteenth day of August one thousand seven hun-
317-   dred and Ninety two Between CHARLES CARTER JUNR. of Fredericksburg of one
318    part and THOMAS VOWLES SENR. of other part; Witnesseth that CHARLES CARTER
        JUNR. for sum of Twenty four pounds current money of Virginia p. annum to be
paid, one half at the expiration of six months and the other half at the expiration of one
year hath bargained rented and demised unto THOMAS VOWLES a parcel of ground containing thirty feet front on CAROLINE STREET and runing back half way to the Back
Street or length of a Lott being opposite the upper part of the Lott of the Estate of THO-
MAS BROWN deced., and now in the occupancy of the said THOMAS VOWLES on which
their stands at present a house which the said VOWLES obliges himself to finish off in a
workman like convenient manner; To have and to hold the said parcell of ground unto
THOMAS VOWLES and his Exrs. during the full term of Fifteen years from the first day of
January one thousand seven hundred and Ninety three ensuing, And THOMAS VOWLES
and his Exrs. shall from time to time during the term at his proper costs and charges
repair and keep the said building in all needfull reparation; In Witness whereof we
have hereunto set our hands and seals the day and year first aforesaid
Sealed and Delivered in the presence of
      RICHD: KENNEY,               CHARLES CARTER JUNR.
      Z. LUCAS; WILLIAM WEST        THOS: VOWLES
  At a Court of Hustings held for the Town and Corporation of Fredericksburg March
22nd 1793     This Deed of Lease between CHARLES CARTER JUNR. and THOMAS VOWLES
was proved by three witnesses thereto and ordered to be recorded
Exd. & deld. THOS: VOWLES SENR.        Teste   JNO: CHEW C. C. H.

p.       THIS INDENTURE made this 9th day of January in year of our Lord one thou-
319    sand seven hundred and ninety three Betweeen PHILIP ROOTES of County of
        FAYETTE in State of KENTUCKY of one part & ELISHA DICKERSON of Town of
Fredericksburg and County of Spotsylvania of other part; Witnesseth that PHILIP
ROOTES for the sum of Six pounds to him in hand paid by ELISHA DICKERSON by these
presents doth bargain sell and confirm unto ELISHA DICKERSON all that lott or parcel of
ground lying in Town of Fredericksburg described by the No. 187, being in a triangular
shape and lies on the Back Street called PRINCESS MARY STREET and the Cross Street
called PRINCESS ELIZABETH STREET; runing along the said Cross Street So. 65 1/2 degrees
West untill it intersects the line that divides the lands of Mr. LEWIS WILLIS and the said
ROGER DIXON, thence along that line along the River to PRINCESS MARY STREET, thence
along that Street to the Begining, containing about 35 square poles; To have and to hold
the described lott to ELISHA DICKERSON his heirs and PHILIP ROOTES the said Lott so
conveyed doth by these presents warrant and defend; In Testimony whereof said
PHILIP ROOTES hath hereunto set his hand and seal the day and year above mentioned
Signed sealed and Delivered in the presence of
      ADAM DARBY,                  PHILIP ROOTES
      JAMES NEWBY, WILLIAM HARVEY
  At a Court of Hustings continued and held for the Corporation of Fredericksburg the
23rd day of March 1793     This Indenture was proved by the oaths of three witnesses
thereto and ordered to be recorded
Exd. & Deld WM. TAYLOR          Teste   JNO: CHEW, C. C. H.

pp.      THIS INDENTURE made this (blank) day of June in year of our Lord one thousand
320-   seven hundred and Ninety one Between JACOB KUHN of Town of Fredericksburg
322    of one part and JOHN LEWIS of County of Spotsylvania of other part; Witnesseth
        that in consideration of the sum of One hundred pounds current money of Vir-

ginia to said JACOB KUHN in hand paid by JOHN LEWIS, by these presents do bargain sell and confirm unto JOHN LEWIS and his heirs, two compleat lotts of land containing half an acre each lott, lying in Town of Fredericksburg and known by the numbers one hundred and five and one hundred and six, bounded Westerly by CHARLES STREET, Northwardly by PITT STREET and Easterly by PRINCESS ANN STREET, they being two lotts formerly sold by aforesaid LEWIS to aforesaid KUHN; Together with all houses, and buildings thereon erected and all previledges profits commodities and appurtenances belonging; To have and to hold the above two lotts of land unto JOHN LEWIS his heirs and JACOB KUHN for himself his heirs doth promise that the premises now are and so shall remain and be free & clear of and from all former and other gifts sales, troubles and incumbrances whatsoever suffered by said JACOB KUHN and his heirs and JACOB KUHN his heirs shall warrant and forever defend by these presents; In Witness whereof JACOB KUHN hath hereunto set his hand and seal the day and year above written Sealed and Delivered in presence of

    WILLIAM  HARVEY,                                JACOB  KUHN
    JOHN  BENSON,  WM. THOMPSON

At a Court of Hustings continued and held for the Corporation of Fredericksburg the 23rd day of March 1793     This Indenture from JACOB KUHN to JOHN LEWIS was acknowledged by the said KUHN and ordered to be recorded

pp.    THIS INDENTURE made this 22d. day of March in the Seventeenth year of the
322-    Commonwealth and in the year of our Lord one thousand seven hundred and
323    ninety two Between GUSTAVUS BROWN WALLACE of Town of Fredericksburg of
    one part and GEORGE W. B. SPOONER of the Town aforesaid of other part; Witnesseth that in consideration of the natural love and affection which he hath & beareth to the said GEORGE and for the sum of Five Shillings in hand paid to GUSTAVUS BROWN WALLACE  by GEORGE W. B. SPOONER, by these presents doth give bargain and sell unto GEORGE W. B. SPOONER his heirs part of two lotts of land commencing at the lower corner thereof at the intersection of CAROLINE and FAUQUIER STREETs runing from thence Two hundred and sixty four feet up FAUQUIER STREET to its intersection with PRINCESS ANN STREET, from thence along PRINCESS ANN STREET forty nine feet and from thence in a direct line through said lots to CAROLINE STREET and from thence down the said Street to the begining; known by the No. 87 & 88; Together with all appurtenances thereunto belonging; To have and to hold the parcel and lot of land hereby granted unto GEORGE W. B. SPOONER his heirs and GUSTAVUS B. WALLACE the said parcel of land against myself my heirs and every other person claiming under me will warrant and forever defend; In Witness whereof I have hereunto set my hand and seal the day month and year above written
Sealed and acknowledged in the presence of

    THOS: GOOSE,                                GUSTAVUS B. WALLCE
    GEO: C. SMOOT, SIDNEY WISHART

At a Court of Hustings continued and held for the Corporation of Fredericksburg the 23rd day of March 1793     This Indenture from GUSTAVUS BROWN WALLACE to GEORGE W. B. SPOONER was acknowledged by the said WALLACE and ordered to be recorded
Examined & deld. G. W. B. SPOONER          Teste   JNO: CHEW, C. C. H.

pp.    THIS INDENTURE Witnesseth that GUSTAVUS RHODES (Son of MARY RHOADS of
324-    County of STAFFORD) hath put himself and by these presents with the consent of
325    his Mother doth voluntarily and of his own free will and accord put himself
    Apprentice to WILLIAM PEARSON of Corporation of Frederickburg, Hatter, to

learn his art trade and mystery, and after the manner of an Apprentice to serve four
years and nine months from the day of the date hereof and in all things behave himself as a faithfull Apprentice ought to do, And the said Master shall use his utmost
endeavour to teach or cause to be taught and instructed the said Apprentice in the trade
and mystery of a Hatter and schooling during his Apprenticeship and at the expiration
of which time to have a new suit of clothes; In Witness whereof the sd. parties have
interchangeably set their hands and seals hereunto dated the 24th day of May in the
year of our Lord one thousand seven hundred and Ninety three
Sealed and Delivered in presence of us
     J. CHEW                        GUSTAVUS his mark  X  ROADES
                                   MARY  her mark  X  ROADES
                                   W. PEARSON

At a Court of Hustings held for the Town and Corporation of Fredericksburg May 24th
1793    This Indenture of Apprenticeship was acknowledged by the parties and ordered
to be recorded
Exd. & deld. WM. PEARSON             Teste  JNO: CHEW, C. C. H.


pp.      THIS INDENTURE made this Twenty sixth day of April one thousand seven hun-
325-    dred and ninety three Between GEORGE WEEDON and CATHARINE his Wife of
327     Town of Fredericksburg in County of Spotsylvania of one part and COLLIN
          MILNE of same Town of other part; Witnesseth that said GEORGE and CATHARINE
in consideration of the yearly rents and covenants hereafter by these presents mentioned and contained on part of COLLIN MILNE to be paid and performed, do bargain
lease & demise ujnto COLLIN MILNE his heirs a certain parcel of land lying in the Town
aforesaid on WILLIAM STREET and is part of Lott number 26; Beginning at the lower
corner of JOSEPH BERRYs Tenement, thence twenty feet fronting on WILLIAM STREET
and extending back sixty seven feet, thence twenty feet parellel with WILLIAM STREET,
thence sixty seven feet adjoining said BERRYs Tenement to the beginning,  To have and
to hold the parcel of land together with all houses commodities and appurtenances to
the said premises belonging; paying for the same on the sixth day of April one thousand seven hundred and ninety four yearly the sum of eight pounds in quarterly
payments, Vizt., one quarter on the sixth day of July next, another quarter on the sixth
day of October next, a third quarter the sixth day of January next, and the fourth on the
sixth day of April next issuing out of the demised premises; to be discharged in Gold at
Five shillings & four pence the pennyweight or in Silver at Six shillings and eight
pence the ounce, unto GEORGE WEEDON his heirs; In Witness whereof the parties to
these presents have hereunto set their hands and affixed their seals the day and year
first above written
Signed sealed and Delivered in presence of         G. WEEDON
    (no witnesses shown)                  CATHERINE WEEDON
                                       COLLEN MILNE
At a Court of Hustings held for the Town & Corporation of Fredericksburg the 26th day
of April 1793  This Deed of Lease between GEORGE WEEDON & COLLIN MILNE was acknowledged by the parties and ordered to be recorded
Exd. & deld. COLLIN MILNE (Commission recorded fo: 344).


pp.      THIS INDENTURE made the 15th day of June in year of our Lord one thousand
327-    seven hundred and Ninety two Between JOHN LEWIS & MARY ANN his Wife of
329     Town of Fredericksburg of one part and GUSTAVUS B. WALLACE of the Town
          aforesaid of other part; Witnesseth that JOHN LEWIS and MARY ANN his Wife for
the sum of One hundred pounds current money of Virginia to them in hand paid by

GUSTAVUS B. WALLACE; by these presents doth bargain sell release and confirm unto
GUSTAVUS B. WALLACE and to his heirs all the state right title and demand of said JOHN
LEWIS and MARY ANN his Wife now have or may hereafter claim or demand in a certain lott of ground lying in Town of Fredericksburg and makred No. 65; bounded by
LEWIS & SOPHIA STREETs, it being the same lott of ground purchased by sd. LEWIS of
RICHARD GARNER & his Wife, who purchased the same of SMITH, YOUNG and HYDE, who
purchased the same of the said JOHN LEWIS & MARY ANN his Wife as the Deeds duly
proved and recorded in the Court of Hustings for the Corporation of Fredericksburg will
more fully appear; Together with all buildings improvements passages, alleys rights
and appurtenances thereunto belonging; To have and to hold the hereby bargained and
sold premises with the appurtenances unto GUST. B. WALLACE his heirs and JOHN LEWIS
and MARY ANN his Wife and their heirs and against every person unto GUSTAVUS B.
WALLACE his heirs shall warrant and forever defend by these presents;  In Witness
whereof the parties to these presents have hereunto interchangeably set their hands
and seals the day and year first above written
Signed sealed and delivered in presence off
     HASLEWOOD FARISH,                        JOHN LEWIS
     K. HURST, BEVERLEY CHEW                  MARY A. LEWIS
Reacknowledged this 7th day of May  1793 before us
     JNO: CHEW,          LAR: STANARD,
     JOHN CHEW JR.,      BEVERLEY  CHEW
At a Court of Hustings held for the Town & Corporation of Fredericksburg the 24th May
1793   This Indenture from JOHN LEWIS to GUSTAVUS B. WALLACE was proved by the
oaths of three witnesses thereto and ordered to be recorded
Examined & deld. G. B. WALLACE              Teste JNO: CHEW C. C. H.
(Commission recorded fo. 334).


pp.     THIS INDENTURE made the eighteenth day of April one thousand seven hun-
330-  dred and ninety three Between JAMES ABBOTT and MILDRED hihs Wife of one
331    Part and DAVID BLAIR of Fredericksburg of other part; Witnesseth that JAMES
     ABBOTT for the sum of Four hundred and nine pounds current money of Vir-
ginia to him in hand paid do bargain and sell unto DAVID BLAIR and his heirs all that
part of the lott of ground lying in the Corporation of Fredericksburg numbered Fifty
three bounded Beginning on PRINCESS ANN STREET at the upper corner of said lott,
thence running down said Street sixty five feet, thence parellel with WOLF STREET
Westerly running through Lott No. Sixty six thence Northerly parellel with PRINCESS
ANN STREET sixty five feet & from thence to the beginning on said PRINCESS ANN
STREET; Together with all appurtenances, To have and to hold the said lott of land with
its appurtenances unto DAVID BLAIR and his heirs and JAMES ABBOTT and MILDRED his
Wife & their heirs the said lott of land unto DAVID BLAIR and his heirs against all
persons will forever warrant and defend; In Witness whereof JAMES ABBOTT and MIL-
DRED his Wife have hereunto subscribed their names and affixed their seals the day
and year above written
Signed sealed & Delivered in the presence of
     WILLIAM LOVELL, GEO: FRENCH,             JAMES ABBOTT
     MARGT. JULIAN, WM. HARVEY,               MILDRED ABBOTT
     ROBERT WALKER, ANTHONY BUCK,
     JOHN ANDERSON
The Commonwealth of Virginia to FONTAINE MAURY,  GEORGE FRENCH and WILLIAM
LOVELL Gent. of Town and Corporation of Fredericksburg Greeting; Whereas (the Com-

mission for the privy Examination of MILDRED, the Wife of JAMES ABBOTT); Witness JOHN CHEW Clerk of our said Court the 18th day of April 1793 and in the 17th year of the Commonwealth                                                                    JNO: CHEW
   In Obedience to the within Commission to us directed by the Worshipfull Court of Hustings (the return of the Execution of the privy Examination of MILDRED ABBOTT); Witness our hands and seals the 18th April 1793          GEO: FRENCH
                                                                WILLIAM LOVELL

   At a Court of Hustings held for the Town & Corporation of Fredericksburg the 24th May 1793   This Indenture from JAMES ABBOTT to DAVID BLAIR was proved by the oath of one witness thereto, And at a Court held for the said Corporation the 22nd. day of November 1793, it was further proved by the oaths of two other witnesses thereto & toge- ther with the Commission annexed & Certificate of Execution thereof indorsed, were ordered to be recorded
Examd. & Delivered DAVID BLAIR                    Teste JNO: CHEW, C. C. H.
Deld. Comm. to this place

pp.      THIS INDENTURE made this Twenty seventh day of March one thousand seven
332-    hundred and Ninety three Between DAVID STEWART, Attorney in fact for GEORGE
333     McCUTCHEN of one part and JAMES ABBOTT of the other part; Whereas as certain
         PHILIP LIPSCOMB did by his Deed of Bargain and Sale bearing date the first day
of May one thousand seven hundred and Eighty seven bargain and sell unto GEORGE McCUTCHEN a certain lott and appurtenances lying in Town of Fredericksburg; To have and to hold the said lott from the first day before the date of the said Deed untill the full term of Twelve years next ensuing; And GEORGE McCUTCHEN being so intitled to and possessed of the said lott did on the tenth day of January last, by his Letters of Attorney, bearing date the same day & year; appoint said DAVID STEWART his lawfull Attorney for sundry purposes and among other things to settle and adjust all accounts and to sell and dispose of all such lands houses and tenements which he was in any manner intitled to in Town of Fredericksburg; And whereas GEORGE McCUTCHEN is indebted to JAMES AB- BOTT in the sum of L 178..8...10, to pay and satisfy which This Indenture Witnesseth that DAVID STEWART in consideration of the premises and also for the sum of Five shillings to him in hand paid for the use of said McCUTCHEN, by these presents doth bargain and sell unto JAMES ABBOTT and assigns a certain lott of land lying in Town of Fredericks- burg beginning on the North end of CAROLINE STREET and joining the said LIPSCOMBs Lot where he now lives, thence running N. E. 58 feet, thence S. E. 132, thence S. W. 58 feet and then N. W. to CAROLINE STREET 65 1/2 feet to the first station; and all buildings commodities and appurtenances to the said lot belonging; To have and to hold the said lot unto JAMES ABBOTT and assigns from the first day of May next ensuing the date of these presents during the full term of Six years paying DAVID STEWART his heirs for the use of said McCUTCHEN the yearly rent of a pepper corn if demanded; In Witness whereof DAVID STEWART hath hereunto set his hand and affixed his seal as Attorney aforesaid the day & year first above written
Signed sealed and delivered in presence of
      JOHN MINOR JR.,                               DAVID STUART
      RD. H. FOOTE, JOHN MUSCHETT
   At a Court of Hustings held for the Town and Corporaltion of Fredericksburg on Fry- day the 26th day of July 1793          This Deed of Lease from DAVID STEWART, Attorney in Fact for GEORGE McCUTCHEN, to JAMES ABBOTT was proved by the oath of the witnesses thereto

pp.      The Commonwealth of Virginia to JAMES LEWIS, THOMAS STRACHAN &
334      EDWARD HERNDON of County of Spotsylvania Gent., Greeting: (the Commission for
         the privy examination of MARY ANN the Wife of JOHN LEWIS for land sold to GUSTAVUS B.
WALLACE by deed bearing date 15th day of June 1792); Witness JOHN CHEW, Clerk of our said
Court the 18th day of October 1793 in the 18th year of the Commonwealth
  Spotsylvania County to wit; Pursuant to the above Commission to us directed, (the return
of the execution of the privy Examination of MARY ANN LEWIS); Certified under our hands &
seals the 19th day of October 1793                        JAMES LEWIS
Truly recorded JNO: CHEW, C.C.H.                          THOMAS STRACHAN
Exd. & deld. Colo. WALLACE

pp.      THIS INDENTURE made this 17th day of Decr. in the Seventeenth year of the
335-     Commonwealth and in the year of our Lord one thousand seven hundred and
336      Ninety three Between GUSTAVUS BROWN WALLACE of Town of Fredericksburg of
         one part and GEO: W. B. SPOONER of said Town of other part; Witnesseth that in
consideration of the natural love and affection which he hath and beareth to said
GEORGE and for Five shillings in hand paid to GUSTAVUS BROWN WALLACE by GEO: W. B.
SPOONER by these presents doth give bargain and sell unto GEO: W. B. SPOONER his heirs
two half acre lotts of land situated on THE HILL, bounded on the North by AMELIA
STREET, on the South by WILLIAM STREET, on the West by LEWIS's Field, and on the East
by two half acre lots heretofore known by the name of NIEL McCOULLs & PHILIP
EVENS's Lotts and known by numbers 142 & 144; Together with all appurtenances
thereunto belonging; To have and to hold the lotts of land unto GEORGE WILLIAM
BARNERDISTON SPOONER his heirs, And GUSTAVUS BROWN WALLACE his heirs will
warrant and forever defend; In Witness whereof I have hereunto set my hand and seal
this day month and year above written
Sealed and acknowledged in the presence of
         RICHD. JOHNSTON,                        GUSTAVUS B. WALLACE
         GEORGE MURRAY, SIDNEY WISHART
  At a Court of Hustings held for the Town and Corporation of Fredericksburg the 24th
day of January 1794   This Deed of Gift from GUSTAVUS BROWN WALLACE to GEORGE W. B.
SPOONER was proved by the oaths of the three witnesses thereto and ordered to be
recorded
Exam'd & Deld. sent G. W. B. SPOONER p note.        Teste   JNO: CHEW, Cl.

pp.      THIS INDENTURE made this Twenty fourth day of October in year of our Lord
336-     one thousand seven hundred and Ninety three Between SUSANNA HEATH and
339      JAMES HEATH of Town of Fredericksburg of one part and THOMAS BARWISE of
         same Town of other part; Witnesseth that SUSANNA and JAMES HEATH in con-
sideration of the Rents and Covenants in this Indenture contained by these presents do
bargain and sell unto THOMAS BARWISE his heirs a certain tract of land in Town of
Fredericksburg being part of the Lott No. 20 and bounded, Beginning at the corner of
HENRY WHITE's Lott and extending from said corner twenty two feet on CAROLINE
STREET, from thence in a right line one hundred & twenty feet from the said Street and
bounded, that is on the left by a part of Lott No. 20 belonging to HENRY WHITE on the
right by the remaining part of Lott No. 20 and on the back part by the said Lott No. 20
making an oblong figure one hundred and twenty feet by twenty two; Together with all
appurtenances thereunto belonging; also a right of way in an Alley twelve feet wide to
be kept open from the back part of said parcel of ground to GEORGE STREET; To have and
to hold the said parcel of ground unto THOMAS BARWISE during the term of Ninety nine
years renewable forever; paying for the same on the third day of December one thou-

sand seven hundred and ninety four and yearly unto SUSANNA and JAMES HEATH their
assigns the rent of Twelve pounds Two shillings specie current money of Virginia at
the rate of Four shillings and six pence Sterling per Dollar discharged of all incumbrances, the Taxes growing due excepted; In Witness whereof the parties hereto have
set their hands and affixed their seals the day and year first above written
Signed sealed and delivered in the presence of
    HENRY WHITE,                           SUSANNA HEATH
    THOS: COCHRAN, BENJN: PARKE       JAMES HEATH
  At a Court of Hustings held for the Town & Corporation of Fredericksburg January 24th
1794   This Indenture of Lease from SUSANNA HEATH and JAMES HEATH to THOMAS
BARWISE was proved by the oaths of the three witnesses thereto & ordered to be
recorded
Exd., & Deld. THOS: BARWISE          Teste   JNO: CHEW, C. C. H.


pp.      THIS INDENTURE made the second day of August in year of our Lord One thou-
339-    sand seven hundred and Ninety three Between CHARLES CARTER and BETTY
341     CARTER his Wife of Town of Fredericksburg of one part and RICHARD DOBSON
        of the City of RICHMOND of other part; Witnesseth that CHARLES CARTER and
BETTY his Wife for sum of One thousand pounds current money of Virginia to the said
CHARLES CARTER in hand paid by these presents do bargain & sell unto RICHARD DOB-
SON his heirs two Lotts of ground lying in Town of Fredericksburg number 85 & 86, on
CAROLINE STREET, thence running up said Street one hundred eighty two feet & a half,
thence up FAQUIER STREET Two hundred and sixty six feet, thence down PRINCESS ANN
STREET one hundred eighty two feet and one half and then adjoining the lotts No. 83 &
84 paralel to FAQUIER STREET two hundred sixty six feet to the beginning; And all
houses improvements and advantages to said lotts belonging; To have and to hold the
aforesaid lotts unto RICHD. DOBSON his heirs and CHARLES CARTER and BETTY his Wife
for themselves their heirs will warrant and forever defend by these presents; In Witness whereof CHARLES CARTER & BETTY his Wife have hereunto set their hands and
affixed their seals the day & year first within written
Sealed and Delivered in presence of
    JOHN MORTIMER,                   CHS: CARTER
    GEORGE CARTER, WILLIAM HARVEY
  At a Court of Hustings held for the Town and Corporation of Fredericksburg January
24th 1794     This Indenture for Lotts from CHARLES CARTER to RICHARD DOBSON was
proved by the oaths of JOHN MORTIMER and WILLIAM HARVEY, two of the witnesses
thereto and ordered to be certified


pp.      THIS INDENTURE made the thirtieth day of December in year of our Lord one
341-    thousand seven hundred ninety three Between ELIZABETH CARTER, Wife of
344     CHARLES CARTER of Town of Fredericksburg of one part and WALKER RANDOLPH
        CARTER, at present of the City of PHILADELPHIA, one of the Sons of said
CHARLES and ELIZABETH CARTER, of other part; Whereas CHARLES CARTER Esquire of
SHIRLEY by his Deed bearing date the sixth day of August one thousand seven hundred
and eighty seven made over to JOSEPH JONES of the Town of Fredericksburg in Trust for
said ELIZABETH CARTER during her life and to such of her Children by her present
Husband as she should by her last Will and Testament as by Deed in Writing declare
concerning the same, Forty three slaves as therein particularly named with their
future issue; And Whereas WALKER RANDOLPH CARTER being now of full age and
serving an Apprenticeship to the Coach Makers Business with HUNTER & CO. in PHILA-
DELPHIA, and CHARLES LANDON CARTER being also engaged in the study of Physick

under a Professor in PHILADELPHIA, and WILLIAM CHAMPE CARTER & GEORGE WASHING-
TON CARTER the other Sons, Surviving Children of said CHARLES & ELIZABETH CARTER,
the one being Apprentice to JOHN FERNEYHOUGH of Town of Fredericksburg and the
other about to enter on the acquiring some business or profession for his future advantage & support, all of which requires an expence dbeyond the ability of said
CHARLES & ELIZABETH, their parents, to support, and the Sons being all of them of such
advanced age as to be in great degree capable of thinking and judging for themselves
what course will most likely promote their future benefit, have requested the said
ELIZABETH, their Mother, to devise some mode whereby such part of the Trust Estate
ultimately intended for their benefit may be applied for their immediate support and
education and the said ELIZABETH conceiving it will be to the advantage of her Children
and promote their laudable efforts to obtain instruction and improvement hath in
consideration of the natural love and affection which shehath for her said Children,
and by virtue of the power given by the before recited Deed from CHARLES CARTER of
SHIRLEY, and by these presents doth grant and make over unto the said WALKER RAN-
DOLPH CARTER and his heirs all the slaves mentioned in the Deed aforesaid now alive, to
wit, Cesar and his Wife, Mary, and their Children Patsey, Sally, Judy, Mary, James,
Betsey, Harry & his Wife Aggey & their Children Sarah, Edmund, Polly, Frank, Abra-
ham and Tom, Troy, Milly, Betsey, Beckey and Nan, Jacob, Tom, Ruth, Jenny, Tobey & his
Wife, Lucy, & their Children Cloe, Tobey, Motly, Jenny, Tim, Nancy, Rose, Beckey, Tom,
Charlotte and her Son Jack, Carrison, John, Cyrus, Godfrey, Marian, Together with
Tonie and Betty, Children of Cesar and Mary, three children of Cloe, Zorn a child of
Molly, Sally, Tom, William, three Children of Milly, Aggey, Jane, Children of Henry and
Aggey, and also two children of Sarah & Toby, the increase of the said slaves since
making the said Deed; To have and to hold the sd. slaves and their issue unto WALKER
RANDOLPH CARTER and his heirs subject to the conditions following, that the said slaves
are to remain in the possession of said ELIZABETH CARTER and for her use during her
life excepting such of them as may be sold under the Power of Attorney to be made by
said WALKER RANDOLPH CARTER unto his Mother, the said ELIZABETH CARTER, and
excepting also John, a Blacksmith, who hath already been sold by the said ELIZABETH &
the purchase money applied to the benefit of her said Sons; and except further that
WALKER RANDOLPH CARTER or his heirs shall on the death of ELIZABETH CARTER make
an equal division between himself and his Brothers if living or the Children of those
who may be dead of all the said slaves remaining unsold; and transmit unto his Mother
and her Husband, a full and ample power of Attorney irrevocable during her life
authorising them so long as they shall live and in every instance with her express
approbation and concurrence in writing to sell such and so many of the said slaves as
she find necessary for maintaing and educating the said WALKER RANDOLPH CARTER
while he remains an Apprentice and the other three Sons untill they shall severally
arrive to their full age and capable of acting for themselves; In Witness whereof the
said ELIZABETH CARTER hath hereunto set her hand and seal the day and year above
written
Sealed and delivered in the presence of
     ANN FITZHUGH,                                    ELIZA: CARTER
     GILBERT  HARROW,  W. FITZHUGH
  At a Court of Hustings for the Town & Corporation of Fredericksburg the 24th day of
January 1794  This Deed of Gift for slaves from ELIZABETH CARTER, Wife of CHARLES
CARTER, to WALKER RANDOLPH CARTER,  CHARLES LANDON CARTER,  JOHN CHAMPE
CARTER and GEORGE WASHINGTON CARTER, was acknowledged by the said ELIZABETH
CARTER, she being first privately examined as the Law directs, and ordered to be
recorded

Exd. & deld to W. R. CARTER          Teste   JNO: CHEW. C. C. H.

pp.      The Commonwealth of Virginia to CHARLES MORTIMER & GEORGE FRENCH of the
344-     Corporation of Fredericksburg Gentlemen, Greeting; Whereas (The Commission for
345      the privy Examination of CATHARINE, the Wife of GEORGE WEEDON by a Deed of Lease
         bearing date 26th of April to COLLIN MILNE); Witness JOHN CHEW Clerk of our said
Court this 27th day of April 1793 in the 17th year of the Commonwealth
 Corporation of Fredericksburg, Sct. Pursuant to the within Commission to us directed
(the return of the Execution of the privy Examination of CATHARINE WEEDON); Given under our
hands & seals the 16th day of November 1793          CHS. MORTIMER
Truly Recorded (Deed page 325)                       GEO: FRENCH
Exd. & deld. COLLIN MILNE


pp.      THIS INDENTURE Witnesseth that ELIZABETH FLETCHER, Mother & next Friend
345-     of CATLETT FLETCHER, hath put him the said CATLETT & by these presents doth
346      voluntarily and of her own free will & accord put him Apprentice to CHARLES
         WARDELL, Hatter, in the Town of Fredericksburg, to learn his art trade &
mystery and after the manner of an Apprentice to serve said CHARLES WARDELL from
the day of the date hereof during the full term of Three years & ten months, and in all
things behave himself as a faithful Apprentice ought to do, And the said Master shall
use the utmost of his endeavour to teach the Apprentice in the trade & mystery of Hat
Making and at the expiration of the said Term shall pay unto him the sum of Three
pounds ten shillings Virginia currency; In Witness whereof the said parties have
interchangeably set their hands and seals thereto dated the 28th day of March in the
year of our Lord one thousand seven hundred and ninety four
Sealed and Delivered in presence of                  CHARLES WARDELL
      (no witnesses shown)                           ELIZABETH her mark X FLETCHER
 At a Court of Hustings held for the Town and Corporation of Fredericksburg the 28th of
March 1794   These Indentures of Apprenticeship between ELIZABETH FLETCHER and
CHARLES WARDELL was acknowledged by the parties and ordered to be recorded
Examd. & deld. C. WARDELL          Teste   JNO: CHEW, C. C. H.


p.       KNOW ALL MEN by these presents that I JAMES M. ADAIR of the Kingdom of
347      Great Britain now a Citizen of the State of Virginia do appoint WILLIAM GLAS-
         SELL & ROBERT MERCER of said State my true and lawfull Attornies to sue for &
prosecute certain claims due by the Estate of JOHN TEMPLE deceased to the Creditors of
JOHN HAMILTON deceased of the Kingdom of Great Britain which said claims I have
power of attorney to receive and for which purpose have power of appointing Sub-
Attornies. Witness my hand & seal this 25th day of April 1794
                                        JAS. M. ADAIR
 At a Court of Hustings held for the Town and Corporation of Fredericksburg the 25th
day of April 1794     This Power of Attorney from JAMES M. ADAIR to WILLIAM GLAS-
SELL and ROBERT MERCER was acknowledged by said ADAIR and ordered to be recorded


pp.      THIS INDENTURE made the first day of February in year of our Lord one thou-
348-     sand seven hundred and Ninety four Between JOHN MAY of one part and HARRY
350      STANARD BEVERLEY of Town of Fredericksburg of other part. Whereas SUSAN-
         NAH & JAMES HEATH of Town of Fredericksburg did by their Deed indented
bearing date the first day of April one thousand seven hundred & Eighty nine for the
consideration of the Rents & agreements in the Indenture mentioned bargain & sell

unto JOHN MAY his heirs a certain parcel of ground in Town of Fredericksburg being one part of lott Number 20, Beginning twenty one feet from the lower corenr of said Lott on CAROLINE STREET, thence running up said Street twenty one feet, thence running back one hundred feet, thence running down the lott paralel to CAROLINE STREET twenty one feet and from thence to the beginning; Together with all ways profits, commodities; To have and to hold said parcel of land to said MAY his heirs paying for the same on the first day of April yearly unto SUSANNAH HEATH her heirs the sum of Ten pounds Ten shillings current money of Virginia issuing out of the premises to be discharged at the rate of Five shillings & four pence a penny weight in Gold or Silver at Six shillings and eight pence the ounce, And Whereas HARRY STANARD BEVERLEY hath purchased the said parcell of ground of said JOHN MAY for the sum of One hundred and Eighty pounds Virga. currencey, NOW THIS INDENTURE WITNESSETH that for the said sum to JOHN MAY in hand paid by HENRY STANARD BEVERLEY, JOHN MAY hath bargained sold and set over unto HARRY S. BEVERLEY and assigns the said Indenture and Lease; To have and to hold under the conditions stipulated in the recited Deed set forth; In Witness whereof the said MAY hath hereunto set his hand and affixed his seal the day and year first above written
Signed sealed and acknowledged in presence of us
    GEO: FRENCH, LAR. STANARD,                              JOHN  MAY
    DAVID OLIVIER
  At a Court of Hustings held for the Town & Corporation of Fredericksburg the 25th day of April 1794  This Indenture for Land from JOHN MAY to HENRY STANARD BEVERLEY was proved by the oaths of three witnesses thereto and ordered to be recorded

pp.     THIS INDENTURE Witnesseth that ELIZABETH KOWIN, Mother & next friend of
351-    JOHN KOWIN hath put the said JOHN and by these presents doth voluntarily and
352     of her own free will & accord put him the said JOHN Apprentice to CHARLES
       WARDELL, Hatter, in Fredericksburg, Virginia, to learn his trade & mystery and after the manner of an Apprentice to serve CHARLES WARDELL from the day of the date hereof during the full term of Six years two months & twenty one days next ensuing and in all things behave himself as a faithful Apprentice ought to do; and the said Master shall use the utmost of his endeavour to teach or cause to be taught and instructed the said Apprentice in the trade and mystery of a Hatter; and also to cause said JOHN KOWIN to be taught to read & write and will at the end of the term pay him Three pounds Ten shillings Virga. currency; In Witness whereof the parties have interchangeable set their hands and seals hereunto dated the 23d. day of May in the year of our Lord one thousand seven hundred and ninety four
Sealed and Delivered in the presence of    CHARLES  WARDELL
    B. W. CHEW               ELIABETH her mark X KOWIN
                          JOHN his mark X  KOWIN
  At a Court of Hustings held for the Town & Corporation of Fredericksburg May 23d. 1794 These Indentures of Apprenticeship was acknowledged by the parties and ordered to be recorded
Examd. & deld. C. WARDELL         Teste  JNO: CHEW C. C. H.

(Notation before the following Deed:  List of Conveyances deld. W. HARVEY to this page.)
pp.     THIS INDENTURE made this twenty first day of June in year of our Lord one
352-    thousand seven hundred and Ninety four Between JACOB KUHN of Town of
354     Fredericksburg, Merchant, of first part and WILLIAM GLASSELL of said Town,
       Merchant, of second part; Witnesseth that JACOB KUHN for sum of Five shillings to him in hand paid by WILLIAM GLASSELL, and for the better payment of sundry sums

of money said JACOB by these presents doth bargain and sell unto WILLIAM GLASSELL a
parcel of ground situated in Town of Fredericksburg on CAROLINE STREET between the
Lotts of WALTER GREGORY and WILLIAM DRUMMOND, bounded, beginning at the lower
corner of Lott No. Twenty eight on said CAROLINE STREET, thence up and along said
Street thirty feet, thence at right angles with said Street one hundred feet Eastwards,
thence parallel with CAROLINE STREET thirty feet to the corner line of said Lott, and
from thence along sd. lower line to the beginning; Together with all houses and appurtenances to said Lott belonging; Also the upper moiety of a Lott number Five
bounded by WILLIAM STREET on the North West by SOPHIA STREET, on the South West
Lott number twenty three, being opposite the same on on the South East by one other
part of said lott number five and on the South East by the RIVER RAPPAHANNOCK, containing one quarter of an acre be the same more or less together with all its appurtenances, Also seven tracts or parcels of land in the County of GREENBRIAR containing
seven thousand acres be the same more or less and particularly described in a Deed of
bargain and sale from WILLIAM HANCHER and ANNE his Wife to said KUHN bearing date
the Twentieth of February one thousand seven hundred and Ninety, now of record in
County Court of GREENBRIAR, together with all appurtenances; To have and to hold the
said lotts lands and premises above mentioned unto WILLIAM GLASSELL his heirs, Provided nevertheless that if JACOB KUHN his heirs truly pay unto WILLIAM GLASSELL the
full sum of Four hundred and Thirty three pounds six shillings & eight pence on or before the first day of February one thousand seven hundred and ninety five, the sum
mof Four hundred and Thirty three pounds Six shillings and eight pence before the
first day of August one thouand seven hundred and ninety five, and Four hundred and
thirty three pounds six shillings & eight pence before the first day of February one
thousand seven hundred and ninety six in gold or silver coin, then everything therein
contained shall cease & be void; In Witness whereof JACOB KUHN hath hereunto set his
hand and seal the day and year first above written
Signed sealed & delivered in presence of
    J. MINOR JR.                              JACOB KUHN
    WILLIAM HARVEY, JOHN GLASSELL
  At a Court of Hustings held for the Town & Corporation of Fredericksburg the 27th
June 1794    This Indenture of Mortgage from JACOB KUHN to WILLIAM GLASSELL was
acknowledged by the said KUHN and ordered to be recorded
Exd. & delivered JACOB KUHN p. note below      Teste   JNO: CHEW C. C.H.
JOHN CHEW Esqr. D. Sir. Deliver Mr. JACOB KUHN his Mortgage to me as it is satisfied
            Signed        WM. GLASSELL
(on the file)


pp.     THIS INDENTURE made the Twenty sixth day of March in year of our Lord one
355-    thousand seven hundred and ninety four Between BENJAMIN HAZLEGROVE of
356     of Town of PORT ROYAL of one part and ADAM DARBY of Town of Fredericksburg
       of other part; Witnesseth that BENJAMIN HAZELGROVE for sum of One Silver
Dollar to him in hand paid by ADAM DARBY, and for other good causes and considerations, said BENJAMIN HAZELGROVE by these presents doth bargin lease and to farm let
unto said ADAM so much of the lott lying in Town of Fredericksburg numbered Fifty
three as is contained in the under mentioned lines and bounded; Beginning at the
lower corner of said lot on PRINCESS ANN STREET, from thence running up said PRIN-
CESS ANN STREET (blank) feet, thence at right angles along the boundary line of that
part of said lot now the property of (blank) BLAIR, (blank) feet, thence along WOLF
STREET to where we began, containing by estimation (blank) be the same more or less,
together with all that Tenement thereon standing with all houses & appurtenances

thereon now standing; To have and to hold the parcel unto ADAM DARBY for the full
term of Fifteen years to be computed from the first day of January ensuing paying
BENJAMIM HAZLEGROVE his heirs the yearly rent of one pepper Corn (excepting that
part of the Lot whereon a Warehouse now stands which is hereby declared to be the
property of the Estate of HUMPHREY McAUSLAND deced., in an agreement bearing date
the 15th August 1792), And the Grave Yard in said lot which is to be kept inclosed by or
at the expence of BENJAMIN HAZLEGROVE; In Witness whereof the parties have hereunto set their hands and seals the day and year first above written
Signed sealed and delivered in the presence of
    JOHN POLLOCK,                              BENJN: HAZLEGROVE
    ALEXR. REDDICK,  JOHN DARE            ADAM DARBY
  At a Court of Hustings held for the Town and Corporation of Fredericksburg 27th June
1794    This Lease from BENJAMIN HAZLEGROVE to ADAM DARBY was proved by the
oaths of three witnesses thereto and ordered to be recorded


pp.     THIS INDENTURE made this Sixth day of February in year of our Lord one thou-
357-   sand seven hundred and Ninety four Between JAMES ABBOTT of County of Spot-
358    sylvania of one part and WILLIAM EDMUNDS of County aforesaid of other part;
      Witnesseth that JAMES ABBOTT in consideration of the Rents and Covenants here
in mentioned on part of WILLIAM EDMUNDS his heirs to be paid and performed hath
demised and to farm let unto WILLIAM EDMUNDS his heirs one fourth part Lott of land
No. 168 in Town of Frederickburg which JAMES ADAMS leased of PHILIP EVANS for ever
together with all profits commodities and appurtenances belonging; To have and to
hold the lott of land unto WM. EDMUNDS his heirs from the present date forever; paying
JAMES ABBOTT his heirs during the time on the sixth day of February in each year the
sum of Five pounds current money of Virginia (at its present value), In Witness whereof the parties to these presents have hereunto set their hands and seals the day and
year first above written
Sealed and Delivd. in the presence of
    WILLIAM BERRY,                              JAMES ABBOTT
    JOHN ROBINSON, FIELDING LUCAS         WM. EDMUNDS
  At a Court of Hustings held for the Town & Corporation of Fredericksburg the 27th
June 1794     This Deed of Lease from JAMES ABBOTT to WILLIAM EDMUNDS was proved
by the oaths of two witnesses thereto and ordered to be certified


pp.     THIS INDENTURE made this ninth day of June in year of our Lord One thousand
358-   seven hundred and Ninety four Between WILLIAM CHAMPE CARTER and MARIA
360    his Wife of County of ALBEMARLE of one part and WILLIAM STANARD of County
     of Spotsylvania of other part; Witnesseth that whereas EDWARD CARTER, late of
the Town of Fredericksburg, Father of WILLIAM CHAMPE CARTER, was in his life time
possessed of certain lotts lying in said Town numbers 83, 84, 95, 96, being a moiety of
eight lotts purchased by said EDWARD of FIELDING LEWIS Esquire deceased, the other
moiety of eight lotts, to wit, Lotts number 85, 86, 97, 98, having been conveyed away
during the life time of the said EDWARD, and said EDWARD being so possessed departed
this life having first made his Will and Testament by which said last Will and Testament
among other things therein contained he devised unto SALLY CARTER, the now Widow
of said EDWARD, all his houses and lotts in Town of Fredericksburg during the term of
her Widowhood or during the term of her natural life; reversion to WILLIAM CHAMPE
CARTER & his heirs; NOW THIS INDENTURE WITNESSETH that WILLIAM CHAMPE CARTER
and MARIA his Wife for sum of One thousand pounds to them secured to be paid by
WILLIAM STANARD by these presents do bargain and sell unto WILLIAM STANARD his

heirs their right interest and estate in the said lotts No. 83, 84, 95 & 96; together with
their appurtenances (excepting that part of Lot No. 83 already sold unto WILLIAM L.
STONE of Town of Fredericksburg); which lotts bounded on the N. E. by CAROLINE or
Main Street, on the N. W.. by Lotts No. d85, 86, 97, 98; on the S. W. by CHARLES STREET and
on the S. E. by LEWIS STREET, PRINCESS ANN STREET intersecting and dividing Lotts 83 &
84 from lotts No. 95 & 96; whereon the said EDWARD CARTER resided in his life time and
whereon his Widow, the said SALLY CARTER, now resides; To have and to hold all the
title and demand of said WILLIAM CHAMPE CARTER and MARIA his Wife (excepting as
excepted) to WILLIAM STANARD his heirs; In Witness whereof WILLIAM CHAMPE CAR-
TER and MARIA his Wife have hereunto subscribed their names and affixed their seals
the day and year above written
Sealed and Delivered in presence of
    WILLIAM C. WILLIS, JAS: SMOCK,      WILLIAM C. CARTER
    LAR: STANARD, FRANS: KERIN MACNAMARA
 At a Court of Hustings held for the Town & Corporation of Fredericksburg June 27th
1794    THIS INDENTURE for Land from WILLIAM CHAMPE CARTER to WILLIAM STANARD
was proved by the oaths of three witnesses thereto and ordered to be recorded
Exd. & deld. WM. STANARD        Teste  JNO: CHEW  C. C. H.
(Commission recorded fo: 364)


pp.     THIS INDENTURE made this 9th day of June in year of our Lord one thousand
361-   seven hundred and Ninety four Between WILLIAM CHAMPE CARTER and MARIA
364    his Wife of County of ALBEMARLE of one part and LARKIN STANARD of Town of
      Fredericksburg of other part; Whereas EDWARD CARTER deceased late of Town of
Fredericksburg did in and by his last Will and Testament among other things devise to
his Wife SALLY CARTER during her Widowhood all his lands and lotts in Town of
Fredericksburg and after her death or marriage to his Son, WILLIAM CHAMPE CARTER
& his heirs, said Will duly proved and recorded in the Court of Spotsylvania County; NOW
THIS INDENTURE WITNESSETH that WILLIAM CHAMPE CARTER & MARIA his Wife for sum
of Two hundred and Seventy pounds to them by LARKIN STANARD in hand paid, doth
bargain and sell unto LARKIN STANARD his heirs the square containing four lotts of
land fronting the LIVERY STABLE & the House occupied as an Office by Mr. JOHN CHEW,
lying in Town of Fredericksburg and numbered 129, 130, 131, 132; and bounded Westwardly by PRINCE EDWARD STREET, Northwardly by AMELIA STREET, Eastwardly by
CHARLES STREET & Southwardly by WILLIAM STREET, being part of lotts devised as
aforesid; To have and to hold said Four lotts to LARKIN STANARD his heirs with all appurtenances thereunto belonging; In Testimony whereof WILLIAM CHAMPE CARTER &
MARIA his Wife have hereunto set their hands and seals the day and year aforewritten
Signed sealed and delivered in presence of
    WILL: STANARD, BENSON,      WILLIAM C. CARTER
    CHS. C. ALLEN, ROB: GALLAWAY,
    JAMES ROSS
 At a Court of Hustings held for the Town and Corporation of Fredericksburg June 27th
1794    This Indenture for Land from WILLIAM CHAMPE CARTER to LARKIN STANARD
was proved by the oaths of three witnesses thereto, Together with the Receipt thereon
indorsed & ordered to be recorded
Exd. & deld. W. S. wth Comm.      Teste   JNO: CHEW, C. C. H.
 The Commonwealth of Virginia to THOMAS BELL & WILLIAM WARDLAW of County of
ALBEMARLE Greeting; Whereas (the Commission for the privy Examination of MARIA, the Wife
of WILLIAM CHAMPE CARTER); Witness JOHN CHEW, Clerk of our said Court the 11th day of
July 1794 in the 19th year of the Commonwealth      JNO: CHEW

ALBEMARLE Sct. In obedience to the within Commission to us directed (the return of the execution of the privy examination of MARIA CARTER); Given under our hands & seals this 17th day of July 1794

                                        THOS: BELL
                                        W: WARDLAW


(On pages 364 and 365, there is another Commission set out in the same manner as above for the land sold to WILLIAM STANARD.  The Commission is undated; the return of the execution thereof is dated the 17th day of July 1794 and signed by THOS: BELL and W. WARDLAW.)

Heritage Books by Ruth and Sam Sparacio:

*Abstracts of Account Books of Edward Dixon, Merchant of
Port Royal, Virginia, Volume I: 1743–1747*

*Abstracts of Account Books of Edward Dixon, Merchant of
Port Royal, Virginia, Volume II*

*Albemarle County, Virginia Deed and Will Book Abstracts, 1748–1752*

*Albemarle County, Virginia Deed Book Abstracts, 1758–1761*

*Albemarle County, Virginia Deed Book Abstracts, 1761–1764*

*Albemarle County, Virginia Deed Book Abstracts, 1764–1768*

*Albemarle County, Virginia Deed Book Abstracts, 1768–1770*

*Albemarle County, Virginia Deed Book Abstracts, 1776–1778*

*Albemarle County, Virginia Deed Book Abstracts, 1778–1780*

*Albemarle County, Virginia Deed Book Abstracts, 1780–1783*

*Albemarle County, Virginia Deed Book Abstracts, 1787–1790*

*Albemarle County, Virginia Deed Book Abstracts, 1790–1791*

*Albemarle County, Virginia Deed Book Abstracts, 1791–1793*

*Augusta County, Virginia Land Tax Books, 1782–1788*

*Augusta County, Virginia Land Tax Books, 1788–1790*

*Amherst County, Virginia Land Tax Books, 1789–1791*

*Caroline County, Virginia Appeals and Land Causes, 1787–1794*

*Caroline County, Virginia Committee of Safety and
Early Surveys, 1729–1762 and 1774–1775*

*Caroline County, Virginia Land Tax Book Alterations, 1782–1789*

*Caroline County, Virginia Land Tax Book Alterations, 1792–1795*

*Caroline County, Virginia Land Tax Book Alterations, 1795–1798*

*Caroline County, Virginia Order Book Abstracts, 1765*

*Caroline County, Virginia Order Book Abstracts, 1767–1768*

*Caroline County, Virginia Order Book Abstracts, 1768–1770*

*Caroline County, Virginia Order Book Abstracts, 1770–1771*

*Caroline County, Virginia Order Book, 1764*

*Caroline County, Virginia Order Book, 1765–1767*

*Caroline County, Virginia Order Book, 1771–1772*

*Caroline County, Virginia Order Book, 1772–1773*

*Caroline County, Virginia Order Book, 1773*

*Caroline County, Virginia Order Book, 1773–1774*

*Caroline County, Virginia Order Book, 1774–1778*

*Caroline County, Virginia Order Book, 1778–1781*

*Caroline County, Virginia Order Book, 1781–1783*

*Caroline County, Virginia Order Book, 1783–1784*

*Caroline County, Virginia Order Book, 1784–1785*

*Caroline County, Virginia Order Book, 1785–1786*

*Caroline County, Virginia Order Book, 1786–1787*

*Caroline County, Virginia Order Book, 1787, Part 1*

*Caroline County, Virginia Order Book, 1787, Part 2*

*Caroline County, Virginia Order Book, 1787–1788*

*Caroline County, Virginia Order Book, 1788*

*Culpeper County, Virginia Deed Book Abstracts, 1795–1796*

*Culpeper County, Virginia Land Tax Book, 1782–1786*

*Culpeper County, Virginia Land Tax Book, 1787–1789*

*Culpeper County, Virginia Minute Book, 1763–1764*

*Digest of Family Relationships, 1650–1692, from
Virginia County Court Records*

*Digest of Family Relationships, 1720–1750, from
Virginia County Court Records*

*Digest of Family Relationships, 1750–1763,
from Virginia County Court Records*

*Digest of Family Relationships, 1764–1775, from
Virginia County Court Records*

*Essex County, Virginia Deed and Will Abstracts, 1695–1697*

*Essex County, Virginia Deed and Will Abstracts, 1697–1699*

*Essex County, Virginia Deed and Will Abstracts, 1699–1701*

*Essex County, Virginia Deed and Will Abstracts, 1701–1703*

*Essex County, Virginia Deed and Will Abstracts, 1745–1749*

*Essex County, Virginia Deed and Will Book, 1692–1693*

*Essex County, Virginia Deed and Will Book, 1693–1694*

*Essex County, Virginia Deed and Will Book, 1694–1695*

*Essex County, Virginia Deed and Will Book, 1701–1704*

*Essex County, Virginia Deed, 1753–1754
and Will Book 1750*

*Essex County, Virginia Deed Abstracts, 1721–1724*

*Essex County, Virginia Deed Book, 1724–1728*

*Essex County, Virginia Deed Book, 1728–1733*

*Essex County, Virginia Deed Book, 1733–1738*

*Essex County, Virginia Deed Book, 1738–1742*

*Essex County, Virginia Deed Book, 1742–1745*

*Essex County, Virginia Deed Book, 1749–1751*

*Essex County, Virginia Deed Book, 1751–1753*

*Essex County, Virginia Land Trials Abstracts,
1711–1716 and 1715–1741*

*Essex County, Virginia Order Book Abstracts, 1695–1699*

*Essex County, Virginia Order Book Abstracts, 1699–1702*

*Essex County, Virginia Order Book Abstracts, 1716–1723, Part 1*

*Essex County, Virginia Order Book Abstracts, 1716–1723, Part 2*

*Essex County, Virginia Order Book Abstracts, 1716–1723, Part 3*

*Essex County, Virginia Order Book Abstracts, 1716–1723, Part 4*

*Essex County, Virginia Order Book Abstracts, 1723–1725, Part 1*

*Essex County, Virginia Order Book Abstracts, 1723–1725, Part 2*

*Essex County, Virginia Order Book Abstracts, 1725–1729, Part 1*

*Essex County, Virginia Order Book Abstracts, 1727–1729*

*Essex County, Virginia Order Book, 1695–1699*

*Essex County, Virginia Will Abstracts, 1730–1735*

*Essex County, Virginia Will Abstracts, 1735–1743*

*Essex County, Virginia Will Abstracts, 1745–1748*

*Fairfax County, Virginia Deed Abstracts, 1799–1800 and 1803–1804*

*Fairfax County, Virginia Deed Abstracts, 1804–1805*

*Fairfax County, Virginia Deed Book Abstracts, 1799*

*Fairfax County, Virginia Deed Book, 1798–1799*

*Fairfax County, Virginia Land Causes, 1788–1824*